LIABILITY OF SCHOOL OFFICIALS AND ADMINISTRATORS FOR CIVIL RIGHTS TORTS

By

RICHARD S. VACCA
Professor of Education
Virginia Commonwealth University

and

H.C. HUDGINS, JR.
Professor of Education
Northern Illinois University

THE MICHIE COMPANY
Law Publishers
CHARLOTTESVILLE, VIRGINIA

COPYRIGHT 1982
BY
THE MICHIE COMPANY

Library of Congress Catalog Card No. 82-62367
ISBN 0-87215-561-7

DEDICATIONS

To my first and most effective teachers — my parents, Marion and Salvatore Vacca — who gave me the gift of life, and

To my current inspiring teachers — my wife Nancy and our children, Richard Steven, Lynn Marie, and John Joseph — whose interest, support, and love helped move this project forward.

— from a grateful R. S. V.

To my immediate family — Mary and Edgar, Irma, and Art and Jessie Marie — who through the years have stimulated, encouraged, and supported my endeavors, and

To my second family — Wanda, Dawne and Joe, and Jane and L.L. — who have created a real sense of family.

— from a grateful H. C. H.

TABLE OF CONTENTS

Page

TABLE OF CONTENTS

FOREWORD

Professors Vacca and and Hudgins have taken a complex, evolving area of the law that is marked nationwide by inconsistencies and subtle distinctions and produced a clear, easy-to-understand and enjoyable-to-read textbook. It is thorough in its scholarship and, refreshingly, places the development of the law governing the civil rights liability of school people in a historical context.

This is a book for school board members, school administrators, school attorneys, and anyone else seriously interested in the enforcement of civil rights in the schools. It is well organized and plainly crafted to provide practical help to the people whose everyday work naturally finds them always on the edge of violating another's civil rights, albeit unintentionally.

The school board member will value this book as significantly useful background information in establishing and enforcing school district policy. The school administrator will see this book as a detailed map guiding one through the maze of the civil rights laws in the day-to-day implementation of school board policy in the schools. The school attorney will like the book because it provides a general overview of the law governing civil rights and contains an encyclopedic/treasury of relevant court case and statute citations. And the other people seriously interested in the enforcement of civil rights in the schools will use the book as a standard against which to measure the civil rights observance and acumen of all school people.

In my judgement, this book is a valuable contribution to the laudable effort by school people to understand better the expanding law on civil rights and to respect both the intent and spirit of that law.

> *Thomas A. Shannon*
> Executive Director
> National School Boards Association
> Washington, D.C.

June, 1982

INTRODUCTION

When the Civil Rights Act of 1871 was enacted by Congress in the decade following the Civil War, the new law was designed primarily to ensure that newly emancipated blacks would be entitled to the same rights as other citizens. The Act was intended to bestow the guarantees of the fourteenth amendment on all black and white citizens.

For many years, the Civil Rights Act of 1871 was largely ignored; but, almost a century later, in 1961, the *Monroe v. Pape* decision initiated what has resulted in two decades of increasing litigation against governmental officials and governmental agencies. It was in 1961 that the provisions of the Act were made applicable to local public school board members and administrators; and, in 1975, the Act was subsequently interpreted by the U.S. Supreme Court as a protection for students. As recently as 1980 the Supreme Court ruled that a local governmental body whose official policy or custom violated a person's constitutional rights is not entitled to any immunity from damages if its officials acted in good faith and in accordance with settled Constitutional law. This case, testing good faith immunity of municipalities, is now held applicable to local public school boards also.

During the past fifteen years the number of court cases in which provisions of the 1871 Act have been applied to school-related issues has increased geometrically. The number of court decisions began to increase steadily in the early 1970's. In 1979, the *Yearbook of School Law* reported an astonishing 1,000% increase during the prior half-decade in court decisions that were based upon provisions of the 1871 Civil Rights Act. Thus, in a short period of our history, this piece of civil rights legislation has become what Thomas Shannon (Executive Director of the National School Boards Association) has referred to as the most significant malpractice law for people in public education in this country.

As the number and bases of constitutional tort cases have expanded, so too have the damages sought (both punitive and compensatory), as well as equitable remedies. When the Act was first applied to school officials, no monetary damages were sought. Since then, however, plaintiffs have sought and been awarded increasing amounts of money, and some settlements have amounted to hundreds of thousands of dollars.

Not unexpectedly, this increasing litigation has been paralleled by a continuing metamorphosis in the interpretations by courts of what exactly constitutes good faith behavior on the part of (1) a school board as a corporate entity, (2) school board members in their official capacities and as individuals, and (3) school administrators in their official capacities and as individuals. For decades the aforementioned were immune to civil rights tort suits under § 1983. That, of course, is no longer true, and the resulting challenge for all concerned is to determine from the hundreds of cases that have been adjudicated since the early 1960's exactly what constitutes good faith behavior for boards and their members today.

For local school districts and their school board members, the dramatic increase in court actions based on the 1871 Civil Rights Act and the apparent ambiguity regarding good faith have had serious repercussions. First, court actions cost money and inevitably divert funds from a district's total educational program. Court settlements of damages can be very costly, and even when cases can be resolved before getting into court, or when they are resolved in favor of the defendants, they will still require substantial expenditures of funds by a district. In addition, districts have had to rely more on legal counsel and pay increased costs for insurance coverage.

Second, litigation has made inordinate time demands on school officials. Involvement in court actions has taken administrators and board members from their primary responsibility — that of planning and operating educational programs — and involved them in hundreds of man-hours that, if spent on a district's educational program, might better serve its school population.

Third, given the fears of suit that it inspires, increased litigation inevitably has reduced the quantity and quality of decisions that school board members and administrators are willing to make. By law, school boards are mandated to engage in stipulated actions or to refrain from engaging in other actions, which leaves a broad spectrum of discretionary behavior. At times it is necessary for board members to make decisions where the law is not fully clear, but where actions are needed to resolve a problem. In view of the increased likelihood of legal action being initiated against them, board members will inevitably be more reluctant to make decisions in these areas of discretionary power.

Fourth, there is great danger that board members and administrators will increasingly spend considerable time in frivolous cases that should never be brought to court. In general, there has been an increased tendency during the past twenty-five years to challenge school authority. With the relative ease of challenge, the chances of winning, and the possibilities of receiving sizeable cash settlements, increasing numbers of individuals are likely to seek redress mistakenly in court for claims that should never have been made and that should not require the attention, time, and dollars of public school officials and public entities.

And fifth, there is likely to be greater reluctance of individuals to become school board members and administrators for fear of being sued in court for any and every decision they make. If this reluctance occurs, it will in turn result in an inferior quality of school board membership and administration and a corresponding decline in the quality of educational programs.

When the parameters of legitimate educational policy and regulations enacted by board members, administrators, and teachers do not conflict with the scope of constitutional activity by students, parents, and those same board members, administrators, and teachers, then a mutual good faith relationship is likely to exist where school district policies and procedures are balanced against an individual's constitutional rights. What is needed to assure this mutual good faith relationship is for each party to understand the confines and limitations within which the other works, for this will tend to mitigate the distrust that can build between decisionmakers and those affected by the decisions.

Unfortunately, given rapid changes in the courts' interpretations of the 1871 Civil Rights Act and its applicability to school districts, many school board members and their administrative officers do not have a full understanding of the balance between their roles as policymakers and the rights of individuals under their jurisdiction. They may believe that a proposed policy is proper and in the best interest of the district, when in fact that policy may conflict with the duly constituted rights of an individual. Conversely, a teacher or student may claim a right that is not deserved or that is to the detriment of the school community, and the board may need to intervene and make a decision that is properly within its province.

Expanding court interpretations of what constitutes constitutionally protected rights in school settings have dramatically altered traditional relationships among school boards, their members, their professional staffs, and their student and parent clients. Despite the hundreds of cases that have been decided in just the past fifteen years, no effort has been made to bring together the case law on point and to analyze those cases and define operationally what constitutes good faith behavior on the part of a school board, a school board member, and a school administrator. Thus, a large gap has appeared in the literature.

By attempting to fill this gap, this book has been written to contribute to promoting equity by examining the cumulative effect on school districts, their policy-making board members, and their administrative officers of judicial decisions rendered during the past two decades on issues related to both teachers and students. Specific attention is paid to good faith behavior, public policy prerogatives, and constitutional rights of individuals. A major contribution of this book will be a clear statement of the law, based on analysis of more than 200 § 1983 cases.

This book will be of special value to specific groups: school board members, school board attorneys, central office administrators and school principals, persons involved in preparing school administrators and teachers, and practicing teachers. With respect to the first group, the research contained in the chapters that follow will increase the knowledge base of school board members and will enable them to enact policy and make decisions consistent with established law; consequently, they should be less likely to become embroiled in litigation. Furthermore, the confidence of the general public in school boards should increase when it is known that board members are both knowledgeable about established law and sensitive to the rights of individuals within their school systems.

With respect to central office administrators, many of whom are often called upon and expected to advise board members, the material in the chapters will also increase their knowledge base, thereby enabling them to act more responsibly as well as give better advice to policymakers. Additionally, the decisions they make in terms of regulations that affect subordinates will be more consistent with settled law. Midlevel administrators will also benefit from the book. Given that the regulations they establish and the school district policies they enforce have a direct bearing on the behavior of both teachers and students, it is critical that they too be knowledgeable about the rights of their subordinates and the parameters of good faith behavior.

With respect to personnel who are involved in preparing school administrators and teachers, the material presented in this book will make them better informed about what constitutes good faith action, and it will therefore increase their ability to inform both prospective and practicing administrators about the limits of their authority and the rights of subordinates; it will also help teachers to understand both their rights and limitations on protected behavior. The end result will be both improved preparation of administrators and teachers and improved practice of both groups of people in the field.

This book should also be informative to teachers. Their rights as citizens under the Constitution and federal laws are clarified, which should make it easier for them to determine what the parameters of their freedom entail. They should understand better when given activities are protected and when they are not protected.

This book has been written, in part, about the public school student, but not intentionally for him. However, those persons who come in daily contact with him, make decisions concerning his conduct, and supervise his activities should be better informed by learning how § 1983 applies to young people in the school setting.

The book has conveniently been organized into five chapters. The first chapter provides the historical perspective for what is to follow in succeeding chapters. It treats the provision of § 1983 and the circumstances under which it was enacted. This chapter also reveals to what extent litigants may recover costs in suits.

The second chapter contains a description of the act as it relates to various agencies and people. These agencies include governmental bodies in general and school boards in particular; the people include school board members and school administrators. The degree to which immunity is applicable to these agencies and people and the context in which damages may be applied are treated.

Chapters 3 and 4 treat the Act in relationship to the key personnel to whom it has been applied. In Chapter 3 the authors examine the degree to which teachers have been protected and have not been protected under § 1983. Likewise, in Chapter 4 the authors examine the Act's applicability to students.

Finally, the concluding chapter puts the whole subject into perspective. In addition to summarizing what has transpired in the courts over the last two decades on this subject, the authors offer a number of global conclusions, supported by discussion, of the meaning and applicability of § 1983 to school officials and school employees.

The authors wish to acknowledge the cooperation and support of their respective institutions in the completion of this project. Professor Vacca completed his research and writing while on study leave from Virginia Commonwealth University. For this opportunity he is greatly indebted to Dean Charles P. Ruch, School of Education. While on leave Professor Vacca was permitted to engage in full-time study at The T. C. Williams School of Law, University of Richmond. For this valuable learning experience he expresses his sincere appreciation to Dean Thomas A. Edmonds and members of his faculty. Professor Vacca owes a special debt of gratitude to Mrs. Susan Goins, whose expert typing skills helped to bring this manuscript to completion.

Professor Hudgins conducted his research and wrote while in the regular employ of Northern Illinois University. He is grateful to Dean John Johansen and Department Chair Getschman for providing him with the freedom and flexibility to complete the manuscript. He is grateful to the personnel of the NIU Law Library and Founders Library for their assistance in providing the resources which made the work easier. And, he is especially grateful to Mrs. Fern Wernick and Mrs. Kathy Panttila whose typing contributed to the completion of the project.

CHAPTER 1

THE CIVIL RIGHTS ACT OF 1871, 42 U.S.C. § 1983

§ 1.0. Introduction.

It is a well established principle of school law that public school boards and their administrative officers possess considerable legal authority in making all policies, rules and regulations for the welfare of the school system. In their official actions, it has traditionally been presumed that school officials act in good faith. When they do, they are generally not subject to suit. This position has been premised on the notion that board members are lay people, not specialized in the work of boardsmanship, and act out of sincere motives, even though they may occasionally make a mistake. This standard has been the holding of courts of law for many decades.

In the recent past, however, legal challenges to school board and administrative authority have become much more numerous. Of all the possible areas of litigation, employee and student matters have received more attention than any others as increasing numbers of civil rights-type complaints have been litigated in both federal and state courts. Having their origins in the mid-1960's, such cases have placed the legal decision-making prerogatives of school officials under both a federal statutory and constitutional overlay, as plaintiff parties have sought both equitable remedy and legal relief. The subject matter of both teacher and student cases is numerous. When viewed in the context of court opinion on these issues, this subject has significant impact on the policy-making functions of boards of education and on the decision-making of administrators. This one area of law and education has opened an entirely new spectrum of the definition of the rights of teachers and administrators as opposed to the prerogatives of school officials. Since more than mere policymaking or administrative implementation of these policies is concerned, a wrong decision can result in a damage suit involving thousands of dollars, tie up school personnel for months or even years in court, and divert considerable time and energy from the heart of an educational program — the instruction of young people. That school systems have been embroiled in a variety and number of court cases is evident by a review of judicial decisions on this topic. A random sampling of case law between 1966 and 1980 follows.

A black public school teacher in North Carolina charged that she was not rehired solely because of her participation in the civil rights movement, a charge which the school board denied. The board alleged that she was incompetent as evidenced by failure to turn in reports on time, to stand outside her door and supervise students as classes changed, and to attend all PTA meetings. A federal circuit court ruled in favor of the teacher and ordered that the school board renew the teacher's contract. The court held that the school board had overstepped its authority by attempting to control the actions of a teacher outside school hours. Such control amounted to a restriction of the teacher's freedom of speech, a guarantee of the first amendment.[1]

A second example also involved a teacher's nonrenewal. Unlike the above case concerning a teacher's behavior outside the classroom, this involved what is central to a teacher's role — actual classroom instruction. The Texas teacher alleged that the sole reason for her nonrenewal was that she used a controversial simulation technique with her American history classes. Again, a circuit court ruled in favor of the teacher, holding that the technique may not receive universal acceptance, but it was a judgmental decision as to its use; furthermore, no one had been injured by it. The teacher's reinstatement was ordered with damage fees plus attorneys' fees awarded, the exact amounts to be determined later.[2]

Like teachers, students have also been successful in suits against school boards. In 1975 the Supreme Court of the United States decided a case in which two high school students in Arkansas charged that their constitutional rights to due process under the fourteenth amendment were infringed by their expulsion from school without a hearing. They had been disciplined for what school officials said was a violation of a school rule prohibiting use or possession of intoxicating beverages at school or school functions. The suit named as defendants not only school board members, but also two administrators and the school district itself. The students sought compensatory and punitive damages, the expungement of any notation of the incident in their records, and reinstatement. The Supreme Court did not

1. Johnson v. Branch, 364 F.2d 177 (4th Cir. 1966).

2. Kingsville Independent School District v. Cooper, 611 F.2d 1109 (5th Cir. 1980).

3

actually settle the issue of damages, but rather held in a landmark opinion that school officials may be liable as individuals for damages if they knew, or reasonably should have known, that their actions would violate the constitutional rights of students, or if they had acted toward the student with the malicious intent to cause such a deprivation or other injury.[3]

In a fourth case, upon the court's decision, a local Virginia school board learned that a teacher's complaint against the principal's actions coupled with a formal grievance against her administrator do not constitute sufficient cause for nonrenewal. Evidence showed that the complaint about her status as a "floating" teacher and the formal grievance were substantial and motivating factors in the school board's decision not to rehire her. At trial, the jury also found that the school board had failed to show that it would have reached the same decision in the absence of her grievance regarding her principal. In agreeing with the teacher, the court acknowledged that her nonrenewal was in retaliation for exercising her constitutionally protected right to freedom of speech. The court ordered the teacher, serving her probationary period with better than satisfactory ratings, to be reinstated with tenure and back pay from the time of termination of her contract until reinstatement (less whatever sums were earned by her during that period and whatever unemployment compensation was received).[4]

A school superintendent in Illinois charged that his local school board forced him to resign his position. At trial, he successfully showed that the board members had acted toward him with malicious intentions. Since his civil rights had been violated, the federal district court declared that the board members were liable for monetary damages.[5]

---

3. Wood v. Strickland, 420 U.S. 308 (1975).

4. Johnson v. Butler, 433 F. Supp. 531 (W.D. Va. 1977).

5. Adelberg v. Labuszewski, 447 F. Supp. 267 (N.D. Ill. 1978).

In another example of case law covering the kinds of suits initiated by school personnel against their superordinates, a suit by a teenage girl charged that her fourth amendment rights were violated when she was subjected to a nude search. The search took place after a specially trained dog, brought into the school by police to assist school officials in enforcing a school policy regarding controlled substances, alerted the officials that drugs were present. After the dog so alerted the officials in the girl's presence, she was then escorted to another part of the building and ordered to undress completely. No drugs were found. The circuit court upheld the use of the dogs but looked with disfavor on school officials conducting a strip search. It ordered the lower court to determine what damages might be appropriate for the girl.[6]

The final example in this section involved a nontenured elementary school teacher who charged that her nonrenewal stemmed from her activism in union matters. The circuit court agreed and ordered school officials to (1) offer her reinstatement with a continuing contract, (2) compensate her for lost earnings, (3) pay attorneys' fees, and (4) pay the costs of her appeal. The teacher convinced both trial and appellate courts that her nonrenewal would not have occurred absent the exercise of her first amendment right which in this instance involved being active and speaking out on union matters, a form of freedom of speech.[7]

A common thread running through the above seven court decisions is that the plaintiffs charged that certain constitutional rights had been denied them, the various courts agreed with their charges, and the courts granted to

---

6. Doe v. Renfrow, 631 F.2d 91 (7th Cir. 1980), *cert. denied,* 49 U.S.L.W. 3880 (May 26, 1981).

7. Hickman v. Valley Local School District Board, 619 F.2d 606 (6th Cir. 1980), *reheard on remand* at 513 F. Supp. 659 (S.D. Ohio 1981).

them certain remedies for the deprivation of those rights. These cases are but a few examples from a new era in school litigation. This era has already had and is continuing to have a profound impact on individuals directly affected by this litigation — local school board members. It affects the kinds and quality of the decisions they make, for board members must now pause and consider whether their decisions will be challenged in court. It influences the preparation that board members must undergo in assuming their offices, for they must now demonstrate substantial knowledge about the rights of persons employed in the school system and students who are enrolled in it. This era of litigation also affects the time allocation of board members, not only in preparation for the job, deliberation in deciding matters, but also in justifying or defending their actions. The thousands of cases filed against school officials, and the hundreds of cases treating the civil rights of staff and student personnel, indicate that no area of the country is exempt from suit; the size or affluence of a school district is not a determinant; nor does the number of years of experience of board members prevent a legal action.

§ 1.1. Emergence of the Civil Rights Tort.

As stated earlier, public school officials possess considerable discretion in making all decisions necessary for the welfare of the school system. The above sampling of court decisions demonstrates, however, that this exercise of discretion is not without legal limitations and challenges by individuals adversely affected by these decisions. The challenges by teachers and students to school officials' authority as a deprivation of their civil rights is grounded in federal legislation enacted after the Civil War. It has been just over the last fifteen-plus years that one law was rediscovered and, when applied to the actions of school officials, has had profound impact on and has changed, in many ways, the legal status and immunity to suit of public school boards as corporate entities, of individual school board members, and of other school officials. The law is the Civil Rights Act of 1871. (More will be said about the intent of this Act in § 1.2 of this Chapter.) Codified at 42 U.S.C. § 1983 (1871), the Act provides:

> Every person who, under color of any statute, ordinance, regulation, custom or usage of any State or Territory, subjects or causes to be subjected any citizen of the United States or other person within the jurisdiction thereof to the deprivation of any rights, privileges or immunities secured by the Constitution and laws shall be liable to the party injured in an action at law, suit in equity or other proper proceeding for redress.

Simply stated, § 1983 was designed as a flexible and broad scoped statute to restrict a wide variety of actions of state officials. When acting in their official capacities, these officials (exercising a portion of the state's authority) cannot move to restrict or deny any person subject to them any right to which an individual is entitled under the Constitution as well as under federal laws. If a state official acts in derogation of one's protected rights, that official may be charged with a court proceeding commonly known now as a *constitutional* or *civil rights tort.*

A distinction must be made, however, between this new tort concept in school law and the traditional concept of the *negligent tort.* Simply stated, a tort is a civil wrong, other than a breach of contract, for which a court will provide a remedy in the form of damages. The wrong grows out of harm to an individual by the unreasonable conduct of others. The remedy is premised on the notion that one should be allowed to recover something, usually money, from the one who harmed him.[8]

---

8. H. C. HUDGINS, JR. & RICHARD S. VACCA, LAW AND EDUCATION:

Generally, actions in tort have been grouped into three types. These types are: (1) intentional interference, (2) strict liability, and (3) negligence. Until the mid-1970's, the case law on point showed clearly that public school system liability for student or teacher injury was limited to the negligent tort, and to matters resulting in physical injury (broken bones, burns, cuts and the like) occurring in certain *high risk* settings (for example, science laboratories, vocational education laboratories, gymnasia, playgrounds and athletic fields).[9]

The current liability arena is expanding gradually to include situations other than physical injury. Section 1983 (the constitutional or civil rights tort) must be placed in this expanding arena.

Section 1983 provides two remedies for a plaintiff injured under the Act. One remedy is equitable relief where the injured party seeks to have the constraints that prompted the injury removed. For example, since the school board in example number one had sought to restrict the teacher's activities outside school and to dismiss her, equitable relief

---

CONTEMPORARY ISSUES AND COURT DECISIONS (Charlottesville, Va.: The Michie Company Law Publishers, 1979), at 69. According to KEMPLIN, *infra*, "no universally acceptable definition of the word 'tort' exists. . . . In practice it indicates some invasion or interference with a right of person, property, or reputation. In order to determine whether a tort exists . . . it is necessary to determine what legally protected rights of person, property, or reputation one has, which are not to be interfered with or invaded. Such a determination is the basis of the whole law of torts." F. G. KEMPLIN, JR., HISTORICAL INTRODUCTION TO ANGLO-AMERICAN LAW IN A NUTSHELL 163 (St. Paul, Minn.: West Publishing Company, 1973), at 163.

9. *See, e.g.,* R. S. Vacca, *Teacher Malpractice,* 8 U. OF RICHMOND LAW REVIEW 447 (Spring, 1974). Simply stated, negligence involves conduct of one person that falls below an established or accepted standard which results in an injury to another person. The injured person must prove that the first person's conduct was the proximate cause of the injury suffered.

would involve in this instance two forms — reinstatement and nonintervention in the teacher's civil rights activities. The second remedy involves damages, a monetary award for the injury. The damages may take one of three forms: nominal; punitive, (sometimes called exemplary damages) or punishment for the wrongful action taken; and compensatory, or an award to compensate for the injury incurred and the suffering resulting from it.

Subsequent chapters of this book will show that in public education local school officials who have deprived employees or students of their federal constitutional and statutory rights may be held corporately and personally liable. First, subsequent sections of this chapter will treat the historical background of § 1983 and then the technical considerations of the application of the Act.

§ 1.2. 42 U.S.C. § 1983: A Historical Perspective.

To understand fully the intent of § 1983, the statute (Civil Rights Act 1871) must be placed within the historical context of the Reconstruction Era (1865-1877). Referred to by some historians as the "Age of Hate," [10] Reconstruction was a very disconcerting period in American history.

In April of 1865 the Civil War ended, but this nation remained in many ways divided. The federal government in Washington was in financial and political trouble. Shortly after Lee's surrender at Appomattox the situation was compounded further by President Lincoln's murder, leaving the nation in a state of political turmoil.

---

10. The historical perspective contained in the paragraphs of the subsection that follow were developed directly from the account given by T. A. BAILEY, THE AMERICAN PAGEANT: A HISTORY OF THE REPUBLIC (2d ed. Boston, Massachusetts: D. C. Heath Company, 1961), Chapter 24, The Ordeal of Reconstruction, at 459-82.

The South was especially hurt by the War, where an entire "way of life" had suffered almost total devastation (social, political and economic). Once rich and powerful, the white landowners of the South's plantation society, many of whom survived the War, found themselves starting over, while more than three million Negroes who had served them as slaves were experiencing the beginning of a new, free life.

The South, therefore, was in a state of total upheaval. Thievery, fraud and physical violence were reported as commonplace activities since pre-Civil War statutes in the southern states were no longer binding. Thus, in once peaceful communities law and order were almost nonexistent. Civil government had to be reconstructed from almost total devastation, and the way was open in the South (and nationally as well) to a struggle for social, political and economic power. It was from this struggle for control and power that in 1866 the infamous Ku Klux Klan came into being with a purpose of reestablishing "white supremacy."

(a) POST-CIVIL WAR CONSTITUTIONAL AMENDMENTS.

Emerging from the Reconstruction Era were three interrelated amendments to the United States Constitution, each one intended to bring the Negroes of the South into full citizenship as Americans. Ratified on December 8, 1865, the thirteenth amendment brought freedom to the slaves.[11] Three years later, in 1868, the fourteenth amendment was ratified.[12] Section One of this addition, considered by legal scholars to have been crucial to the task of bringing full civil rights to the newly freed Negroes, states:

---

11. UNITED STATES CONSTITUTION, Amend. XIII, ratified December 8, 1865.

12. UNITED STATES CONSTITUTION, Amend. XIV, ratified July 23, 1868.

10

All persons born or naturalized in the United States, and subject to the jurisdiction thereof, are citizens of the United States and of the State wherein they reside. No State shall abridge the privileges or immunities of citizens of the United States; nor shall any State deprive any person of life, liberty, or property, without due process of law; nor deny to any person within its jurisdiction the equal protection of the laws.[13]

Intended to protect all citizens (especially the newly freed Negroes) from unwarranted *state action,* the last two clauses of this amendment *(due process* and *equal protection)* planted the seeds of potential civil rights litigation which were realized in the years to follow.

Negro suffrage became a constitutional fact with the ratification of the fifteenth amendment in 1870.[14] It was in that same year that each of the southern states had reestablished civil government and each one was back in the Union. As one historian reported, however, "[t]he white South, for many decades, openly and defiantly flaunted the 14th and 15th Amendments." [15] Thus Congress needed to take additional statutory steps (a provision made in all three amendments) to enforce the intent of these constitutional mandates.[16]

(b) Post-Civil War Congressional Acts.

In 1870 Congress reenacted the Civil Rights Act of 1866

---

13. *Id.*

14. United States Constitution, Amend. XV, ratified March 30, 1870.

15. Bailey, *supra* note 10, at 478.

16. D. G. Engdahl, Constitutional Power Federal and State (St. Paul, Minn.: West Publishing Company, 1974). "The thirteenth, fourteenth, and fifteenth amendments ... each contain a section providing ... that 'Congress shall have power to enforce, by appropriate legislation the provisions of this article.' ... These enforcement sections have become increasingly significant sources of federal power in recent years." *Id.* at 237.

(codified at 42 U.S.C. § 1981) with the intent that "all persons within the jurisdiction of the United States should enjoy the same rights as white citizens and be subject only to like punishment, pains and penalties . . . ." [17] Through § 1981 the intent of the thirteenth amendment could be realized and, at the same time, enforcement of the guarantees of the fourteenth amendment would be assisted.

Also related to assisting the enforcement of the guarantees of the thirteenth and fourteenth amendments was another piece of legislation emerging from the Congress of 1866. Section 1982 of the United States Code declared "that all citizens shall have the same right to convey personal and real property," [18] free from both private and public discrimination.

(c) THE CIVIL RIGHTS ACT OF 1871: 42 U.S.C. § 1983.

Originally enacted as § 1 of the Civil Rights Act of 1871, what is now referred to as 42 U.S.C. § 1983 (hereafter referred to as § 1983) was intended to enable the enforcement of the guarantees of the fourteenth amendment to the United States Constitution.[19] Referred to as the Ku Klux Klan Act, A. E. Dick Howard tells us, in his treatise, that § 1983 "grew out of the period of Civil War and Reconstruction, during which antebellum assumptions about the nature of the federal system were superseded by a greater emphasis on national power." [20] This period in our country's history, he continues, was permeated with a

---

17. 42 U.S.C.A. § 1981, at 212.

18. 42 U.S.C.A. § 1982, at 251.

19. 42 U.S.C.A. § 1983, at 252-60. *See also* 15 AMERICAN JURISPRUDENCE 2d (Rochester: The Lawyer's Co-Operative Publishing Company) at 305.

20. A. E. DICK HOWARD, I'LL SEE YOU IN COURT: THE STATES AND THE SUPREME COURT (Washington, D.C.: National Governors' Association Center for Policy Research, 1980), at 3-4.

"spirit of nationalism" and was one marked by an "explosive expansion of federal judicial power." [21]

The language of the Civil Rights Act of 1871 was directed at acts of misconduct and abuse by state officials (in the southern states) who deprived citizens of their constitutional entitlements. In effect, the purposes of the law were three. These were: "to provide a remedy where state law is inadequate, to provide a federal remedy where a theoretically adequate state remedy is not available in practice, and to provide a remedy in the federal courts supplementary to any remedy which any state might provide." [22] To put it another way, and bring it up-to-date, the statute has existed for the past century to supplement state remedies and private civil rights remedies where they appear inadequate, and to provide remedy to aggrieved persons apart from those available as state guarantees put into practice. [23]

As is true of statutory law in general, the provision and guarantees of § 1983 lacked practical meaning and remained legal abstractions until interpreted by courts of law in adjudicating actual cases. For more than seventy-five years, however, § 1983 was used very little, and lay virtually dormant in the United States Code. Between 1871 and 1920, reports A. E. Dick Howard, in his book, twenty-one cases were brought under this section of the Code. He also states it wasn't until 1939 that "[t]he seed of more ambitious use for Sec. 1983 was planted." [24] Moreover, over the past twenty years "section 1983 has

---

21. *Id.* at 17.

22. 15 Am. Jur. 2d, *supra* note 19, at 305.

23. *Id.* For an excellent article on point, see N. H. Cambron-McCabe, *School District Liability Under Section 1983 for Violations of Federal Rights,* 10 NOLPE Sch. Law J. 99 (1982).

24. Howard, *supra* note 10, at 5.

13

become a staple of litigation in the federal courts." [25]

The current status of court suits taken by plaintiffs against public school systems is best summarized by F. G. Delon and R. E. Bartman in *The Yearbook of School Law.* In their view, "[t]he number of actions under 42 U.S.C. § 1983 of the Civil Rights Act of 1871 continues to increase at a dramatic rate. It appears that more attorneys who represent school employees now realize the importance of this federal statute. . . ." [26]

The chapters of this book that follow are intended to demonstrate the application of § 1983 to public school issues involving both employees and students. To gain a better understanding of § 1983 it is necessary to look briefly at certain legal-technical dimensions of the law before examining specific cases on point. The remaining sections of this chapter are intended to present *four* such dimensions: Attorneys' Fees in § 1983 Actions, Costs in § 1983 Actions Other than Attorneys' Fees, Exhaustion of State Remedies in § 1983 Actions, and Statutes of Limitations in § 1983 Actions.

§ 1.3. Attorneys Fees in § 1983 Actions.

At the very heart of our nation's legal system is the basic principle of law that for every *wrong* done to a person by either government or another person or persons there must

---

25. *Id.* at 6. To Whitman, *infra,* § 1983 acts as an affirmer of rights, a deterrent to rights abuse, a vehicle for punishment, and as a way of gaining compensation. C. Whitman, *Constitutional Torts,* 79 MICH. LAW REV. 5 (November, 1980).

26. F. G. Delon & R. E. Bartman, *Employees,* THE YEARBOOK OF SCHOOL LAW 1979 (P. K. Piele ed. in chief, Topeka, Kan.: NOLPE, 1979), at 123.

be a *remedy* (a means by which a violation of rights is prevented, redressed or compensated) provided. Thus, under our system of law individuals who claim that they have been wronged are able to go to court seeking the appropriate remedy from those who have wronged them.

Plaintiffs taking § 1983-type cases to court seek specific remedy. As demonstrated in the previous pages, both teachers and students have gone to court seeking equitable as well as legal relief from public school boards and administrators. Taking such cases to court costs money and a major portion of that expense is the payment of attorneys' fees. What individual parties (plaintiff and defendant) in a civil rights suit may not be aware of, however, is that they may find themselves liable for paying the fees of their opponent's attorney if they do not in some way prevail (win) in their quest for remedy.

(a) CIVIL RIGHTS ATTORNEYS' FEES ACT OF 1976.

In *Monell v. Department of Social Services,*[27] the United States Supreme Court opined that the Civil Rights Attorneys' Fees Act of 1976 [28] allows prevailing parties (as determined by the court's discretion) to obtain attorneys' fees in § 1983-type suits. The portion of the Act cited as authority for these awards states, in part, that "the court, in its discretion, may allow the prevailing party, other than the United States, a reasonable attorney's fee as part of the costs." [29]

Writing in 1975, E. W. Williams stated that the

---

27. Monell v. Department of Social Services, 436 U.S. 658 (1978). In *Monell* the majority held that local governments were not wholly immune from suit under section 1983.

28. The Attorneys' Fees Act of 1976, amended 42 U.S.C. § 1988 (1970).

29. A. Berkovitz, *A Summary of Issues Involving Attorneys' Fees in Civil Rights Cases,* 13 CLEAR REV. 282 (August, 1979). *See, e.g.,* Brubaker v. Board of Educ., 502 F.2d 973 (7th Cir. 1974).

15

"allowance of attorney fees and litigation expenses is part of a federal court's traditional equity powers." [30] Citing *Edelman v. Jordan*[31] and *Skehan v. Board of Trustees*[32] as controlling, he added that "it has been held that any differences between attorneys' fees and damages is irrelevant." [33]

Since *Monell,* however, the Attorneys' Fees Act (hereafter referred to as § 1988) has been the subject of mixed court interpretations. This judicial inconsistency results from the inability of judges to "agree on criteria for deciding when federal law is in need of supplementation, or when state rules, once examined, nevertheless may be ignored as undermining civil rights policy." [34]

To some experts, however, § 1988 has emerged from recent litigation with a limited scope. "The new approach," suggests Eisenberg, "leaves federal courts room to maneuver, while undertaking a careful analysis of the propriety of borrowing the state rule in the particular case." [35]

The Supreme Court's recent decision in *Maine v. Thiboutot*[36] (a non-education case) reaffirms the *Monell*

---

30. E. W. Williams, Liability of Public Schools and Public School Officials for Damages Under 42 U.S.C. § 1983, (Harvard University Law School: An unpublished paper, 1975), n.173, at 73. *See, e.g., Brubaker, supra* note 29.

31. *Id.* Edelman v. Jordan, 415 U.S. 651 (1974).

32. *Id.* Skehan v. Board of Trustees, 501 F.2d 31 (3d Cir. 1974).

33. *Id.*

34. T. Eisenberg, *State Law in Federal Civil Rights Cases: The Proper Scope of Section 1988,* 128 U. OF PENN. LAW REV. 499 (January, 1980), at 499. The implication here is that the availability of attorneys' fees may be determined in a particular case by application of appropriate state law.

35. *Id.* at 543.

36. Maine v. Thiboutot, 448 U.S. 1 (1980). Commenting on this case, Smith, *infra,* has said "the Supreme Court held that § 1983 in fact does authorize a person whose rights under a federal statute have been

rule that attorney's fees, pursuant to § 1988, may be awarded to the appropriate prevailing party in § 1983 actions. Additionally, the high court broadened its holding by extending § 1983 to apply both to constitutional and statutory claims. In a companion case, *Maher v. Gagne,*[37] the majority further expanded the holding by rejecting the state's claim that § 1988 authorized attorney's fees only in § 1983 actions where civil or equal rights were at issue.[38]

With the Supreme Court's holding in the *Maine* case, new and broader based possibilities for § 1983-type litigation were created. Thus, the applicability of the Attorneys' Fees Act was also extended. To show this, C. Hukill, in his article, has summarized into eight categories the types of court actions where § 1988 applies. These are: (1) equal right to contract, (2) equal rights in property transactions, (3) violations of protected rights by state and local officials, (4) conspiracy to interfere with civil rights, (5) failure to prevent conspiracies to interfere with civil rights, (6) racial discrimination in federally assisted program, (7) discrimination in federally funded educational programs, and (8) matters involving the Internal Revenue Code.[39]

Five of the above eight types of actions have already found their way into the school law arena (equal right to contract, violations of protected rights, conspiracy to interfere with civil rights, racial discrimination in federally assisted programs, and discrimination in federally funded educational programs). Subsequent chapters of this book

---

violated to sue for damages." M. R. Smith, *School Board Liability for Violations of Federal Rights,* 12 SCH. LAW BUL. 10 (January, 1981).

37. Maher v. Gagne, 448 U.S. 122 (1980).

38. *Id.*

39. C. Hukill, *Opponents' Attorney's Fees in Civil Rights Cases,* 10 SCH. LAW BUL. 1 (January, 1979), at 3.

will demonstrate this influx in both employee and student matters.

(b) PREVAILING PARTIES.

Following the passage of § 1988, some confusion existed regarding the notion of prevailing parties. What was not always clear was who actually prevailed in civil rights cases, since both plaintiff and defendant may have won on some of the issues while losing on others. To A. Berkovitz, in her article, the issue of prevailing parties was ultimately resolved

> in favor of maintenance of a "dual standard" under which prevailing plaintiffs should receive fees as a matter of course, while prevailing defendants are eligible for fees only if plaintiffs are found to have brought suit vexatiously, for purposes of harassment, or otherwise in bad faith.[40]

Additionally, she states, "the parties can be considered to have prevailed in litigation when they 'vindicate rights through a consent judgment or without formally obtaining relief.'"[41] As the Supreme Court held in *Maher,* there is "no reason to discriminate in awarding fees between parties who prevail in full litigation and those who win in settlement."[42] Finally, the "success on 'any significant issue' which achieves some benefit which had been sought

---

40. Berkovitz, *supra* note 29, at 282. For an example of a school case where a teacher was judged not to be the prevailing party, see Harrington v. Vandalia-Butler Board of Education, 585 F.2d 192 (6th Cir. 1978). For a recent case (non-school matter) where defendants were entitled to attorney's fees because plaintiff's claims were judged "frivolous or meritless," see Ellis v. Cassidy, 625 F.2d 227 (9th Cir. 1980).

41. Berkovitz, *supra* note 29, at 283.

42. Maher, *supra* note 37.

is sufficient to consider the plaintiffs prevailing parties." [43] In fact, attorneys' fees "have also been granted to plaintiffs who ultimately prevailed at the administrative level." [44]

As the above information demonstrates, school officials would be wise to take their potential liability for attorneys' fees into consideration before a matter becomes either a court suit or a formal administrative grievance. Likewise, those who take legal and administrative actions against school officials should recognize that if they do not ultimately win their case or grievance, they too may be held liable for the prevailing opposition's attorneys' fees.

(c) TIMELINESS OF REQUESTS FOR FEES.

School officials are cognizant of the importance of meeting deadlines. Reports are due, budgets are due, and school must open on a specific date; these and many other such examples underscore the importance of *time* in school work. Missing a deadline can cause a school system problems. The timeliness of requests for attorneys' fees may also be an issue in court. So far, the courts are not in agreement on setting a definite time limit on when such requests must be filed prior to entry of a judgment.

Whether § 1988 is retroactive or not (that is, does it apply to actions begun before the passage of the Act) has been another key question before the courts. To some legal scholars, however, this question was answered in *Bradley v. School Board of the City of Richmond.* Interpreting *Bradley* (a case involving the attorneys' fees provisions of the Emer-

---

43. Berkovitz, *supra* note 29, at 284. In a recent higher education case, Jacobs v. Stratton, 615 P.2d 982 (N.M. 1980), the court held that the prevailing party in a damage action based on an alleged violation of civil rights should ordinarily receive attorneys' fees absent special circumstances.

44. Berkovitz, *supra* note 29, at 284.

gency School Aid Act of 1972), one writer has concluded that "a court is to apply the law in effect at the time it renders its decision, unless doing so would result in manifest injustice or there is legislative history to the contrary." [45]

In *Williams v. Anderson,*[46] (a case involving alleged racial discrimination in teacher employment), the Eighth Circuit Court awarded attorney's fees to the prevailing plaintiff since the Attorneys' Fees Awards Act was passed while the appeal was pending. Similarly, in *Webster v. Redmond,*[47] the plaintiff school principal was judged entitled to recover an amount for the payment of reasonable attorney's fees, although the case was pending when the statute was adopted.

Not inconsistent with the opinions in *Williams* and *Webster* above is a somewhat different view of *Bradley* voiced by Hukill in his article. In his opinion, "[t]he simple fact that a case was pending when the Attorneys' Fee Act was passed, however, does not ensure that the act will be applied retroactively." [48] He cites *Peacock v. Drew Municipal Separate School District* (a challenge to a school district's policy which inhibited employment of unwed parents) as an example of a case that was pending at the time the Act was passed; but, since plaintiff did not begin to request fees until after enactment of the statute, fees were denied.[49]

Bacica v. Board of Education [50] offers another example of a case where a court denied the award of attorney's fees. In

---

45. *Id.* at 283. Bradley v. School Board of the City of Richmond, 416 U.S. 696 (1974).

46. Williams v. Anderson, 526 F.2d 1081 (8th Cir. 1977).

47. Webster v. Redmond, 443 F. Supp. 670 (N.D. Ill. 1977).

48. Hukill, *supra* note 39, at 4.

49. *Id. See* Andrews v. Drew Municipal School District, 371 F. Supp. 27 (N.D. Miss. 1973).

50. Bacica v. Board of Education, 451 F. Supp. 882 (W.D. Pa. 1978).

this case, however, the court refused to make the award citing the following rationale:

> Because the award of counsel fees is a discretionary matter and because we do not feel that the relevant facts necessary for our determination were properly marshaled or presented in an orderly and timely fashion we shall deny the award of attorney's fees to the plaintiffs.[51]

(d) LIMITS ON FEE AMOUNTS.

Generally, there is no one definite scale that sets specific amounts for attorneys' fees in civil rights actions. Several factors will have an impact upon the amount charged by the attorney. For example, how complex and complicated is the legal matter? How much time (usually calculated by the hour) will be involved in researching and preparing the briefs? How long does it take (in hours) to actually process the case from initial interviews with the client through final settlement? What is the potential size of the final settlement? What is the professional stature (training, background, experience, skill and reputation) of the attorney handling the case?

Some courts have attempted to "limit attorneys' fees to the actual work performed only on issues on which plaintiffs were sucessful. . . ." [52] Other courts have set attorneys'

---

51. *Id.* at 889.

52. Berkovitz, *supra* note 29, at 284. District courts are not completely free of constraints in setting and explaining fee amounts awarded. For example in a recent public school case, Brown v. Bullard Independent School District, 640 F.2d 651 (5th Cir. 1981), the Fifth Circuit remanded the matter back for reconsideration of the attorney's fee sum, because the district court failed to explain how it had arrived at the figure and it had made no reference to guidelines set by the Fifth Circuit in a previous case.

21

fees on an hourly basis.[53] Still other courts have added
yearly interest to the attorney's usual hourly rate.[54] Thus,
the actual amounts vary from case to case. For example,
$4,500 may be considered reasonable attorneys' fees in one
public school situation, while $10,000 may be considered
reasonable in another, and $35,000 may be considered rea-
sonable in another. Parties in school cases must keep in
mind that they may be held liable for payment of such
amounts.

(e) ELEVENTH AMENDMENT CASES.

The awarding of attorneys' fees in eleventh amendment
cases (this amendment precludes suits by citizens of one
state against another state and suits by citizens against
their own state without the state's consent) is another
unsettled area of law. There is one major exception, however, where attorneys' fees are awarded as a part of costs.
According to A. Berkovitz in her article:

> The eleventh amendment issue was disposed of by the
> Supreme Court in *Hutto v. Finney* last year. The Court
> pointed out that the Act imposes attorneys' fees "as a
> part of costs," and costs have traditionally been
> awarded without regard for the states' eleventh amend-
> ment immunity.[55]

Chapter Two, plus the cases presented in subsequent

---

53. Barham v. Welch, 478 F. Supp. 1246 (E.D. Ark. 1979).

54. Harkless v. Sweeny Independent School District, 466 F. Supp. 457
(S.D. Tex. 1979).

55. Berkovitz, *supra* note 29, at 282-83. *See* Hutto v. Finney, 437 U.S.
678 (1978). In the matter of possible Eleventh Amendment bars and
plaintiff claims of monetary damages instead of seeking equitable relief,
Howard has stated: "The plaintiff may, of course, seek damages against
an officer without concern of the Eleventh Amendment. But if he seeks
a monetary judgment which will be satisfied out of the State Treasury,
an Eleventh Amendment issue arises." HOWARD, *supra* note 20, at 13.

chapters will treat the applicability of eleventh amendment immunity to public school matters involving both employees and students.

(f) IMPACT AND RAMIFICATIONS OF 42 U.S.C. § 1988.

The impact and ramifications of the Attorneys' Fees Awards Act of 1976 on school officials are several. As C. Hukill has concluded, in his article, "it may become economically wise for school administrators to enter into consent decrees and out-of-court settlements in some cases they think they would win but cannot afford to litigate because of the risk that they will also have to pay the opponent's attorney's fees." [56]

§ 1.4. Costs in § 1983 Actions: Other than Attorneys' Fees.

Generally, courts have held that prevailing parties may, as a part of the award, receive reimbursement for reasonable expenses and costs incurred during litigation. As the previous section illustrates, attorneys' fees are sometimes awarded prevailing parties as a part of costs.

In addition to attorneys' fees, courts have the discretion to make awards to cover other expenses and costs (for example, the production of maps, charts, and documents; travel expenses, food and lodging), including out-of-pocket costs incurred by the prevailing party as a *direct* part of litigation. As a rule, courts will not award costs to cover those expenses not having a *direct* relationship to the success of the litigation. *Williams, Webster,* and *Hickman* [57] offer recent, representative examples of precedent existing

---

56. Hukill, *supra* note 39, at 1.

57. *Supra* notes 7, 46 and 47. For a more recent case wherein plaintiff was awarded "out of pocket expenses," see Schreffler v. Board of Education, 506 F. Supp. 1300 (D. Del. 1981).

in public school cases for courts making awards of costs, in addition to attorneys' fees, to cover the direct expenses of prevailing parties.

§ 1.5. Exhaustion of State Remedies in § 1983 Actions.

Generally, every state provides legislative, administrative and judicial remedies for aggrieved citizens. What is more, the avenues of remedy available to citizens in pursuit of their civil rights are too numerous to list. Every now and then, however, a person will attempt to take his or her civil rights grievance directly to a federal court where remedy will be requested. The question then becomes: Will a federal court ask that plaintiff first seek remedy through existing state procedures before taking that case?

According to C. A. Wright, in his book, the traditional rule holds that a "litigant must normally exhaust state 'legislative' or 'administrative' remedies before challenging the state action in federal court." [58] However, he adds, a litigant "need not normally exhaust state 'judicial remedies.' " [59] When a federal statute so provides, however, then state judicial remedies must be exhausted.[60]

Recent interpretations of the exhaustion requirement indicate flexibility in the rule, especially where § 1983 actions are under review. Referring specifically to § 1983, D. P. Currie has said, in his book, "the statute does not require exhaustion if state remedies are 'ineffective' to protect petitioners rights." [61] Also, not only was § 1983

---

58. C. A. WRIGHT, LAW OF FEDERAL COURTS (St. Paul, Minn.: West Publishing Company, 1976), at 210.

59. *Id.* According to HOWARD, *supra* note 20: "There may be special circumstances when a federal court ought to abstain . . . to permit a state court to clarify a question of state law." *Id.* at 1.

60. *Id.* at 211.

61. D. P. CURRIE, FEDERAL JURISDICTION IN A NUTSHELL (St. Paul, Minn.: West Publishing Company, 1976), at 73.

intended to supplement existing state remedies, but to override existing state remedies if they are judged to be inadequate.[62]

Since the possibility exists that some § 1983 matters may come to the federal courts after settlement in a state court, a question may arise whether the *res judicata* principle may or may not apply.[63] Res judicata is an important tenet of our system of civil law. Translated, the term means "a thing decided," or "a matter adjudged." As applied in our system of jurisprudence the phrase refers to matters finally settled by court judgment. In other words, once a court finally decides a case (res judicata) the matter between the parties of that case is finally decided and, as a general rule, no "new suit" on the same subject may be brought by those parties.

It should be emphasized, however, that courts decide specific cases and the particular matters present in those cases. Thus, a court may dispose of an individual case (res judicata), but this may not necessarily mean the final resolution of the legal controversy represented in that case.

Speaking directly to § 1983 actions and res judicata, L. L. Levenson opines in his article that

> [t]here is little reason to fear that allowing 1983 actions after state court proceedings will permit double recovery. Section 1983 was designed, in part, to provide remedies that are not available or not commonly sought in the state forum. Further, the majority of 1983 cases which follow state proceedings are brought precisely because the state judgment did not prove satisfactory.[64]

Levenson points out, however, that the United States Supreme Court has yet to speak to this point of law.

---

62. 15 Am. Jur. 2d, *supra* note 19, at 305.

63. L. L. Levenson, *Res Judicata and Section 1983: The Effect of State Court Judgments on Federal Civil Rights Actions*, 27 U.C.L.A. Law Rev. 1977 (October 1979).

64. *Id.* at 187.

School officials should keep in mind that federal courts have limited jurisdiction. The presumption is that a federal court lacks jurisdiction unless a plaintiff can show that court that the issue presented for review involves a federal question. If no federal question is present, the matter will not be heard. As such, plaintiffs in § 1983-type suits (constitutionally or statutorily based) must establish their standing in federal court. According to M. R. Smith, in his article, "[t]he federal jurisdictional statute that empowers the federal courts to consider most Section 1983 claims is 28 U.S.C. 1343(3), but it permits only lawsuits to recover for the deprivation of rights 'secured by the Constitution of the United States or by any act of Congress providing for equal rights. . . .' " [65]

What about suits against school officials involving federal statutes that do not cover "equal or civil rights claims?" Smith suggests that these may be taken into federal court under another federal statute. "Federal statute 28 U.S.C. 1331(a) permits federal district courts to consider lawsuits involving a federal statute — including Section 1983 — if the amount in controversy exceeds $10,000. Thus, a plaintiff must claim damages greater than $10,000 in order to recover in federal court for the violation of a federal statute that does not involve equal or civil rights." [66]

One possible tactic for school boards to "avoid the $10,000 jurisdictional amount requirement," suggests Smith, "is to take the 1983-type action in a state court." [67] "State courts," he points out, "are authorized to consider lawsuits brought under Section 1983. . . ." [68] In his opinion the same tactic

---

65. M. R. Smith, *School Board Liability for Violations of Federal Rights,* 12 Sch. Law Bul. 10 (January, 1981).

66. *Id.*

67. *Id.* at 11.

68. *Id.*

may be used by plaintiff parties "to avoid the prohibition of the Eleventh Amendment. . . ."[69]

Current case law seems to indicate that exhaustion of state *administrative* remedies is more consistently held a necessary prerequisite under § 1983, unless requiring such exhaustion would, in the court's view, actually leave the plaintiff without a remedy. Such was the case in *Wagle v. Murray.*[70]

A teacher case, the United States Supreme Court vacated *Wagle*[71] and sent the case back to the Ninth Circuit Court for reconsideration in light of *Mt. Healthy v. Doyle.*[72] The fact that plaintiff teacher had not exhausted administrative remedies did not deny the teacher federal judicial review, "[s]ince such a denial would have, in fact, left the teacher without remedy."[73]

In a 1979 decision from the United States District Court, Eastern District of Virginia, the matter of exhaustion of legislative and administrative remedies was an issue. The case, *Harris v. Campbell,*[74] involved a suit brought by a parent, on behalf of her emotionally disturbed child, claiming (among other things) that school officials failed to provide her child with an appropriate education in violation of the Education for All Handicapped Children Act.[75]

As a part of his holding in the matter Judge Merhige ruled that the claims were premature. To him, "[t]he determination of whether defendants violated the Act and what

---

69. *Id.*

70. Wagle v. Murray, 546 F.2d 1329 (9th Cir. 1976).

71. *Vacated* at 431 U.S. 935 (1977).

72. Mt. Healthy City School District Board of Education v. Doyle, 429 U.S. 274 (1977), *aff'd on remand,* 670 F.2d 59 (6th Cir. 1981).

73. *Wagle, supra* note 70.

74. Harris v. Campbell, 472 F. Supp. 51 (E.D. Va. 1979).

75. *Id.* at 52.

steps they must take to correct any such violations must be brought before the local and state agencies, as required by law." [76] To put it another way, a plaintiff is required to exhaust administrative remedies under the Act before maintaining suit.

In a 1980 case involving a charge of sex discrimination against Texas A&M University, a United States district court in that state also commented on the exhaustion rule. The court said that individual plaintiffs are not required to exhaust administrative remedies before filing suit under § 901 of the Educational Amendments of 1972.[77] It is important to note that case law exists requiring finality of administrative action prior to filing suit in federal court. For example, in *Hardwick v. Ault* final school board action on a teacher dismissed was considered a prerequisite to taking an action in court under § 1983.[78]

§ 1.6. Statutes of Limitations in § 1983 Actions.

Generally, to be successful, litigation must be initiated in court within a certain period of time following an incident. This time limitation is crucial. One must look to applicable state statutes of limitations to find what the time limitations are on processing § 1983-type actions. According to *A.L.R. Federal,* "[t]he general rule ... is that state statutes of limitations are applicable to section 1983 actions. ... Ordinarily, the forum state and the state in which the action arose will be the same." [79] Where they are not, the statutes of the state where the action arose will most often be the applicable statutes.

The selection of a particular statute of limitation applicable to the matter under review has been an issue in

76. *Id.* at 55.

77. Zentgraf v. Texas A & M University, 492 F. Supp. 265 (S.D. Tex. 1980).

78. Hardwick v. Ault, 517 F.2d 295 (5th Cir. 1975).

79. 45 A.L.R. Fed. 553 (1979).

some court cases. So far the United States Supreme Court has not enumerated "standards which lower courts can consider in selecting and applying state statutes of limitations to federal civil rights actions."[80] Thus, the court hearing the matter will decide the applicability issue.

The general rule is that "state law governs the question whether an applicable statute of limitations has been tolled in a section 1983 action." [81] Some authority exists, however, that holds, "under certain circumstances a federal court in a section 1983 case may apply a federal tolling rule."[82]

In a 1976 case, *Chambers v. Omaha Public School District*,[83] a guidance counselor claimed that his employment was terminated because he was black, and because he had spoken out against the school system. Regarding the latter allegation, he claimed that the school system retaliated against him for his exercise of his first amendment right of freedom of speech. In *Chambers*, the applicability of a Nebraska three-year statute of limitation was an issue.

In upholding the applicability of the Nebraska statute, the Eighth Circuit Court ruled that

> federal courts must apply the most analogous state statute of limitations to those federally created causes of action; in making that determination, court selects the state period of limitations which best effectuates the federal policy underlying the claim.[84]

In addition to selecting a reasonable period of time to litigate the matter, the Eighth Circuit Court also stressed the selection of a statute that will "not be shown to discriminate against the plaintiff. . . ." [85]

---

80. *Id.* at 554.
81. *Id.*
82. *Id.*
83. Chambers v. Omaha Public School District, 536 F.2d 222 (8th Cir. 1976).
84. *Id.* at 223.
85. *Id. See* Clark v. Mann, 562 F.2d 1104 (8th Cir. 1977).

§ 1.7. Summary.

At a time when the courts (federal and state) are exhibiting a reluctance to exercise jurisdiction over public school employment and student matters and, at the same time, are insisting that aggrieved parties seek remedy through established administrative channels, 42 U.S.C. § 1983 represents somewhat an exception to the rule. Since the late 1960's and early 1970's, § 1983 has shown almost unlimited possibilities as both employee and student plaintiffs have successfully sought judicial remedy for what they were able to prove were invasions by public school officials of their civil rights (both constitutional and statutory).

During the coming years, as public school officials (boards and administrators) carry out their legal functions, the potential for becoming involved in a § 1983-type suit will remain a real possibility. In the opinion of the authors, 42 U.S.C. § 1983 cannot be taken casually. It may have the most potential for taking public school officials into court.

School officials who once believed that a matter of controversy (involving an employee or a student) was settled finally and firmly by either an administrative procedure or by a local or state court decision can no longer think that. Now, or at some point in time subsequent to such a decision, these same school officials may find themselves facing a § 1983-type action taken in a federal district court by that same employee or student.

Recent decisions of the Supreme Court dealing with the possible *immunity* claims of public school officials from such suits, and their employing the affirmative defense of *good faith,* have in many ways made school officials even more vulnerable in civil rights tort suits.

Chapter Two discusses in detail this expanding arena of official liability. Chapters Three and Four treat recent examples of case law on point and illustrate the application of § 1983 to teacher and student matters.

CHAPTER 2

THE ACT'S APPLICATION TO PUBLIC SCHOOL BOARDS, BOARD MEMBERS, AND ADMINISTRATORS

§ 2.0. Introduction.

Thirty years ago school board members were very secure in not fearing suits against them for the decisions they made. Although individuals challenged board members occasionally, these challenges were more often than not resolved by the courts in favor of the board members. Invariably, judges reasoned that they would not question the wisdom of board members unless it could be shown that the action taken was arbitrary, capricious or unreasonable. Judges reasoned also that a better route to overturn a school board decision would be through the ballot box rather than in a court room.

Thirty years ago school boards were not sued for negligence. The maxim "the king can do no wrong" applied to a state and its local agencies, such as local school districts. Thus, if a student was seriously injured in an accident at school, negligence could not be imputed to the board as a corporate body.

Within the past thirty years, many states have abandoned the notion that school boards do not act negligently. Whether by an act of the state legislature or through a court decision, many states now allow school boards as corporate entities to be sued when their negligent acts harm others.

As Chapter 1 illustrates, another development has transpired in approximately the last fifteen years which has changed the character of lawsuits brought against school boards and school board members. That development is the interpretation of § 1983 of the Civil Rights Act of 1871 and its application to both school boards and school board members. As demonstrated in the previous chapter, through its interpretation and because of the number and variety of court suits it has spawned, § 1983 is now responsible for a considerable part of the litigation brought by teachers and students against school boards and school board members.

The focus of this chapter is on the Act as it pertains to school boards as corporate bodies and on school board members as individuals. Initially, the Act applied only to the actions of individual school board members; later it was extended to include also the actions of the school board as a corporate body. The evolution of this development will be treated.

This chapter will cover only incidentally the wrongs which resulted in court action under § 1983. Instead, the emphasis is placed on the nature and character of decisions by school boards and school board members which prompted a court suit. The facts of a case have been included where they help in framing the legal issue before the court, but the real issue in this chapter is the nature of liability of officials or the body the officials represent.

Since the major historical developments in court of § 1983 have been determined by the Supreme Court, the major thrust of this chapter is on decisions by that court. Lower court opinions, along with those of the Supreme Court, will be treated in the next two chapters.

§ 2.1. Immunity of Governmental Officials.

(a) ELEVENTH AMENDMENT IMMUNITY.

(1) *In General.*

Tort law involving the immunity or liability of governmental officials and governmental bodies has undergone considerable change in our nation's history. At the time of the adoption of the federal Constitution, neither the range of litigious issues nor the avenues for relief were as clearly thought through as they have been since.[1] The eleventh amendment served as the basis for individuals who sought relief in court for wrongful acts committed on them by government, as well as the basis for government not entertaining suits against it by individuals.

The eleventh amendment provides:

> The Judicial power of the United States shall not be construed to extend to any suit in law or equity, com-

---

1. Article 1, § 6 of the federal Constitution grants absolute immunity to members of both houses of Congress with respect to any speech, debate, vote, report, or action taken in session. *See* Gravel v. United States, 408 U.S. 606 (1972); United States v. Brewster, 408 U.S. 501 (1972); and Kilbourn v. Thompson, 103 U.S. 168 (1881). Immunity for the executive and judicial branches of the federal government grew out of common law. *See, e.g.,* Spalding v. Vilas, in which the Court stated, "In exercising the functions of his office, the head of an Executive Department, keeping within the limits of his authority, should not be under an apprehension that the motives that control his official conduct may, at any time, become the subject of inquiry in a civil suit for damages. It would seriously cripple the proper and effective administration of public affairs as entrusted to the executive branch of the government, if he were subjected to any such restraint." 161 U.S. 483, at 637 (1896).

menced or prosecuted against one of the United States by Citizens of another State, or by Citizens or subjects of any foreign State.[2]

Historically, the amendment has been interpreted as prohibiting lawsuits in federal court against a state and its agencies, although the precise language of the amendment does not expressly provide that. Beyond that and through the years, the amendment has been interpreted to mean that it places two major restrictions on individuals who have sought to initiate suits against state government. In the first instance, it has meant that no citizen may sue a state in federal court without its consent. Second, it has also meant that no citizen may sue a state in his own state court without the state's consent.

(2) *Immunity of Local Governmental Bodies.*

Unlike states, which have enjoyed considerable immunity under the eleventh amendment, local governmental bodies have not been similarly shielded from liability. Thus, a county, municipality or local school board has not been historically immune under the amendment. Like other local governing bodies, school boards have sought to avoid liability under the eleventh amendment by claiming to be an arm of the state and, in effect, the state itself. Under this line of reasoning, when a local board of education makes a decision, it is the state itself which has acted. In general, both states and local school districts have adopted this point of view, and basic texts in local school organization and administration have supported this stance.[3] This position is

---

2. UNITED STATES CONSTITUTION, art. XI, ratified 1798.

3. Edwards has often been cited for his treatment of this relationship. He wrote: "[S]ubject to constitutional limitations, the state legislature has plenary power with respect to matters of educational policy. In the absence of constitutional prohibitions, the ends to be attained and the

also taught in many basic educational administration courses. Recently, however, courts have examined this stance, and it is currently undergoing a metamorphosis of interpretation. Within the past decade the Supreme Court has spoken on this matter, both directly and indirectly, as it applies to § 1983 suits. Specifically, in two decisions treated here briefly, the justices exploded the myth that equates a school district with a state.

In a case that did not involve a § 1983 suit, the Supreme Court examined the state-local school district relationship over the issue of local school desegregation.[4] The justices concluded that a school district and a state are not always one and the same, that is, the actions of a local school district are not necessarily the actions of a state. Based on this reasoning, the Court held that the state of Michigan was not liable or accountable for the segregation that existed in

---

means to be employed are wholly subject to legislative determination. The legislature may determine the types of schools to be established throughout the state, the means of their support, the organs of their administration, the content of their curricula, and the qualifications of their teachers. Moreover, all these matters may be determined with or without regard to the wishes of the localities, for in education the state is the unit and there are no local rights except such as are safeguarded by the curriculum. N. EDWARDS, THE COURTS AND THE PUBLIC SCHOOLS (rev. ed. Chicago: University of Chicago Press 1955) at 27. See E. C. BOLMEIER, THE SCHOOL IN THE LEGAL STRUCTURE (2d ed. Cincinnati: W. H. Anderson Co. 1973) for an extensive treatment of the American school systems in the federal, state, and local spheres; H. C. HUDGINS, JR. & RICHARD S. VACCA, LAW AND EDUCATION: CONTEMPORARY ISSUES AND COURT DECISIONS (Charlottesville: The Michie Company 1979). For treatment of this subject in general texts in educational administration, see, e.g., STEPHEN J. KNEZEVICH, ADMINISTRATION OF PUBLIC EDUCATION (3rd ed. New York: Harper and Row Publishers 1975); RONALD F. CAMPBELL, THE ORGANIZATION AND CONTROL OF AMERICAN SCHOOLS (4th ed. Columbus: Charles E. Merrill Publishing Company 1980); RALPH B. KIMBROUGH & MICHAEL Y. NUNNERY, EDUCATIONAL ADMINISTRATION: AN INTRODUCTION (New York: Macmillan Publishing Company, Inc. 1976).

4. Milliken v. Bradley, 418 U.S. 717 (1974).

Detroit, one of the state's local school districts. That reasoning is at variance with what has long been recognized, that when a local school district speaks or acts, it is the state that is speaking or acting.

More directly, the Supreme Court spoke on this matter in *Mt. Healthy,* a 1977 decision.[5] On the specific issue of whether a local school board is subject to the eleventh amendment, the Court responded: "The issue here thus turns on whether the Mt. Healthy Board of Education is to be treated as an arm of the State ... or is instead to be treated as a municipal corporation or other political subdivision to which the Eleventh Amendment does not extend." [6] The Court next concluded that "a local school board such as petitioner is more like a county or city than it is an arm of the State ... it was not entitled to assert any Eleventh Amendment immunity from suit in the federal courts." [7] The Court justified its position on the fact that, even though the school board received money and directions from the state, it had extensive powers to issue bonds and to levy taxes, making it more like a city than an arm of the state.

Since the *Mt. Healthy* decision, some lower courts have followed the thinking of the Supreme Court. For example, the Fifth Circuit ruled that a Louisiana school board is an

---

5. Mt. Healthy City School District Board of Education v. Doyle, 429 U.S. 274 (1977), *aff'd on remand,* 670 F.2d 59 (6th Cir. 1981). For a detailed treatment of this decision, *see* E. Gordon Gee, *Constitutional Rights: A View from Mt. Healthy,* SCHOOL LAW IN CONTEMPORARY SOCIETY (M. A. McGhehey, ed. Topeka: National Organization on Legal Problems of Education 1980), at 73-93.

6. *Mt. Healthy, id.* at 280.

7. *Id.* at 280-81.

autonomous political subdivision rather than an arm of the state and thus not eligible for any immunity under the eleventh amendment.[8] To date the notion that a school district and a state are not legally one and the same has not gained universal acceptance. This may be due in part to the Supreme Court's not yet having been asked to rule specifically on the question. To date the court holdings have been germane to the issue but not the central issue itself.

(3) *Immunity of Local Governmental Officials.*

Scheurer v. Rhodes[9] is a swing decision in that it distinguishes between a suit against a governmental body and a suit against a governmental official. In making its decision, the Supreme Court established that officials have considerably less protection in § 1983 suits than does a governmental body, when that suit is premised on the eleventh amendment. That is, the amendment protects a governing body — in this case, the state — when it does not protect an officer of the state.

The case involved a suit by representatives of three students killed by the National Guard in a well-publicized incident at Kent State University at the height of the student protest movement. In naming the governor and other state officials as defendants, the plaintiffs charged that they "intentionally, recklessly, wilfully, and wantonly caused an unnecessary deployment of the Ohio National Guard members to perform allegedly illegal actions which resulted in the death of plaintiffs' decedents."[10] In an unanimous opinion, the Supreme Court ruled that the defendants were sued in their individual capacities and

---

8. Moore v. Tangipahoa Parish School Board, 594 F.2d 489 (5th Cir. 1979).

9. Scheuer v. Rhodes, 416 U.S. 232 (1974).

10. *Id.* at 235.

thus were not protected by the eleventh amendment's prohibition of suits against the state.

In *Scheurer* the Supreme Court traced the historical development of the doctrine of official immunity. It cited two reasons as justification for granting immunity to public officials under the amendment: "(1) the injustice, particularly in the absence of bad faith, of subjecting to liability an officer who is required by the legal obligations of his position, to exercise discretion; (2) the danger that the threat of such liability would deter his willingness to execute his office with the decisiveness and the judgment required by the public good." [11]

Next, the Court addressed the issue of the reluctance of officials to make decisions for fear of suit. The Court's response was that timid or suit-conscious officials do not fully discharge their duties when they shun their responsibility for making decisions. School officials must also have some protection for the decisions they make, for the Court recognized that: "Implicit in the idea that officials have some immunity — absolute or qualified — for their acts, is a recognition that they may err. The concept of immunity assumes this and goes on to assume that it is better to risk some error and possible injury for such error than not to decide or act at all." [12] Two purposes will determine whether or not officials will be protected by immunity: (1) the functions and responsibilities of the defendants, and (2) the purposes of § 1983. When the Court measured these two purposes against the factual circumstances of the Kent State incident, it held that governmental officials, acting under color of state authority, could not be totally exempt from immunity.

The *Wood* decision [13] both modified and clarified

---

11. *Id.* at 240.
12. *Id.* at 242.
13. Wood v. Strickland, 420 U.S. 308 (1975).

Scheurer, which it followed. In rejecting the school board members' claim to absolute immunity in *Wood,* the Supreme Court instead adopted the standard of qualified good faith immunity. That standard, as well as the treatment of *Wood,* will be discussed in a later section of this chapter.

(4) *Immunity of State Officials.*

For a number of years § 1983 suits were initiated against various other categories of public officials before they were against school officials. Initially these suits tested the immunity of state officials, then local officials and following that, local school board members. In treating the immunity of state officials, the Supreme Court held as early as 1951 in *Tenney v. Brandhove* [14] that state legislators had absolute immunity from damages when they act in their official capacity. The plaintiff in this case had sought damages against members of the California Senate Fact-Finding Committee on Un-American Activities. He invoked § 1983 as being applicable in what he claimed to be wrongful interrogation and prosecution in the committee's investigation. The Supreme Court, speaking through Justice Frankfurter, disagreed with the plaintiff and ruled that state legislators, acting in their official capacity, enjoy immunity from suit. The Court's majority did not state what specific kinds of action are protected or might be protected, neither did the justices identify what classes of governmental officials might also be immune because of their actions.

Monroe v. Pape, [15] decided ten years after *Tenney,* extended as well as helped to clarify the applicability of § 1983 to local governmental bodies and their agents —

---

14. Tenney v. Brandhove, 341 U.S. 367 (1951).
15. Monroe v. Pape, 365 U.S. 167 (1961).

local officials. This decision has often been referred to as a pivotal case involving an interpretation of § 1983 and its applicability to local governmental bodies. Until the time of this suit, the Supreme Court had considered local governmental bodies as not being "persons" within the meaning of the Act, and consequently not liable to suit. In *Monroe* the Court distinguished between a local governmental body and a local governmental official. It held that municipal corporations cannot be held liable under the Act; however, local governmental officials could be held liable.

In treating the question of the liability of local governmental officials, the justices established in *Monroe* that there are degrees of immunity. On one level there is the degree of absolute immunity. This kind of immunity shields an individual or a governmental body from any kind of liability. The behavior of that individual or body is protected even to the degree that any kind of inquiry into the defendant's state of mind regarding his thinking or intentions is not allowed. State legislators, judges and prosecutors fall into this category and, in actions growing out of their official behavior, receive full immunity from suit.

A second degree of immunity is qualified immunity. This kind of immunity protects a defendant to a lesser degree than that covered by absolute immunity, for it allows inquiry into a defendant's state of mind after a § 1983 cause of action has been established.

An alleged illegal search by police officers instigated the *Monroe* suit. The plaintiffs charged that police officers, acting without a warrant, broke into their home early one morning, ransacked the premises, and arrested one of them. When they were charged with making an unlawful search, the police claimed not to be subject to § 1983. The Supreme Court rejected their claim of not having acted under color of the state law of Illinois and held that § 1983 provided individuals with a remedy in federal court.

In writing for the majority and in interpreting the statute, Justice Douglas, who had dissented in *Tenney*, recognized that § 1983 has three purposes: (1) to override or to supersede state laws calling openly for racial discrimination; (2) to provide individuals with a remedy in federal court where the state remedy, though adequate in theory, was not available in practice; and (3) to provide individuals with a remedy where state law is inadequate.[16] These purposes allow a complainant to initiate an action in a federal court without having to go first through a state court. At the same time, both state and federal laws can provide alternate routes to recovery for the same wrongful act.

In a later decision, the Supreme Court established in *Pierson v. Ray*[17] that state judicial officials have absolute immunity. The Court held that judges must be absolutely immune from damages for actions within their official scope of authority, a position consistent with the holding of immunity for legislators in *Tenney*.[18] The Justices took the position that the legislative history of § 1983 did not reveal any intent to abolish the common law immunity of judges.

---

16. *Tenney, supra* note 14.

17. Pierson v. Ray, 386 U.S. 547 (1967).

18. The Court stated in *Pierson* that "Few doctrines are more solidly established at common law than the immunity of judges from liability for damages for acts committed within the judicial jurisdiction, as the Court recognized when it adopted the doctrine in Bradley v. Fisher, 13 Wall. 335 (1872). This immunity applies even when a judge is accused of acting maliciously and corruptly, and it 'is not for the protection or benefit of a malicious or corrupt judge, but for the benefit of the public, whose interest it is that the judges should be at liberty to exercise their functions with independence and without fear or consequences.'" *Id.* at 554. A judge is liable for injury caused by a ministerial act; he is not liable for injury caused by a judicial function. *Ex parte* Virginia, 100 U.S. 339 (1880).

The *Pierson* suit grew out of an arrest by Mississippi policemen of fifteen white and Negro clergymen who were charged with violating a statute on breach of the peace. When they attempted to use segregated facilities at a bus terminal in Jackson, local police officers ordered them to "move on." They refused to do so, were arrested and jailed. They waived a jury trial and were each sentenced to four months in jail and fined $200. Following their vindication on appeal, the citizens (clergymen) then sued for false arrest and imprisonment.

The Supreme Court denied the petitioners' claims. Chief Justice Warren, speaking for the Court, held that common law has never granted police officers an absolute and unqualified immunity. They are entitled, however, to a defense of good faith and probable cause. The Court also held that the judge could not be held for damages under the Civil Rights Act for an unconstitutional conviction. The Court did hold that the clergymen were entitled to use the facilities of the bus terminal.

As a result of the three decisions of *Tenney, Monroe* and *Pierson,* the courts began to develop a clearer position of official immunity. That position affirmed that state officials are protected from any torts they might commit in the course of their official responsibilities. The question was no longer whether or not the Act protected state officials, but rather the degree to which the Act applied to these officials. The federal courts gradually began to provide some answers to this question. Initially, the rulings were mixed; there was no unanimity among the courts of appeal that ruled on this question. For example, in 1964 the Fifth Circuit held that absolute immunity applied when an official acted within the scope of his employment when he took the action involved.[19] In contrast, the Eighth Circuit provided for no

---

19. Norton v. McShane, 332 F.2d 855 (5th Cir. 1964).

immunity for any public official sued under the Act.[20] The reasoning of the Third Circuit followed more closely that of the Fifth Circuit rather than the Eighth Circuit when, in 1974, it allowed absolute immunity to all public officials who performed discretionary acts.[21]

By the mid-1970's the doctrine of immunity had been established, but it was less than clear as to who was clothed with immunity and, when clothed, for what kinds of action. The *Wood* decision of 1975 brought into focus these conflicting rulings.

(b) QUALIFIED GOOD FAITH IMMUNITY.

The *Wood v. Strickland* decision,[22] which followed the decisions treated in the previous section of this chapter, helped to clarify to some extent the reach of the law with respect to local school board members and their liability. It is a significant case in that, unlike the previous decisions in this chapter which treated the liability of state officials and local officials other than school board members, this case spoke directly on the issue of the liability of local school board members. The Court's holding made it possible for students to sue school board members for a violation of their constitutional rights. For the first time the Supreme Court addressed the degree of protection that local school board members have under § 1983 as well as the conditions under which they may lose their immunity. Unlike previous decisions affirming absolute immunity for selected state officials, *Wood* enunciated a new standard of immunity, qualified good faith immunity, a condition that provides

---

20. Board of Trustees v. Davis, 396 F.2d 730 (8th Cir. 1968).

21. Fidtler v. Rundle, 497 F.2d 794 (3d Cir. 1974). The Fifth Circuit has held that state officials cannot assert a qualified good faith immunity when their actions clearly violate established state law. William v. Treer, 50 U.S.L.W. 2590 (April 13, 1982).

22. *Wood, supra* note 13.

some degree of security. At the same time, that standard of immunity serves as a warning to school board members that their actions will be carefully scrutinized.

(1) *The Due Process Issue.*

The central issue of the *Wood* case was the plaintiffs' contention that their procedural due process rights had been violated. The students made this charge after the school board expelled them for the remainder of the school term without a proper due process hearing. The students charged that they were entitled to this right under the fourteenth amendment.

The facts of the *Wood* case involved three secondary school students who, in violation of school policy, brought alcoholic beverages to their campus, mixed them with soft drinks, and served the mixture at a social hour. The teacher-sponsor learned of the incident ten days after it happened, confronted the girls, and they confessed. After reflection, the teacher advised the girls to report the matter to the principal, which they did. The principal promptly suspended the girls for the maximum two-week period, subject to a decision by the school board.

The same day of the suspension, the school board met in the evening and considered the matter. At this meeting neither the girls nor their parents attended. Both the teacher and the principal recommended leniency until it was learned that one of the girls had been in a fight that same evening at the school's basketball game. The leniency recommendation was withdrawn and the school board voted to expel the girls for the remainder of the semester — approximately three months. The school board made its decision on the basis of information the members received from school officials; there was no presentation of facts from the girls and their parents, nor was there any opportunity for them to make a statement or rebut any of the charges. In short, the girls did not have any procedural due process.

The school board also voted to consider the exclusion matter at a meeting two weeks hence. This time the girls, their parents, and counsel attended and requested that the school board lighten its punishment. The board refused to do so; instead, it reaffirmed its earlier decision. The issue was resolved the second time without any of the elements of a due process hearing; rather, there was evidence that the board had already arrived at its decision prior to the meeting.

Following the school board action, the girls brought a § 1983 suit against the school board members as individuals, as well as against two administrators. The administrators were later dropped from the suit, leaving only the school board members as defendants. The suit charged that these individuals had denied the students their rights to due process under the federal Constitution.

The lower federal courts disagreed over the standard of immunity that should apply in this case. At the district court level,[23] the jury failed to reach a verdict and the judge entered a directed verdict for the school officials. The judge applied a subjective standard-of-immunity test. This test involves proof of malice on the part of the defendants, that is, showing that the defendants actually intended to harm the plaintiffs. Since this element could not be proven, the defendants were held to be immune from suit.

On appeal, the Eighth Circuit reversed,[24] rejected the subjective standard applied by the district court, and relied

---

23. Strickland v. Inlow, 348 F. Supp. 244 (W.D. Ark. 1972).
24. Strickland v. Inlow, 485 F.2d 186 (8th Cir. 1973).

on an objective standard-of-immunity test. This test involves a showing that one has not violated another's settled constitutional rights. One of these rights is that of due process, found in the fourteenth amendment. In applying the objective standard to the specific case, the court ruled that the students had been denied due process and remanded the case for a new trial on the issue of damages.

The school board then appealed to the Supreme Court and a decision was rendered in early 1975. In deciding whether the objective or the subjective standard should be used in determining liability, the Court actually elected not to take either polar position. Instead, the majority stated:

> As we see it, the appropriate standard necessarily contains elements of both. The official must himself be acting sincerely and with a belief that he is doing right, but an act violating a student's constitutional rights can be no more justified by ignorance or disregard of settled, indisputable law on the part of one entrusted with supervision of students' daily lives than by the presence of actual malice.[25]

(2) Standards of Immunity for School Board Members.

While the *Wood* decision established that students in public schools are entitled to due process, it pronounced a more noteworthy standard. In its narrowest sense, the Court held that failure to recognize and honor the rights of students in exclusionary hearings could result in the liability of school board members. In a much broader sense, *Wood* established a new standard in determining if board members were subject to liability under § 1983. Justice White, who wrote the majority opinion, held that board members would not be held liable for knowing and respecting the constitutional rights of their students. In addressing the

---

25. *Wood, supra* note 13, at 321.

immunity standard, White stated:

> To be entitled to a special exemption from ... 1983 ... a school board member, who has voluntarily undertaken the task of supervising the operation of the school and the activities of the students, must be held to a standard of conduct based not only on permissible intentions, but also on knowledge of the basic, unquestioned constitutional rights of his charges. Such a standard imposes neither an unfair burden upon a person assuming a responsible public office requiring a high degree of intelligence and judgment for the proper fulfillment of its duties, nor an unwarranted burden in light of the value which civil rights have in our legal system.[26]

Next, the Court applied the standard to instances where school board members lose their immunity, specifically with respect to the discipline of students.

> [I]n the specific context of school discipline, we hold that a school board member is not immune from liability for damages under § 1983 if he knew or reasonably should have known that the action he took within his sphere of official responsibility would violate the constitutional rights of the students affected, or if he took the action with the malicious intention to cause a deprivation of constitutional rights or other injury to the student.[27]

What emerged from the above statement of the Court was a declaration of three conditions that may result in a board member's liability:

(1) Knowingly violating a student's constitutional rights. Disregard of what is recognized as settled law is no defense; a board member is legally bound to make decisions consistent with current law.

---

26. *Id.* at 322.
27. *Id.* at 322.

(2) Unknowingly violating a student's constitutional rights. That is no excuse if a school board member should have known what the law was on a given subject. Ignorance of settled constitutional law is no more excuse than intentional violation of what is settled law. Impliedly, there is a burden on school board members to know what current law is.

(3) Acting on the basis of malice. A board member will lose any immunity he might otherwise have had if he sets out intentionally to harm a student, acts out of vindictiveness, or decides an issue on a spiteful motive.

After affirming the rights of students to bring suit against school board members, the Court then sought to reassure board members that not every decision they make on student disciplinary matters will result in a tort suit. The Court set forth the following two conditions, one that may and one that may not result in a board member's liability. A board member may be liable for compensatory damages if he acted "with such an impermissible disregard of the student's clearly established constitutional rights that his action cannot reasonably be characterized as being in good faith." [28] The Court did not explain what constitutes "established constitutional rights" and what is the meaning of "good faith." On the other hand, board members are not expected to anticipate how courts will rule on constitutional matters not yet decided. This position is consistent with the Court's holding in *Pierson v. Ray* when Chief Justice Warren wrote, "We agree that a police officer is not charged with predicting the future course of constitutional law." [29]

The key element of the *Wood* decision is its standard of liability. The Court adapted the standard of "good faith" from *Scheuer v. Rhodes,* decided one year earlier, and cre-

28. *Id.* at 322.
29. *Pierson, supra* note 17, at 557.

ated a new one, a "qualified good faith" standard. The latter standard recognizes that school board members do and must have some immunity for their actions. They are entitled to errors for, in making decisions, it may be better for them to make some mistakes as opposed to avoid making any decision. The Court affirmed this stance in stating that "action taken in the good-faith fulfillment of their [school board members] responsibilities and within the bounds of reason under all the circumstances will not be punished and that they need not exercise their discretion with undue timidity." [30] Thus, when board members act sincerely and with a belief that they are doing right, they are protected in § 1983 suits by the standard of qualified good faith immunity.

The *Wood* decision has raised a number of questions about the meaning of qualified good faith immunity. The decision has been criticized for its lack of specificity in describing the areas whereby a board member may be held liable. In addition to the meaning of "qualified good faith," the definition of "settled indisputable law" has been perplexing to those affected by the decision. The Court enunciated these standards but failed to define them with any degree of precision. The elusiveness of the phrase, "settled indisputable law" has given rise to a number of hypothetical questions, questions that any conscientious board member should ponder.

Are board members required to be familiar with the latest decisions handed down by various courts? Is there a reasonable period of time between a decision's being handed down and before board members have the opportunity to become familiar with it? Is a board member expected to be more familiar with a court decision from a higher court than

---

30. *Wood, supra* note 13, at 321.

he is from a lower court? If courts are in disagreement on
the same basic issue, is a board member bound only by the
jurisdiction of the court in which he resides? If one's own
court has not ruled on an issue, is a board member expected
to be familiar with the holding of a court in a different
jurisdiction? For purposes of a board member's knowledge of
settled law, do holdings of inferior (lower) courts carry the
same weight as the decisions of higher courts? Does the
weight of a decision have any effect on a school board member's immunity, that is, are there degrees of decisions,
ranging from major to minor, with board members
expecting to be more familiar with the major decisions than
with the minor decisions? If a board member makes a
discretionary decision rather than a directory decision,[31] is
a board member subjected to the same standard of qualified
good faith immunity? Is there such a thing as a minor violation of the constitutional rights of another person? Some of
these questions will be answered in the next two chapters
in the context of suits brought by teachers and students.

The justices in the minority held that the Court had not
been faithful to the holding of *Scheuer.*[32] Speaking through

---

31. HUDGINS & VACCA, *supra* note 3, at 54, define a discretionary decision as "one which requires judgment of the board. Such action involves
debate and discussion, and it is expected that a board deliberate fully
before agreeing on an issue. Most of the board's actions fall within this
category. Discretionary action cannot be delegated to a committee of the
board, to subordinate educators, or to other agencies." A directory decision is "a provision in a statute, rule of procedure, or the like, which is
a mere direction or instruction of no obligatory force, and involving no
invalidating consequence for its disregard as opposed to an imperative or
mandatory provision, which must be followed." Blacks Law Dictionary
(rev. 4th ed. St. Paul: West Publishing Co.). More recent decisions supporting this holding are: Whiteside v. State, 534 F. Supp. 774 (E.D. Wash.
1982) and Starstead v. City of Superior, 533 F. Supp. 1365 (W.D. Wisc.
1982).

32. Justice Powell wrote a dissenting opinion with whom the Chief

Justice Powell, the minority charged that too harsh a burden is placed on school officials which requires of them sufficient knowledge of what is characterized as settled, indisputable law. The minority also objected to the fact that the majority did not describe just what constitutes settled, indisputable law. In the third instance, the minority charged that school officials are being held to a standard of behavior that involves forecasting what conduct will be constitutionally protected.

Although the justices were divided on the meaning of good faith immunity, they were unanimous on another issue in *Wood.* On the second issue they rejected the notion that school board members have absolute immunity under § 1983. The justices observed that absolute immunity is not necessary. If board members were to have it, "it would not sufficiently increase the ability of school officials to exercise their discretion in a forthright manner to warrant the absence of a remedy for students subjected to intentional or otherwise inexcusable deprivations." [33] What resulted from *Wood* was a standard of immunity for reasonable conduct, but no immunity for other kinds of conduct. That is the essence of the term "qualified good faith immunity."

§ 2.2. Liability of School Boards as Persons.

When § 1983 was first made applicable to education, the class of defendants was limited. *Monroe* in 1961 established the precedent that while officials within a governmental body could be held liable, the governmental body that the officials represent could not be held liable. That reasoning grew out of the Supreme Court's interpretation of the Act that reads "every person . . . ." In *Monroe* the Court

---

Justice, Justice Blackmun, and Justice Rehnquist joined, concurring in part and dissenting in part.

33. *Wood, supra* note 13, at 321.

51

interpreted that phrase to attach only to individuals and not to the corporate body. Insofar as school boards are concerned, the distinction was a crucial one. It meant that school boards *qua* school boards could not be sued, but school board members could be sued in their individual capacities. Thus, if a teacher's or student's constitutional rights were violated, that individual could have legal recourse against school board members but not against the board.

The *Monroe* principal remained the law of the land from 1961 to 1978. In 1978 the Supreme Court reversed itself and held that municipalities and other local governmental bodies, including school boards, can be sued under § 1983. Specifically, *Monell v. Department of Social Services* [34] held that the above local entities are not immune from suit if, out of law or custom, they violate the constitutional rights of their employees.

The *Monell* ruling is a limited one in that the Court refused to impute liability to a municipal corporation solely because it employs an individual who violates another's constitutional rights. Sarah W. J. Pell points out, in her article, that the Court suggested two justifications for its holding: "(1) if an employer knew that actions could be held up to legal scrutiny, and that employer, if indeed in error, could be held liable for violations of an individual's Constitutionally protected rights, the employer might avoid 'accidents' in judgment; and (2) liability costs *can* be paid." [35]

Monell originated as a class action suit in New York City by female employees of the Department of Social Services

---

34. Monell v. Department of Social Services, 436 U.S. 658 (1978).

35. Sarah W. J. Pell, *Liability of School Board Members,* SCHOOL LAW FOR A NEW DECADE (Topeka: National Organization on Legal Problems of Education 1981), at 19.

and the city Board of Education. The plaintiffs sought injunctive relief and back pay for the defendants' actions in compelling them, as pregnant employees, to take unpaid leaves of absence from their jobs before they were medically required to do so.[36]

The district court ruled [37] that the plaintiffs' claim for equitable relief was moot because both the Department of Social Services and the Board of Education had changed their policies after the suit had been initiated. On the issue of back pay, the court ruled that, based on the *Monroe* holding, the city could not be required to award the plaintiffs monetary damages. The court of appeals affirmed.[38]

On appeal to the Supreme Court, and speaking through Justice Brennan, the justices overturned the lower court's holdings. They held that a local governmental body can be sued if the action alleged to be unconstitutional was a result of a "government's policy or custom, whether made by its lawmakers or by those whose edicts or acts may fairly be said to represent official policy, inflicts the injury that the government as an entity is responsible under § 1983." [39] The Court did not define what kinds of official policy or

---

36. This practice had been ruled unconstitutional by the Supreme Court four years earlier in Cleveland Board of Education v. La Fleur, 414 U.S. 632 (1974). The court held that an arbitrary cutoff date by school officials violates due process since the provisions create a presumption that every teacher who is four or five months pregnant is incapable of continuing her duties. A cutoff date is more reasonable when determined by the teacher and her physician.

37. Monell v. Department of Social Services, 394 F. Supp. 853 (S.D.N.Y. 1975).

38. Monell v. Department of Social Services, 532 F.2d 259 (2d Cir. 1976).

39. *Monell, supra* note 34, at 694.

customs would result in liability of local governmental bodies for their unconstitutional actions. The only clues the Court gave for an interpretation of "policy" or "custom" was that the action would be "responsible for" or the "moving force" behind the constitutional violation. The kind as well as the degree of involvement necessary to establish the liability of a municipality was left unanswered.

To a limited degree, the Court explained what constitutes "custom." Even though a custom may not have received formal or official sanction through a local government's legislative channels, it may involve "persistent and widespread . . . practices . . . of officials." [40] Beyond that, the Court did not make a statement on the precise nature of these practices.

Ken Ballen suggests in his article that there are three kinds of conduct which can render a local governmental body subject to liability under § 1983. They include affirmative denials of protection, passive denials of protection, and unacceptable standards of conduct.[41]

(1) *Affirmative denials of conduct.* This kind of conduct involves the enactment of unconstitutional legislation. For example, a dress code for faculty that would require all females to wear dresses and forbid their wearing slacks and would forbid males from growing beards would be in conflict with § 1983.

(2) *Passive denials of protection.* This kind of conduct involves the failure of local government to protect the constitutional rights of another. For example, the repeated insistence of building school administrators in enforcing a dress code as stated above, with the knowledge of school

---

40. *Id.* at 691.

41. Adapted from Ken Ballen, *Municipal Liability Under Section 1983: The Meaning of "Policy or Custom,"* 79 COLUMBIA LAW REVIEW 315 (March 1979).

board members, and the acquiescence of the board to this practice, would constitute a passive denial of protection.

(3) *Unacceptable standards of conduct.* This kind of conduct involves also the failure of local government to protect the constitutional rights of another. For example, if local school board members knew that a dress code was to become effective at one or more schools, and if the members refused or neglected to take any action to prevent a constitutional violation, they may be subject to a § 1983 suit. This third kind of conduct differs from the second in that it focuses on preventing from being enacted a constitutionally impermissible action rather than stopping an action that had already been adopted.

The significance of *Monell* can be seen in that it now allows individuals whose rights have been violated by a governmental agency to sue that agency for equitable and monetary relief. The agencies potentially liable for this holding include, among others, local school boards, for the Supreme Court specifically held that school boards are not to be distinguished from a municipality for the purposes of a § 1983 suit. Consequently, like municipalities, school boards are now considered as being "persons" under § 1983 and can be held liable for their policies and customs if either or both of them cause an individual to be deprived of his constitutional rights.

The Supreme Court in *Monell* did not address the question of the entitlement of local governmental units to the qualified good faith immunity accorded public officials under the *Wood* holding until it treated the matter only one year later. In the meantime, a number of lower courts acted on this issue after *Monell* in which judges extended the good faith immunity to include not only individuals but also local governmental entities. That is, these local governing bodies were held to be immune if the officials acted without malice and consistent with settled, indisputable law. That trend in the lower courts was very short-lived, however, when the Supreme Court was faced with that issue and rejected that position in *Owen.*

In *Owen v. City of Independence* [42] the Supreme Court established that local governing bodies are more vulnerable to suits under § 1983 than are their officers. They are not entitled to the standard of good faith immunity. The Court held that, unlike governmental bodies, governmental officials may continue to enjoy the good faith immunity. Thus, on this latter issue, the justices acted consistently with their holding in *Wood.*

The facts of *Owen* are rather involved and, for the purposes of understanding the case, bear repeating here. Owen had been serving an indefinite term as police chief when an investigation into his managerial competencies revealed some administrative irregularities but no violations of criminal law. Owen's superordinate, the city manager, reviewed the report of the investigation and gave the police chief two choices: accept a lower position or be fired. Alberg, the city manager, then submitted a report on the matter to the mayor and city council without making any reference in the document to Owen. In the meantime, Owen consulted an attorney and, based on the attorney's advice, demanded of the city manager a written notice of charges and the opportunity to respond at a public hearing. During this time Roberts, one of the city councilmen, requested and received a copy of the report. At the next council meeting he presented a prepared statement containing four allegations: (1) Owen had taken television sets belonging to the police department; (2) there had been a mysterious disappearance of narcotics and money from Owen's office;

---

42. Owen v. City of Independence, 445 U.S. 622, *rehearing denied,* 446 U.S. 993 (1980).

(3) he had manipulated traffic tickets; and (4) there had been inappropriate requests of the police court by high-ranking police officers. Unlike the city manager's report, the councilman's report directly implicated Owen by name. Following the Roberts' presentation, the council then decided to release the investigative reports to the news media, the grand jury, and the city manager, and for Alberg to "take all direct and appropriate action" against those persons "involved in illegal, wrongful, or gross inefficient activities brought out in the investigative reports." [43]

The next day Alberg dismissed Owen. None of the above four charges had been proven and the city manager gave no reasons for his action. However, the news media linked Owen's dismissal with the investigation of the property losses in the department. In the meantime the grand jury, upon receipt and investigation of the report, did not return an indictment. Neither the city manager nor the city council took any further action; neither released the investigative reports to the public.

Owen initiated a suit in which he charged the city, the city manager, and the city council members in their official capacity with a deprivation of liberty and property without due process. He asked for a hearing on the reasons for his discharge, back pay effective from the date of his discharge, and attorneys fees.

The trial court ruled against Owen.[44] It held that he had no property interest in his job, that he had no continued right to public employment, and thus was not entitled to notice and a hearing. It ruled also that his discharge did not deprive him of a liberty interest. There had been no stigma

---

43. *Id.* at 628-29. Councilman Roberts' statement is reproduced in full at 421 F. Supp. 1110, 1116 (W.D. Mo. 1976).

44. Owen v. City of Independence, 421 F. Supp. 1110 (W.D. Mo. 1976).

attached to his dismissal since no question had been raised about any illegal or immoral conduct. Having established these conditions, the court held that Owen was not entitled to a hearing for purposes of clearing his name.

Following his adverse ruling, Owen then appealed to the court of appeals. The Eighth Circuit disagreed in part with the district court's holding, principally on the interpretation of Owen's liberty interest.[45] It held that Owen had been deprived of his liberty interest without due process, based on the fact that the city council had released false charges against Owen at the time of his dismissal. That rationale did not justify, however, the circuit court's overturning the district court's decision; on the contrary, the court of appeals sustained the lower court's judgment that the dismissal was proper. It declared that the city was entitled to immunity because its officers had acted in good faith and without malice. Owen's appeal followed.

The Supreme Court held that local governmental bodies are not entitled to qualified good faith immunity.[46] When these bodies violate, either through policy or custom, a person's constitutional rights, the governmental body is not entitled to immunity from damages. Further, the governmental body may not rely on the good faith of its officers as a defense to its own liability under § 1983. The officers are entitled to immunity if they acted in good faith, a position the Court took in *Wood* and which was not altered by the

---

45. Owen v. City of Independence, 560 F.2d 925 (8th Cir. 1977) and 589 F.2d 335 (8th Cir. 1978). The court of appeals concluded that the primary justification for a qualified immunity — the fear that public officials might be reluctant to discharge their duties for fear of the possibility of personal liability — does not exist where the relief would be borne by the governmental entity rather than by the individual officer.

46. The Court ruling was 5-4 with Justice Powell filing a dissenting opinion, in which Justices Stewart, Rehnquist, and the Chief Justice concurred.

Owen decision. But, the good faith immunity of public officers does not extend to the governing body. Even if the officers could not predict that their actions would be declared unconstitutional, the governing body they represent can still be held liable, according to the *Owen* holding.

Speaking for the Court and specifically to the immediate question in Owen's case, Justice Brennan found that the city councilman's harmful statements at the council meeting and the council's resolution — although neutral on its face, occurring nevertheless at the time of Owen's discharge — constituted official governmental action. These circumstances harmed Owen's reputation and resulted in a deprivation of his liberty without due process of law.

The Supreme Court saw that the city council had erred in meddling in personnel affairs that were not properly within its jurisdiction. Neither the council nor any one of its members had any authority over Owen's discharge. In fact, only the city manager had the exclusive authority to discharge Owen. The council also overstepped its authority when it released to the public allegedly false statements that damaged Owen's reputation. That action entitled Owen to a name-clearing hearing, a guarantee of due process of law.[47] One is not ordinarily entitled to such a hearing when there is no public disclosure of the reasons for the employee's discharge.

The city council did not directly damage Owen's reputation. However, council members indirectly

---

47. In a decision handed down approximately three months prior to Owen's discharge, the Supreme Court ruled that a discharged public employee is entitled to a hearing to clear his name if his employer makes a public statement that might severely damage his reputation and standing in the community. Roth v. Board of Regents, 408 U.S. 564 (1972).

contributed to the problem with the way the council reacted to the behavior of one of its members. That member's independent accusations of Owen in public were never proven and they directly injured his reputation. Following the accusation, the council discussed the matter and adopted a motion by the accusing councilman to turn over the investigative reports to the news media, an action which implicated them by association. Unlike the one councilman directly and the corporate council indirectly, the city manager did not damage Owen's reputation by any public disclosure.

The *Owen* decision is a strong statement for the protection of individuals' constitutional rights, in this instance, the right of due process. Had the Supreme Court ruled differently, it would have left individuals without the legal remedy which Congress intended in enacting § 1983. Furthermore, a contrary ruling may not have deterred local governments from enacting policies and engaging in practices likely to violate one's rights.

One of the significant outcomes of the *Owen* decision is that liability for official governmental action is now concentrated more in the governmental body than in its employees. The decision makes it easier for an individual to sue the governmental body rather than its officers. As applied to a public school district, this means that a school board member, acting in good faith and without malice, is immune from suit while, for the same action, a school board member may be held liable. One of the trends to look for in the 1980's in court cases involving § 1983 is an increasing number of suits filed against school boards rather than against board members.

In order to prevent the possibility of a number of lawsuits against school boards made possible by the *Owen* holding, Michael R. Smith, in his article, offers two suggestions to board members. Both suggestions affect the behavior of board members at an open session of a board meeting. (1) School board members and administrators should say nothing at open sessions of board meetings that might damage an employee's reputation. Such discussions should transpire only in executive session. (2) If a board member makes a defamatory statement about an employee at a board meeting, the other board members should take some official action to indicate that the member is not speaking for the board; they may even go so far as to disassociate themselves with the statement. Smith suggests that the Supreme Court may have ruled differently in *Owen* had the city councilman adopted a different strategy from what he used. Instead of presenting his charges at an official meeting of the council, he could have called a press conference and denounced the police chief at it. By adopting the councilman's motion, the city council gave tacit approval to his defamatory charges which were aired prior to the resolution which led to the termination of Owen.[48]

The final case in this section involved, like *Owen,* a 1980 decision in which the Supreme Court interpreted § 1983. It went beyond *Owen,* however, in making it easier for individuals claiming deprivations under § 1983 to seek relief in court. Whereas the Act had previously been interpreted as affording a remedy to individuals whose *constitutional rights* had been violated, *Maine v. Thiboutot*[49] extended that interpretation to be applicable also to individuals whose federal *statutory rights* had been violated.

The Supreme Court decision stopped short of holding that all federal laws come under the penumbra of § 1983.[50] The

---

48. Michael R. Smith, *School Board Liability for Violation of Federal Rights,* 12 Sch. Law Bul. 11 (January 1981).

49. Maine v. Thiboutot, 448 U.S. 1 (1980).

50. *See, e.g.,* Rosado v. Wyman, 397 U.S. 397 (1970) in which the Court

justices ruled that where a federal statute provides an exclusive judicial remedy, § 1983 does not apply. Conversely, § 1983 suits may be premised on violations of federal statutory laws that do not provide equitable or compensatory relief to employees from their employers.

The plaintiffs in this case challenged the state of Maine for the actions of the state's Department of Human Services in computing welfare benefits. The plaintiffs were advised that they were entitled to benefits for only three of their children; they were not entitled to benefits for the remaining five.[51] The parents disagreed with the ruling, charged that the defendants had incorrectly interpreted the Social Security Act, and initiated a § 1983 suit. The Supreme Judicial Court of Maine agree with them.[52] Appeal followed.

In deciding for the parents, the Supreme Court increased the scope of protection to individuals under federal law. Individuals may now have access to redress for violations of both constitutional provisions and selected statutory laws. The Supreme Court made this possible through its interpretation of that part of § 1983 that reads, "secured by the

----

held that suits in federal court under § 1983 are proper in securing compliance with the Social Security Act on the part of participating states; Edelman v. Jordan, 415 U.S. 651 (1974); Monell v. Department of Social Services, 436 U.S. 658 (1978) in which the Court ruled that § 1983 was intended to provide a remedy, broadly construed, against all forms of official violation of federally protected rights, presumably to include federal statutes.

51. The married couple had eight children, three of them were the husband's by previous marriage. The Maine Department of Human Resources determined that the couple was entitled to benefits under the Social Security Act only for the three children exclusively his, even though the husband was legally obligated to support the other five as well.

52. Thiboutot v. State, 405 A.2d 230 (Me. 1979).

Constitution *and laws*. . . ." (Emphasis added.) The question was whether the phrase "and laws" referred to a subset of laws such as acts of Congress or whether it referred only to provisions of the Constitution. After examining the congressional history and debate on the Act and after concluding that the intent of Congress could not be determined, the Supreme Court ruled that "and laws" was intended to include acts of Congress.

The Court's decision increases the likelihood of more people filing § 1983 suits, particularly in view of the Court's interpretation of the expanded scope of the Act. There are, however, conditions which govern the initiation of such suits. These conditions govern jurisdiction, the nature of the deprivation, and the amount of damages sought. First, one must show that a federal statute authorizes the federal courts to entertain such a suit. Second, a § 1983 suit must be premised only on the deprivation of a right secured by the Constitution or by an act of Congress involving equal or civil rights.[53] If a plaintiff claims damages in excess of $10,000 he must assert that the claimed deprivation did not involve equal or civil rights, in which case a different statute applies.[54]

§ 2.3. Liability of School Administrators.

Case law on suits under § 1983 has been directed much more against policymakers than against policy implementers. Suits have been filed against those whose laws or policies were responsible for the constitutional violation rather than against those individuals who implemented them.

In determining where officials or administrators might be

---

53. 28 U.S.C. § 1343(3).
54. 28 U.S.C. § 1331(a).

culpable, courts look more to the nature of the act rather than the status of the person. If school officials have absolutely no authority under state law to engage in conduct outside their sphere or responsibility, then they may be liable for doing so when that activity leads to the denial of a protected right of a teacher or student. For example, in *Lucia v. Duggan* a teacher was dismissed for having grown a beard.[55] Although there was no published policy on this matter, the school committee gave the teacher a choice — remove the beard or be terminated. There was no evidence that the teacher's performance was anything but satisfactory. The court held the school committee as individuals and the superintendent liable, and they were ordered to compensate the teacher for his salary for the time during the school term when he was out of work.

School administrators are protected under § 1983 when they act in implementing state laws and school board policies. When they act in this capacity, school administrators serve as the agents of others — the state and the school board. Where a clear violation can be established under law or policy, it is the body or the individuals of that body making the law or policy who are responsible rather than the executioners of the law or policy.

To date, the great preponderance of § 1983 suits have been filed against school boards and school board members rather than superintendents and principals. Plaintiffs in these suits have alleged, successfully or not, that laws and policies were designed to restrict rights to which they were otherwise entitled. School administrators may feel somewhat secure in the limited number of suits against them; they should also be fully aware that they are not immune from such suits.

---

55. Lucia v. Duggan, 303 F. Supp. 112 (D. Mass. 1969).

§ 2.4. Damages.

The purpose of awarding damages under § 1983 is to compensate those who have been injured through a violation of their constitutional rights. "To the extent that Congress intended that awards under § 1983 should deter the deprivation of constitutional rights, there is no evidence that it meant to establish a deterrent more formidable than that deterrent in the award of compensatory damages." [56]

This section will treat the issue of damages as the Supreme Court has examined it. An extensive treatment will not be given here, for the subject has already been considered in Chapter 1 and it will also be considered in the next two chapters in conjunction with suits brought by teachers and students. The focus of this section will be specifically on damages assessed officials in their individual capacity and damages assessed a corporate body. The criteria used in determining under what conditions damages can be assessed will also be treated. Three cases in particular will be reviewed: *Carey v. Piphus*, decided in 1978; *Owen v. City of Independence*, decided in 1980; and *Fact Concerts v. Newport*, decided in 1981.

Both *Carey* and *Owen* considered the issue of compensatory damages, but each case involved a different class of defendants. *Carey* [57] involved damages against school board members as individuals; the suit did not seek damages against the board in its corporate capacity.

---

56. Imbler v. Pachtman, 424 U.S. 409, 442 (1976). *See also* United States *ex rel.* Tyrrell v. Speaker, 535 F.2d 823 (3d Cir. 1976); United States *ex rel.* Larkins v. Oswald, 510 F.2d 583 (2d Cir. 1975); Magnett v. Pelletier, 488 F.2d 33 (1st Cir. 1973); Stolberg v. Members of Board of Trustees, 474 F.2d 485 (2d Cir. 1973); Donovan v. Reinbold, 433 F.2d 738 (9th Cir. 1970).

57. Carey v. Piphus, 435 U.S. 247 (1978).

Owen [58] involved damages against a corporate body and not
against the members of that body. *Fact Concerts* involved
punitive rather than compensatory damages. Each case will
be treated in turn with applications to school board members
and to the board itself.

(a) DAMAGES ASSESSED INDIVIDUAL BOARD MEMBERS.

Section 1983 clearly provides that a litigant may bring
suit under the Act for compensatory damages as well as for
equitable relief. When the Act was first interpreted as being
applicable to school personnel, only equitable relief was
asked for, but in more recent years both relief as well as
compensatory awards have been sought. In order to establish a compensatory award, it must first be proven that a
plaintiff was entitled to the exercise of a constitutionally
protected right and that that right was denied him. After
these two conditions have been met, the court must then
determine if one is entitled to an award for damages. *Carey*
addressed the question of damages as it relates to the deprivation of rights of students. The Supreme Court has not yet
addressed the question of damages as it relates to the deprivation of rights of teachers, but it has been addressed in a
number of lower courts, as will be seen in Chapter Three.

Carey treated two issues: the conditions that warrant the
awarding of damages to students, and the amount of damages that can be assessed local school officials for having
violated a student's constitutional rights. It was a consol-
idation of two cases that resulted from the suspension from
school of two students in unrelated incidents. The common
element of them was that each student was suspended
without first being given due process. This lack of due process was the basis for the court action.

---

58. *Owen, supra* note 42.

In one of the incidents, a freshman was believed to be smoking marihuana on campus. The principal saw two students passing back and forth an irregularly shaped cigarette and, approaching the boys unnoticed, he detected what he believed was an odor of burning marihuana. He also saw one boy try to pass off a packet of cigarette papers to the other student. In observing the principal, the boy threw the cigarette into a nearby hedge. The principal directed a twenty-day suspension for the boy's having violated the school's rule against use of drugs on campus. The school sent a suspension notice to the boy's mother and a conference was later held with her. It should be noted, however, that the conference was held, not to determine the guilt or innocence of the boy, but to explain the reasons for the suspension. The boy denied that he had been smoking marihuana, and his suit which followed sought damages in the amount of $3,000.[59]

The second incident involved a sixth-grade boy who wore an earring to school, a violation of a school regulation. The principal justified the rule on the basis that the prohibition tended to minimize the activity of gangs within the school. The student asserted that wearing the earring bore no relationship to membership in a gang, rather it was a symbol of black pride. The principal informed the boy and his mother that failure to remove the earring would result in a twenty-day suspension. When the youngster refused to remove the earring, the principal imposed the suspension without first conducting a due process hearing. Through his

---

59. The suit named as defendants, individually and in their official capacities, the school principal, the General Superintendent of Schools, the City of Chicago, and the members of the Board of Education of the City of Chicago.

parents, he sued and sought damages in the amount of $5,000.[60]

The federal district court [61] held that both students had been denied procedural due process. It also held that the school officials were not entitled to good faith immunity because they should have known that a suspension of this length without any hearing would be a violation of due process. The court refused, however, to award damages because there was no evidence in the record to quantify their damages.

The court of appeals reversed.[62] It held, substantively, that the students would not be entitled to recover damages for the time missed in attending school if school officials could (1) show that there was just cause for the suspension, and (2) establish that they would have been suspended even if a proper hearing had been held. The court ruled further that even if suspensions had been justified, the students would still be entitled to recover substantial nonpunitive damages because they had been denied due process.

On appeal before the Supreme Court, the major question was whether a plaintiff must prove that he was actually injured by a deprivation of a right to which he is entitled before he can recover substantial nonpunitive damages. These kinds of damages cover such elements as emotional distress and similar harms. In answer to this question, the Court agreed 8-0 that the students were entitled only to nominal damages in the absence of any proof of actual

---

60. The suit named also the above parties as defendants as well as the Illinois Superintendent of Public Instruction. The District Court granted the latter party's motion to dismiss.

61. Data are from the opinion of the Court of Appeals in that the decision of the district court is apparently unreported.

62. Piphus v. Carey, 545 F.2d 30 (7th Cir. 1976).

injury.[63] As Justice Powell, writing for the Court, observed, any kind of deprivation of procedural due process may cause some injury, but compensation should be tailored to the interests protected by the particular right in question. Since the right to procedural due process is absolute, its denial should be cause for action without proof of actual injury. The Court then held that, if the action of school officials was justified, the students should be entitled to damages of one dollar. The Court's decision was thus an affirmation for the protection of the rights of students, but it was also a warning to students that they could not expect to win damage awards for mere denial of constitutional rights. There must also be a showing that the student was actually injured by the denial of the right. Since no showing could be made in either instance, the damages of one dollar became a symbolic award.[64]

(b) DAMAGES ASSESSED THE CORPORATE BODY.

The *Owen* decision [65] of 1980 also treated the issue of damages, but it was not the pivotal issue in the case. The pivotal issue was whether governmental bodies, like their officers, are entitled to good faith immunity. A more comprehensive statement of the facts of the case, which were very involved and which relate to the major question before the Court, appeared earlier in this chapter. For a

---

63. Justice Blackmun took no part in the consideration or decision of this case.

64. The awarding of nominal damages is not without precedent. A number of lower federal courts have approved the awarding of nominal damages under § 1983 where actual injury was not shown, even though constitutional rights had been violated. See Thompson v. Burke, 556 F.2d 231 (3d Cir. 1977); United States *ex rel.* Tyrrell v. Speaker, 535 F.2d 823 (3d Cir. 1976); Magnett v. Pelletier, 488 F.2d 33 (1st Cir. 1973); Bell v. Gayle, 384 F. Supp. 1022 (N.D. Tex. 1974); United States *ex rel.* Myers v. Sielaff, 381 F. Supp. 840 (E.D. Pa. 1974).

65. *Owen, supra* note 42.

wrongful dismissal from his job, a police chief brought charges against various city officials as well as the city as a coporate body. With respect to whether the dismissed police chief was entitled to damages, the Supreme Court applied the following standard: a local government may be liable only if the constitutional violation is caused by public officers or employees in the execution of official governmental policy or custom made by the governmental body or by someone whose acts may be said to represent official policy. More specifically, as applied to Owen's case, the Court held that a city may be required to pay damages for depriving a public employee of liberty without due process of law if the employee is discharged without a public statement of reasons by the officer who has the sole authority to discharge that individual. The city may also be required to pay damages if a city officer, without responsibility to discharge employees, makes independent statements at the time of the termination of the employee that injures his reputation.

The Court's determination of when a governmental body may be liable for damages has three distinct applications to local boards of education.

(1) A school board may be liable for damages if it violates the constitutional rights of teachers or students. The violation may have resulted either from the board's official policy or custom.

(2) A school board may be liable for damages if one or more of its members, acting in an official capacity, violate the constitutional rights of teachers or students. This standard is explained more fully in another section of this Chapter.

(3) A school board may be liable for damages if an employee (for example, a principal) assumes responsibility not rightfully his and violates the constitutional rights of teachers or students.

70

Although *Owen* sought damages against both the city and various city officials, the Supreme Court held that the officials were entitled to good faith immunity and thus were not liable. No such immunity attached to the city.

Another major Supreme Court decision on the issue of damages arose out of Newport, Rhode Island.[66] It raised the issue of whether § 1983 was intended to allow punitive damages against a municipality. Since the Court had already determined that compensatory damages could be awarded against a corporate body,[67] *Newport* sought to extend previous rulings. The Court divided 6-3, the majority holding that punitive damages could not be assessed.[68] Speaking for the majority, Justice Blackmum held that neither a history of the Act nor policy considerations justify "exposing a municipality to punitive damages for the bad faith actions of its officials." [69]

The case arose over a concert scheduled for the city by Blood, Sweat and Tears. The group had been booked as a replacement for another group which had cancelled. When they learned of the appearance of Blood, Sweat and Tears, the mayor and the city council sought to cancel the performance on the basis of possible disturbances in the city. Fact Concerts, a corporation promoting the concert, justified the group's appearance on the grounds that it is a jazz band and not a rock group, and that it had appeared in Carnegie Hall and other symphony halls throughout the world.[70] In spite of this defense, the council voted to cancel

---

66. City of Newport v. Fact Concerts, Inc., 101 S. Ct. 2748 (1981).

67. *Monell, supra* note 34.

68. Justice Brennan filed a dissenting opinion and was joined by Justices Marshall and Stevens.

69. *Newport, supra* note 66, at 2757.

70. Under the terms of the contract, Fact Concerts was to retain control over the choice of performers and the type of music played. The city reserved the right to cancel the license if, in its opinion, the interests of public safety demanded it.

the program unless Blood, Sweat and Tears were removed from it. Council later relented and agreed to the group's appearance if it did not play rock music. The day before the scheduled performance, the mayor advised the council that it had two options: (1) allow Blood, Sweat and Tears to perform, subject to its not playing rock music, or (2) cancel the concert. Council decided to cancel the concert for two reasons.[71] Fact Concerts then successfully enjoined the mayor and the council from interfering with the performances, and the concerts were held without incident. However, only half the tickets were sold.

In bringing suit, Fact Concerts named the city, mayor, and six council members as defendants, charging content-based censorship and a violation of rights under § 1983. It sought compensatory and punitive damages under § 1983 and claims for tortious interference under state law.

At trial, the jury awarded the plaintiffs compensatory damages of $72,910 and punitive damages of $275,000.[72] Following this decision, the city asked for a new trial on two grounds. First, it argued that punitive damages cannot be awarded under § 1983 against a municipality; even if they can, the amount was excessive. Second, the city challenged the judge's charge to the jury awarding punitive damages, but this objection had transpired at the time of post-trial motions and not at the time the judge formally charged the jury. This prompted the district court to rule that the charge was untimely. The district court elected not to distinguish

---

71. Council asserted that Fact Concerts had not fulfilled all its agreement in that it had not fully wired together the spectator seats and it had not put an auxiliary generator in place.

72. Of the $275,000, $200,000 was charged the city and $75,000 was charged among the 6 councilmen and the mayor.

between fines against a municipality and fines against an individual.

The court of appeals affirmed.[73] Although it noted that the challenge to the damage award was flawed, that matter should be overlooked only when there is a plain error that has seriously affected the fairness and integrity of a judicial proceeding. The court did not find these conditions present.

Before the Supreme Court, the justices in the majority agreed to hear the case on both the procedural question and on its merits. The procedural question was disposed of quickly and the justices moved to the merits of the case. In doing so, they examined two elements: the history of § 1983 and public policy considerations.

With respect to the history of § 1983, Justice Blackmun noted that there was nothing in the record to indicate that Congress had intended to do away with the immunity of state officials; instead, there had been "immunities of varying scope applicable to different officials sued under the statute."[74] Section 1983 was designed to expose certain state and local officials to a new form of liability. When § 1983 was enacted, the immunity of a municipal corporation for punitive damages was not seriously considered and that notion has persisted to today. "In general, courts viewed punitive damages as contrary to sound public policy, because such awards would burden the very taxpayers and citizens for whose benefits the wrongdoer was being chastised."[75]

The Court then distinguished between two kinds of damage awards. There are, first, damages to compensate for injuries received, those damages being shared by the

---

73. Fact Concerts, Inc. v. City of Newport, 626 F.2d 1060 (1st Cir. 1980).

74. *Newport, supra* note 66, at 2759.

75. *Id.*

offending officer and the municipality. Second, there are vindictive damages as punishment for bad faith conduct, those damages being assessed only against the offending officer. Justice Blackmun concluded that the public was protected from unjust punishment and the municipalities from undue fiscal restraints.

The Court concluded that, had Congress wished to abolish the Act, it would have specifically done so.

With respect to public policy considerations, the Court noted that punitive damages serve a limited purpose. They are directed, not at the injured party, but to the tort-feasor in order to deter him and others from engaging in like conduct. Consequently, punitive damages against a municipality punishes the taxpayers, not the wrongdoer. When a municipality is taxed, it is likely that there will be either an increase in taxes or a reduction of services for citizens.

Under § 1983, if a governmental official maliciously or knowingly deprives another of his civil rights, that official may be the object of the municipality's vindictiveness. "A municipality can have no malice independent of the malice of its officials. Damages awarded for punitive purposes are not sensibly assessed against the governmental entity itself." [76]

Rather than penalize a municipality for the wrongful actions of one or more of its agents, the Court suggested that a more appropriate alternative might be to discharge the offending official, or, punitive damages could be assessed directly against the offending official.

The three justices in the minority would not have considered the matter since the petitioners had failed to raise

---

76. *Id.* at 2760.

the issue until after the trial court had rendered its decision. They did not see anything unique about the case that would warrant the Court's review under the notion of "special circumstances." The justices would have affirmed the holding of the court of appeals.

§ 2.5. Summary.

The last two decades have resulted in a significant number of changes with respect to court interpretation of the litigious nature of school boards and school board members. During the period encompassing 1961 to 1981, court decisions have increased considerably the vulnerability of both school boards and school board members for the actions either may have taken which resulted in a deprivation of rights of a teacher or a student. The courts established this vulnerability through a series of interpretations of § 1983 of the Civil Rights Act of 1871 as it applies to state and local officials serving in a superordinate capacity and to governmental bodies as corporate entities.

Initially, § 1983 was interpreted as meaning that only individuals were subject to suit under the Act. This interpretation grew out of the meaning of the word "person" in the Act. Later, the word "person" was interpreted to include also corporate bodies, in this instance, local boards of education. Thus, as of 1981, both school boards and school board members as individuals can be sued for depriving one in their employ of his duly protected rights.

Suits against school boards and school board members can take one of two tacts. They can be premised on specific action that either of them took or the failure of either of them to take appropriate action. The action can involve a specific denial of a right, or it can involve the failure to correct a subordinate for not respecting the rights of those whom he is supervising. Impliedly, board members must be cognizant of the rights of teachers and students, must observe these rights, and must be knowledgeable of the extent to which administrators are also observing and respecting these rights.

It is now possible for individuals to bring suit against school boards and school board members for a deprivation of both constitutional and statutory rights. So long as it can be established that an individual has a right under the federal Constitution and that a governmental official acted in some way to deny the exercise of that right, the harmed individual can bring suit. To be successful in a § 1983 suit on a deprivation of a right secured by federal law, it must be established that the act in question does not provide one with an exclusive remedy. That is, if the act provides a specific mechanism for redress, one cannot initiate a § 1983 suit. Section 1983 is applicable only in those instances in which one has no other recourse.

The relief that teachers and students can get under a successful § 1983 suit takes two forms. First, one can bring a suit in equity in which an injured individual can seek merely to have the deprivation removed. Second, a successful litigant can also seek damages. The Supreme Court has not spoken definitively on the awarding of damages to teachers; it has held that students are entitled only to a symbolic award if their rights have been violated and if they suffered no injury from the deprivation. Lower courts have awarded damages in a number of instances and for a variety of deprivations. Compensatory damages may be assessed against an individual or against the corporate body; punitive damages may be assessed against an individual but not against the corporate body for the wrongful actions of one of its officials.

The criteria for determining liability of school boards and school board members vary. School boards are subject to stricter standards than are board members. Whereas board members are entitled to a qualified good faith immunity, the board as a corporate body is not. Furthermore, the board may be liable not only for its official policies, but also for its customs which have been a part of its decision-making and practices. Unlike boards, school board members are subject to a less rigorous standard of liability. They are entitled to a standard of qualified immunity, also known as good faith immunity. That standard shields a board member from suit if he acted sincerely, with a conscientious belief that he was doing right, consistent with settled law, with no intent to harm anyone, and with no malice. Given these conditions, the criteria allow board members considerable opportunity to reflect on whether they are doing right.

Courts have made it clear that school boards should not be hesitant in making decisions as opposed to their risking the possibility of a lawsuit. In fact, avoiding decision-making may reflect a dereliction of duty. In spite of this reassurance, courts have not recently given school boards the security they need in making decisions. Instead, recent opinions have created a climate whereby board members must wonder if the actions they take will result in a challenge in court.

Courts have made it increasingly clear that local school boards cannot continue to seek the protective security of the state, for no longer do courts automatically equate a local school district with a state. Whereas a state may not be subject to a suit on the basis of the eleventh amendment, a local school district may be subject to such a suit. The immunity of a state may not mean the immunity of a local school district.

Unlike school boards and school board members, school administrators are considerably less vulnerable to § 1983 suits. When they follow duly enacted board policies in good faith, superintendents and principals are unlikely to be

sued; it is the makers of the policies who are more subject
to suit. However, when administrators make decisions
which have the effect of policy and these decisions remove
or curtail a teacher's or a student's constitutional rights,
these administrators are subject to suit.

CHAPTER 3

TEACHERS AND § 1983

§ 3.0. Introduction.

Until recent years, nonintervention of judges in public school personnel matters stood as a case hardened principle of school law. The period beginning in the late 1960's and ending in 1976, however, marked an era of increased judicial involvement in public school personnel administration. Beginning with the Supreme Court's famous statement in the landmark student rights case, *Tinker v. Des Moines, Independent Community School District,* that "teachers and students do not shed their rights at the school house gate,"[1] school boards and administrators, in addition to

---

1. 393 U.S. 503 (1969). As Delon, *infra,* reminds us, "[p]rior to the 1960's, restrictions on school authorities' handling of personnel matters were minimal. If, for example, a school board decided to dismiss an overly critical teacher or principal for insubordination, the courts would seldom intervene. About the only basis for a successful challenge of these actions was the board's failure to follow procedures specified in state statutes." F. G. Delon, *Coping Legally with Teachers' Criticisms,* 9 NOLPE SCH. LAW BUL. 99 (1981).

adhering to state mandated tenure guarantees, found that their personnel decisions had to comply with emerging federal civil rights employment decrees.

Referred to as the post-*Roth* and *Sindermann* era (so named to reflect the United States Supreme Court's landmark teacher rights decisions in *Board of Regents v. Roth* [2] and *Perry v. Sindermann* [3]), the period had a conditioning effect on the once unlimited discretionary authority of public school officials over personnel. Tenured and nontenured professionals alike who could establish a clearly implied promise of continued employment (property interest), or who could establish some legitimate claim of entitlement to continued employment (property interest), or who could show that their termination imposed a stigma that foreclosed on their freedom to pursue their profession (liberty) found that they were entitled to basic procedural due process (notice, cause, hearing) as a part of the termination process.

The United States Supreme Court's decision in *Bishop v. Wood*,[4] however, marked a turning point in teacher rights. A non-school case decided originally by a United States district court in North Carolina, *Bishop* had a direct bearing on teacher statutory and constitutional protections. Writing for the majority, Justice Stevens set in place a posture of non-interference in school personnel decisions by federal judges when he said:

> The federal court is not the appropriate forum in which to review the multitude of personnel decisions that are made daily by public agencies. We must accept the harsh fact that numerous individual mistakes are inevitable in the day-to-day administration of our affairs. The United States Constitution cannot feasibly

2. 408 U.S. 564 (1972).
3. 408 U.S. 593 (1972).
4. 426 U.S. 341 (1976).

be construed to require federal judicial review for every such error. In the absence of any claim that the public employer was motivated by a desire to curtail or to penalize the exercise of an employee's constitutionally protected rights, we must presume that official action was regular and, if erroneous, can best be corrected in other ways. The Due Process Clause of the Fourteenth Amendment is not a guarantee against incorrect or ill-advised personnel decisions.[5]

Numerous cases have been heard by the lower federal courts since *Bishop.* Emerging from the decisions in such cases is a definite pattern of judicial attitudes toward public school personnel decision-making. Some of these attitudes are: a reluctance of federal judges to take school personnel cases; an insistence that aggrieved parties seek remedy elsewhere before bringing their complaint in federal court; an initial presumption that personnel actions taken by school officials were taken in good faith; and a reluctance to intervene in the decisions made by school officials absent a showing that their actions were motivated by an intent to curtail, violate or penalize an employee's exercise of constitutionally or statutorily protected rights.

Decided on September 18, 1980, *Lee v. Washington County Board of Education*[6] (a case wherein an Alabama Teachers Association, with the NEA as plaintiff-intervenor, sought review of certain local school board decisions to determine whether they were in accord with a prior desegregation order), offers an excellent statement demonstrating the typical attitude of contemporary federal courts regarding matters of faculty and staff employment. In the opinion of the Fifth Circuit,

> The internal affairs of a local school system should be administered by its elected or appointed authorities,

---

5. *Id.* at 349.
6. 625 F.2d 1235 (5th Cir. 1980).

not by federal courts. . . . However, where a local school authority discriminates unconstitutionally against an individual or a class of individuals, it becomes the court's duty to fashion appropriate relief.[7]

In recent years, § 1983 (when applicable) has become alternative action for advocates in their attempts to take teacher cases into the federal courts. Since the mid-1970's, § 1983-type cases have proliferated as teachers have claimed that they have been wronged by *abuses* of board and administrative authority.

§ 3.1. Teacher Rights and § 1983.

Generally, public school teachers have had success in seeking remedy under § 1983 as an alternative action. According to K. Alexander in his book:

> Traditionally, teachers could recover damages or ask for judicial relief in specific performance in accordance with contract law, but more recently the Civil Rights Act of 1871 has come into play as an alternative action. As with students' denial of a constitutional right, a teacher is protected by the Act and violation may result in damages. Monetary damage is not difficult to prove for the teacher who has been deprived of employment by denial of a right or interest. If, for example, the future employability of the teacher is harmed by action of a school board or official, the damages could be quite substantial.[8]

The applicability of § 1983 is not dependent upon a teacher's holding bona fide tenure status in a public school system. As the Seventh Circuit held in *McLaughlin v. Tilendis* even though plaintiff teachers did not have tenure, the Civil Rights Act of 1871 gives them remedy if their

---

7. *Id.* at 1237.

8. K. ALEXANDER, SCHOOL LAW (St. Paul, Minn.: West Publishing Co., 1980), at 629-30.

contracts were not renewed because of their exercise of constitutional rights.[9] To nonrenew, dismiss, or otherwise punish a teacher (tenured or not) for constitutionally impermissible reasons will not stand.

More recently, a federal district court in Minnesota heard a suit brought by a former superintendent of schools. Employed for one year under an annual contract, at the time of his nonrenewal the superintendent had been in the field of education for thirty years (fifteen of which he had served as a superintendent of schools).[10]

Alleging a cause of action for violation of his civil rights and for breach of contract, he sought remedy under § 1983. His claim failed.

Since plaintiff was untenured, and since he had neither an express nor implied contract for reemployment, said the court, he had no property interest in jeopardy. Also, no evidence was introduced at trial to show that his "good name, reputation, honor or integrity" were at stake. Finally, in the court's opinion, no evidence was introduced that the superintendent's termination "was based on vindictive or maliciously inspired reports without basis in fact." [11] Generally, the burden of proof rests on the plaintiff to establish that this condition exists.

To put it another way, even though the superintendent could not demonstrate a property interest in continued employment, his cause of action would have been successful had he either demonstrated a violation of liberty, or if he could have demonstrated by the preponderance of evidence

---

9. 398 F.2d 287 (7th Cir. 1968). *See* Cherry v. Burnett, 444 F. Supp. 324 (D. Md. 1977).

10. Tatter v. Board of Education, 490 F. Supp. 494 (D. Minn. 1980).

11. *Id.* at 496. "An act or failure to act is maliciously done if promoted or accompanied by ill will, or spite or grudge, toward the injured person." Schreffler v. Board of Education, 506 F. Supp. 1300 (D. Del. 1981).

that the board's nonrenewal decision did not rest on fact, or that its decision was made either maliciously or vindictively.

§ 3.2. The *Mt. Healthy* Causation Standard.

A § 1983-type case involving the nonrenewal of a nontenured male teacher in Ohio, *Mt. Healthy City School District Board of Education v. Doyle* [12] established a judicial standard that has greatly conditioned school board authority in personnel matters. The standard, created by Justice Rehnquist, is commonly referred to as the *test of causation* and has brought much needed clarity to situations associated with the issues of teacher nonrenewal and dismissal.

In 1971, Mr. Doyle had been advised by his school board that he would not be rehired because of his "lack of tact in handling professional matters." The board's decision not to rehire was based upon the following incidents: an altercation between Doyle and another teacher; an argument between Doyle and some school cafeteria workers; Doyle's swearing at students and using obscene gestures to female students; and his conveying to a radio station the substance of a principal's memorandum relating to teacher dress and appearance, whereupon the radio station announced, in the form of a "news item," the adoption of the dress code.[13]

Doyle brought a § 1983 action in federal district court seeking reinstatement and damages. In his complaint he alleged that the board's refusal to rehire him violated his rights under the first and fourteenth amendments. The district court granted Doyle relief, convinced that the telephone call was "clearly protected by the First Amendment"

---

12. 429 U.S. 274 (1977), *aff'd on remand,* 670 F.2d 59 (6th Cir. 1981).

13. *Id.* at 274.

and, because it had played a "substantial part" in the decision not to rehire Doyle, he was entitled to reinstatement with back pay. The United States Court of Appeals for the Sixth Circuit affirmed that decision and the United States Supreme Court granted certiorari.[14]

After considering several jurisdictional questions, Justice Rehnquist proceeded to consider Doyle's claim under the first and fourteenth amendments. Relying on *Roth* and *Sindermann* he began with the following statement concerning Doyle's nontenured status:

> Doyle's claims under the First and Fourteenth Amendments are not defeated by the fact that he did not have tenure. Even though he could have been discharged for no reason whatever, and had no constitutional right to a hearing prior to the decision not to rehire him ..., he may nonetheless establish a claim to reinstatement if the decision not to rehire him was made by reason of his exercise of constitutionally protected First Amendment freedoms.[15]

In an effort to evaluate whether or not the speech of a government employee is "constitutionally protected," said Justice Rehnquist, a need exists to strike

> a balance between the interests of the teacher, as a citizen, in commenting upon matters of public concern and the interest of the State, as an employer, in promoting the efficiency of the public services it performs through its employees.[16]

Thus, since Doyle's communication to the radio station had violated no established board policy, and since the board's response to the communication was *ad hoc* in nature, the Supreme Court agreed with the district court decision that

---

14. *Id.* at 276.
15. *Id.* at 283-84.
16. *Id.* at 284. Here Justice Rehnquist is quoting directly from Pickering v. Board of Education, 391 U.S. 563 (1968).

found Doyle's communication as protected by the first and fourteenth amendments.[17] However, said Justice Rehnquist, the Court was not "entirely in agreement with that court's manner of reasoning from this finding to the conclusion that Doyle was entitled to reinstatement with back pay." [18]

To answer the question as to whether an employee has a right to reinstatement to his or her position, Rehnquist suggests that courts must apply a three-part "test of causation." First, a court must be shown by the employee that his or her conduct was constitutionally protected. Second, the court must determine whether an employee's exercise of that constitutionally protected right (*e.g.,* speech) played a "substantial part" in the board's actual decision not to renew his or her contract. Third, the board and administration must demonstrate to the court that they not only could, but in fact would have reached the same decision not to rehire the employee had the exercise of the constitutionality protected conduct not existed.[19] Application of the test of causation, states Rehnquist, helps a court "distinguish between a result caused by a constitutional violation and one not so caused." [20]

In rendering the Court's final decision to vacate the judgment of the appeals court and to remand *Doyle* for further proceedings, Justice Rehnquist made it clear that in such cases as this one it is proper for a court to place the burden of proof on the employee to show that his conduct was constitutionally protected. It is also proper to require the employee to show that his exercise of constitutionally protected behavior was the "motivating factor" in the board's

---

17. *Id.* at 284.
18. *Id.*
19. *Id.* at 285.
20. *Id.*

decision not to rehire him. Finally, a court must determine, based upon evidence presented, whether the board has shown that it would have reached its decision not to rehire the employee absent the employee's exercise of constitutionally protected conduct.[21]

§ 3.3. Freedom to Speak and § 1983.

Of the basic civil rights afforded all citizens of this nation, the first amendment right to speak remains one of our most cherished freedoms. Similarly, the freedom to speak has always held an exhalted place in the academic community — especially in American public education.

A review of teacher litigation from the past fifteen years reveals that this basic first amendment entitlement has been the subject of numerous § 1983-type cases involving teacher activity both inside and outside school. What makes these first amendment teacher issues complex is that while some cases involve speech as verbal expression, others involve speech in written form, and still others involve instances of symbolic speech (*i.e.,* appearance). A common thread running through these cases, however, is that plaintiff teachers must not only be prepared to show that the board's decision had a discriminatory *impact,* but also that the board's *intent* was to discriminate against the teacher.[22]

(a) THE *PICKERING* STANDARD.

More than a decade ago, the Supreme Court created a standard to be employed by the courts below to balance a teacher's first amendment right to speak with a school

---

21. *Id.* at 287. For a more recent case on point involving the standard of causation and the allocation of the burden of proof, see Avery v. Homewood City Board of Education, 674 F.2d 337 (5th Cir. 1982).

22. G. A. Caplan, *Employment Discrimination: A Survey,* SCHOOL LAW FOR A NEW DECADE (M.A. McGhehey ed., Topeka, Kan.: NOLPE, 1981), at 38.

board's countervailing interest to limit that right. The benchmark case on point was *Pickering v. Board of Education*. Not a § 1983 case, *Pickering* involved a public school teacher in Illinois who was dismissed from employment for sending a letter to a local newspaper critical of his school board and district superintendent.[23]

Deciding in favor of the teacher-appellant (that he could not constitutionally be dismissed from his teaching position because of his letter writing), the Supreme Court established the following standard. To uphold a school board's action in such cases, evidence would need to establish that either the teacher's exercise of speech was detrimental to the efficient operation and administration of the school district, or that the teacher knowingly and recklessly made false statements about his board and administration.[24]

Also significant in *Pickering* is the Supreme Court's statement that teachers should be free to speak in school "without fear of retaliatory dismissal."[25] The notion of "retaliatory dismissal" has played a significant role in subsequent first amendment cases, and will be discussed further in subsequent sections of this chapter.

(b) Verbal Expression as Speech.

No court has ever held that one's right to speak is absolute. Such factors as time, place and manner join together with content to produce a definite conditioning effect on one's right to speak. Similarly, no court has ever ruled that academic freedom is not without reasonable limitations. As E. C. Bolmeier said more than a decade ago in his book:

---

23. *Pickering, supra* note 16.

24. *Id.* at 571-72.

25. *Id.* For an excellent discussion of the *Pickering* standard and teacher citicisms, see Delon, *supra* note 1.

A public school teacher possesses certain rights and freedoms enjoyed by all citizens. As a citizen he has the legal right to speak, think, and believe as he wishes. As a public school teacher, however, he must exercise these and other legal rights with due consideration of the effects upon others — particularly school children.[26]

In 1973, a federal district court in Texas ordered a teacher reinstated with lost salary after he had been dismissed for public remarks to a city council and board of trustees about his concern over community and economic problems affecting teachers and students in the district. Granting relief under § 1983, the court was of the opinion that teachers should be entitled to relief even if the board action was only partially in retaliation for constitutionally protected activities.[27] Similarly, in a 1977 case, a teacher was dismissed for openly criticizing the school board and administration. At a board meeting the school board alleged that her dismissal was based on her classroom performance, not as a result of her public statement. Brought in federal district court under § 1983, the district court held that violations of state law and the state's constitution were present, not violations of federal law and the United States Constitution. Therefore, remedy was to be found in a state court.[28]

More recent case law has established that a teacher's freedom to exercise his or her right to speak out must not be inhibited under the *guise* of "protecting the children," or because of some *unfounded fear* of disruption of the daily activities of the school; one's constitutional protection is not limited solely to public speech but is applicable to private

---

26. E. C. BOLMEIER, TEACHERS' LEGAL RIGHTS, RESTRAINTS AND LIABILITIES (Cincinnati, Ohio: W. H. Anderson Company 1971), at 1.

27. Lusk v. Estes, 361 F. Supp. 653 (N.D. Tex. 1973).

28. Branch v. School District, 432 F. Supp. 608 (D. Mont. 1977).

settings as well. An excellent case on point is *Givhan v. Western Line Consolidated School District.*[29]

A case actually tried before *Mt. Healthy (see* § 3.2, *supra), Givhan* came to the United States Supreme Court in much the same posture as that case did. While *Givhan* was pending an appeal before the Fifth Circuit, however, *Mt. Healthy* was decided, and the *causation standard* ultimately played an important part in the final resolution of that matter.

Bessie Givhan was dismissed from her employment as a junior high school English teacher at the end of the 1970-71 school year. At the time of her termination, her school district was the subject of a desegregation order entered by the United States District Court for the Northern District of Mississippi. Ms. Givhan filed suit as an intervenor in the desegregation suit and complained that she had been terminated by reason of her exercise of first amendment rights.[30]

At trial, in an effort to show that its termination decision was justified, the school district introduced evidence of, among other things, a series of private encounters between Ms. Givhan and her school principal in which she allegedly made "petty and unreasonable demands" in a manner described by the principal as "insulting," "hostile," "loud," and "arrogant."[31] In two footnotes in the *Supreme Court Reporter,* the following information is included:

> In a letter to petitioner dated July 28, 1971 District Superintendent C. L. Morris gave the following reasons for the decision not to renew her contract:
>
> > (1) [A] flat refusal to administer standardized national tests to the pupils in your charge; (2) an

---

29. 439 U.S. 410 (1979).

30. *See* Ayers v. Western Line Consolidated School District, 404 F. Supp. 1225 (N.D. Miss. 1977).

31. Givhan, *supra* note 29, at 412.

announced intention not to co-operate with the administration of the Glen Allan Attendance Center; (3) and an antagonistic and hostile attitude to the administration of the Glen Allan Attendance Center demonstrated throughout the school year. In addition to the reasons set out in the District Superintendent's termination letter to petitioner ... the School District advanced several other justifications for its decision not to rehire petitioner . . ."(1) that Givhan 'downgraded' the papers of white students; (2) that she was one of a number of teachers who walked out of a meeting about desegregation in the fall of 1969 and attempted to disrupt it by blowing automobile horns outside the gymnasium; (3) that the school district had received a threat by Givhan and other teachers not to return to work when schools reopened on a unitary basis in February, 1970; and (4) that Givhan had protected a student during a weapons shakedown ... in March, 1970, by concealing a student's knife until completion of a search. . . ."[32]

Regarding the above four justifications, evidence on the first three was later shown as "inconclusive;" and, even though Givhan admitted the fourth incident, there was no evidence ever presented at trial that the principal "relied on it in making his recommendation" not to renew the contract.[33]

After a two-day bench trial, the United States District Court ordered that Bessie Givhan be reinstated. In that court's view, Givhan's termination had violated the first amendment. The court found that she had made her demands on but two occasions, and that the demands were neither "petty" nor "unreasonable." All of her complaints involved employment policies and practices at the school

---

32. The information included in both paragraphs of this quotation is taken directly from *Givhan, supra* note 29, at 411-12, nn.1, 2.

33. *Givhan, supra* note 29, at 412, n.2.

which Givhan conceived to be racially discriminatory in purpose or effect.[34]

In its concluding statement the district court said,

> the primary reason for the school district's failure to renew [petitioner's] contract was her criticism of the policies and practices of the school district, especially the school to which she was assigned to teach.[35]

Thus, the district court held that the dismissal violated the first amendment.

The United States Court of Appeals for the Fifth Circuit reversed the decision.[36] Not finding the lower court's findings clearly erroneous, the appellate court concluded, however, "that because petitioner had privately expressed her complaints and opinions to the principal, her expression was not protected under the First Amendment." [37] In that court's opinion *Pickering, Perry,* and *Mt. Healthy* contain the strong implication "that private expression by a public employee is not constitutionally protected." To give this protection to public employees, the judges said, "would in effect force school principals to be ombudsmen, for damnable as well as laudable expressions." [38]

The United States Supreme Court granted certiorari and ultimately reversed the Fifth Circuit Court of Appeals. *Givhan* was remanded so that the contentions of the parties could be considered, freed from "[t]his erroneous view of the First Amendment." Said Mr. Justice Rehnquist, for the majority,

---

34. *Givhan, supra* note 29, at 411-12.

35. The district court is quoted at 439 U.S. 412-13 in the *Givhan* opinion.

36. *See* Ayers v. Western Line Consolidated School District, 555 F.2d 1309 (5th Cir. 1977).

37. *Givhan, supra* note 29, at 413.

38. *Id.* Here the court utilized the previous decisions of *Pickering, supra* note 16; *Perry, supra* note 3; and *Mt. Healthy, supra* note 12.

The First Amendment forbids abridgment of the "freedom of speech." Neither the Amendment itself nor our decisions indicate that this freedom is lost to the public employee who arranges to communicate privately with his employer rather than to spread his views before the public. We decline to adopt such a view of the First Amendment.[39]

In the high court's view, the *Mt. Healthy* claim in this case called for a factual determination which could not be resolved by the court of appeals.[40]

Aebisher v. Ryan [41] is a 1980 decision of the Second Circuit wherein both *Givhan* [42] and *Pickering* [43] were seen as controlling.

Decided on June 2, 1980, *Aebisher* involved an appeal taken by two public school teachers of a summary judgment by a United States district court in favor of school officials. The teachers brought their action seeking remedy for what they claimed was a violation of their first amendment rights. More specifically, the two teachers said that letters of reprimand had been placed in their personnel files by their principal in retaliation for their having spoken out in the press.

One of the teachers, a tenured junior high school teacher, had been attacked by a fourteen-year-old female student as she attempted to put the student out of her classroom. The student dragged the teacher out into the hallway "scratching and beating her about the face. . . ." The teacher "suffered facial scratches and face wounds and allegedly permanent injuries to her neck and thumb." [44]

---

39. *Id.* at 415-16.
40. *Id.* at 417.
41. 622 F.2d 651 (2d Cir. 1980).
42. *Supra* note 27.
43. *Supra* note 16.
44. *Aebisher, supra* note 41, at 652.

Not long after the incident a reporter for a local newspaper telephoned the injured teacher. The reporter and the teacher discussed the situation, but the teacher never named the student nor did she give the student's age.[45] The reporter next contacted the other of the two appellants (a tenured social studies teacher who was also serving as president of the local teachers union). She also discussed the incident with the reporter.[46] The reporter later contacted the superintendent of schools with regard to the incident. Based upon his conversations, the reporter wrote a news release for publication in the local paper. The article appeared on June 30, 1977.[47]

When the two teachers returned to their jobs in September, 1977, they were summoned separately to their principal's office. The principal told each that she "had acted unprofessionally and with poor judgment in discussing the attack with a reporter."[48] Subsequently, in October the principal delivered to each a letter criticizing their conduct. These "letters of reprimand" were placed permanently in their personnel files.[49]

The two teachers were unsuccessful in their attempts to have the letters removed. They obtained a lawyer and ultimately filed suit under §§ 1983 and 1985, "alleging conspiracy to violate and violation of their First Amendment free speech rights and their Fourteenth Amendment due process rights."[50] Remedy sought consisted of both declaratory and injunctive relief, removal of the letters from their files, formal public apologies from defendant school officials, and monetary damages. The district court judge

---

45. *Id.*
46. *Id.*
47. *Id.* at 653.
48. *Id.*
49. *Id.*
50. *Id.* at 654.

ruled in favor of the school officials and held that the "minimal discipline imposed" was justified.[51] An appeal was then taken to the Second Circuit.

Beginning its opinion with a reiteration of the traditional attitude that the federal courts are "reluctant to intervene in conflicts that arise in the daily operation of the public schools . . .,"[52] the Second Circuit assumed a typical post-*Bishop* attitude. Judicial intervention in such conflicts, said the court, is warranted whenever "basic constitutional values" are "directly and sharply implicated."[53] In this case, said the court, the first amendment rights of these teachers were at issue. Citing both *Pickering* and *Givhan* the Second Circuit held,

> [w]hen those rights are at issue, the court must balance "the interests of the teacher, as a citizen, in commenting upon matters of public concern and the interest of the State, as an employer, in promoting the efficiency of the public services it performs through its employees."[54]

Clearly, the Second Circuit was influenced by the admission of the principal that the letters were "official reprimands," and by the "threatening tone" of the principal that if appellants went to the press again "he would be very angry."[55] In the court's view, "[t]he exercise of First Amendment freedoms may be deterred almost as potently by the threat of sanctions as by their actual application."[56] Thus, the court reversed the district court and remanded the case back for a factual determination of whether or not

---

51. *Id.*
52. *Id.*
53. *Id.*
54. *Id.* at 654-55.
55. *Id.* at 655.
56. *Id.*

the principal's acts had "a chilling effect sufficient to trigger First Amendment inquiry. . . ."[57]

Swilley v. Alexander is another 1980 case wherein a teacher's comments on school matters, which ultimately appeared in the press, precipitated § 1983 litigation.[58] Swilley was a teacher employed by the Mobile County School System in Alabama. He also served as President of the Mobile Federation of Teachers AFL-CIO, Local 777.

In July of 1977, in his role as President of Local 777, Swilley informed the school board (in a closed session) about an unnamed principal whose alleged conduct "exposed children to risk of serious physical harm."[59] The school board told Swilley that it would "investigate the allegations and would take proper action."[60]

It seems, however, that Swilley had given a release to the press, prior to the closed meeting, telling about the nature of the session. This prior press release "caused a small stew in the area and various members of the School Administration became upset."[61]

On August 9, 1977, the assistant superintendent, at the direction of the school board president, wrote Swilley a letter accusing him of releasing the information after the July 27 meeting in disregard of the school board's supposed request to remain silent on the matter.[62] The letter "labelled Swilley as 'unethical and unprofessional' and officially reprimanded him in his capacity as an employee

---

57. *Id.*

58. 629 F.2d 1018 (5th Cir. 1980).

59. *Id.* at 1019. According to the record, the principal "had allegedly caused young children to go outdoors for tornado drills during lightning storms and had sent home unattended small children without notifying the childrens' parents."

60. *Id.*

61. *Id.*

62. *Id.*

of the school system."[63] A copy of the letter was placed in his personnel file.

One day later, the school board "chastised" Swilley at a public meeting, "for furnishing the news media with information of the discussion at the July 27 meeting."[64] In the Board President's words, "Swilley's actions had questioned the good character and reputation of all eighty-four principals within the Mobile County School System."[65] Thus, he continued, "Mr. Swilley will never again attend any executive conference on personnel that we have . . . ."[66]

Swilley filed suit in federal court under both § 1983 and § 1985. He claimed violations of his first and fourteenth amendment rights. Basically, Swilley's first amendment complaint stated that

> (1) he has a right to disclose truthful information of public concern, therefore, the School Board had no right to reprimand him; (2) the School Board conspired to inhibit his right to free speech and association, as a union representative and teacher, by publicly humiliating him and damaging his reputation; and (3) the School Board conditioned his continued employment, in the letter of reprimand, upon the relinquishment of his right to speak on matters of public importance regarding the school system.[67]

Regarding alleged violations of his fourteenth amendment due process rights Swilley claimed that

> (1) the School Board had no right to reprimand him, because the Board's reprimand was based on incorrect

---

63. *Id.*

64. *Id.*

65. *Id.*

66. *Id.* According to the case report, "The record is not clear, but it seems that the President of the School Board knew by August 10 that Swilley had issued the press release to the July 27 meeting."

67. *Id.* at 1019-20.

assumptions of fact; (2) the reprimand of him, as a
school employee, was wrongful since his actions of
informing the news media were performed in his capacity and in furtherance of his duty as a representative of
the teacher's union — not as a school employee; (3) the
reprimand letter was written and placed in his
personnel file at the direction of the President of the
School Board, without the concurrence of the School
Board and therefore, without legal right; and (4) all of
the above was done without notice or hearing in violation of his property and liberty interests guaranteed by
the Fourteenth Amendment.[68]

The United States district court granted defendant's
motion to dismiss for failure to state a claim for which relief
could be granted.[69] Also, the district court did not consider
"Swilley's claims, even if all facts were taken as true, . . . of
sufficient Constitutional magnitude to be actionable as a
matter of law." [70] Finally, in the district court's view, the
Swilley matter was different from that presented to the
Supreme Court in *Pickering.*

On appeal, the Fifth Circuit's opinion centered on two
points. First, *Monell v. Department of Social Services* had
been decided by the Supreme Court, opening the way to
§ 1983 suits against school boards as entities.[71] Second, and
most important, the appellate court found the distinction
drawn between *Swilley* and *Pickering* as unwarranted.[72] It

---

68. *Id.* at 1020.

69. *Id.* at 1020. A footnote reveals that the trial court relied on Monroe
v. Pape, 365 U.S. 167 (1961) to reach the conclusion that a political
subdivision of a state (*e.g.,* school board) could not be sued as an entity.
This ruling was made prior to Monell v. Department of Social Services,
436 U.S. 658 (1979).

70. *Id.*

71. *Monell, supra* note 69.

72. *Swilley, supra* note 58, at 1021.

was on this last point that the Fifth Circuit developed its major rationale for reversing the lower court decision.

According to the circuit court, there was no evidence presented that the principal, about whom Swilley's comments were directed, would have daily and frequent contact with Swilley. Even if the principal had been his immediate superior, there was no evidence that "severe discipline or personality problems would arise to the extent of undermining the employer-employee relationship and the teaching abilities of Swilley." [73] Finally, the Fifth Circuit was convinced that Swilley's press release involved matters of public concern and was not merely a petty personal attack. On this last point the court was of the opinion that

> the Supreme Court did not intend to stifle discussion on matters of legitimate public importance concerning the professional conduct of school employees. Surely, the physical safety and well-being of our school children is as important an issue for public scrutiny as is the allocation of school funds between athletic and educational programs. Indeed, our experience tells us that the more important the subject matter is to the public, the sharper the reaction will be by those whose conduct may be called into question. It is precisely the probability of oppressive over-reaction by the powers that be which requires our constant vigilance of the First Amendment protections accorded all public employees. Therefore, we hold that the District Court erred in finding Swilley's press release beyond the protection of the First Amendment as a matter of law. [74]

The Fifth Circuit next focused its attention on the issue of the "letters of reprimand" placed in Swilley's personnel file. The pivotal point of the issue concerned whether or not the letter would be "merely present" in the folder and kept

---

73. *Id.*
74. *Id.*

confidential. Citing a previous decision in *Sims v. Fox* [75] the court reiterated its position "that liberty is not infringed by the *mere* presence of derogatory information in *confidential* files and that the government has not infringed liberty unless it perpetuates *untrue* charges." [76]

In *Swilley,* said the Fifth Circuit, there was absolutely no evidence showing that the letter of reprimand would be merely present and remain confidential. Moreover, defendants conceded that the letter contained some false information.[77] Thus, the court held that the district court had erred. Swilley's due process rights had been violated.[78]

Welch v. Barham [79] is another case decided in 1980 involving, among other things, comments made by a public school employee which appeared in a local newspaper. In this case, however, the employee charged school officials with "prejudice," thus their decision to terminate his contract was reached unfairly. The facts of the case are as follows.

A public school superintendent in an Arkansas school system brought this action, under § 1983 and state law, against his school board and its members, seeking reinstatement, equitable relief and damages. He alleged that his contract had been prematurely terminated, depriving him of free speech and due process.

It seems that Superintendent Barham was rehired for a third year in his position. Subsequent to that rehiring a disagreement developed between the school board and Barham. The disagreement grew from budgetary matters. After a special meeting to discuss finances, the board

---

75. 505 F.2d 857 (5th Cir. 1974).
76. *Swilley, supra* note 58, at 1022.
77. *Id.*
78. *Id.*
79. 635 F.2d 1322 (8th Cir. 1980).

decided "to supervise Barham's expenditures more closely." [80] Ten days later an article appeared in the local newspaper in which Superintendent Barham "defended his school expenditures." Three days following publication of the article, the board met to discuss a "serious personnel problem," namely, Barham.[81]

Superintendent Barham and his attorney attended the meeting. The board discussed finances, the newspaper article, Barham's outside teaching activities (at Arkansas Tech University), and his work as a deputy sheriff for Yell County. The record indicates that some board members were aware of his outside activities before his new contract was offered. After Superintendent Barham said that he would not be resigning from those activities, the board met in executive session and decided to hold a hearing to consider terminating his contract.[82]

Superintendent Barham was notified of the following charges against him:

> (1) violation of his employment contract by his outside teaching activities at Arkansas Tech University;
>
> (2) violation of his contract by his outside duties as deputy sheriff;
>
> (3) irresponsibility in the management of the financial affairs of the school district; and
>
> (4) bringing discredit on the school board and the community through public utterances to the media (his comments about school finance were in a newspaper article about a drug raid in which Barham participated.)[83]

---

80. *Id.* at 1323-24.
81. *Id.* at 1324.
82. *Id.*
83. *Id.*

Barham argued that his actions in no way warranted his termination. In his view his outside teaching did not impair his responsibilities as superintendent; his uncompensated duties as deputy sheriff benefited the community; his financial management had improved the quality of education in the school district; and his statement to the press "was a justified response to untruthful rumors. . . ." [84]

At trial, the district court concluded that Barham was deprived of property (his job) without due process of law, because the board of education "was not sufficiently impartial . . . ." [85] The Eighth Circuit did not agree.

In the opinion of the Eighth Circuit, "in the absence of a claim of personal animosity, illegal prejudice, or a personal or financial stake in the outcome, school board members are entitled to this presumption of honesty and integrity." [86] Citing *Hortonville*[87] as controlling, the court added: "Merely by its involvement in the events preceding Barham's discharge, the Board did not become so tainted as to lose this presumption." [88] The appellate court entered a judgment of dismissal on the plaintiff's § 1983 action.

In dissent, however, Judge Heaney emphasized that the *Hortonville* standard suggests that "mere familiarity" with the facts does not disqualify a board member. In his view this was not the case with Barham. Two board members, he said, had taken a position prior to the termination hearing that they would not change their minds on Barham, and took such a position before Barham had a chance to present his version of the facts. Their minds were "closed on the

---

84. *Id.* at 1325.

85. *Id.*

86. *Id.* at 1326.

87. Hortonville School District v. Hortonville Educ. Association, 426 U.S. 482 (1976).

88. *Welch, supra* note 79, at 1326.

factual disputes. . . ." To Judge Heaney, the district court decision should have been affirmed.[89]

Comments made by public school employees in newspapers have not been the only source of § 1983 litigation. Decided September 19, 1980, *Lemons v. Morgan* [90] presented the Eighth Circuit with the appeal of a public school teacher in Missouri (his claim had been dismissed by the trial court) who alleged that he had been removed from his jobs as manager of the school's radio station and as broadcast technology teacher because of an editorial he broadcast and with which the school board disagreed. Manager-teacher Lemons claimed that the board's decision deprived him of first and fourteenth amendment guarantees.

At the time of the broadcast incident (August, 1976) Lemons had been employed for eleven years in the same school system, as teacher of broadcast technology. He had also been manager of the school system owned and operated radio station.[91]

At the beginning of the 1976-77 school year Lemons was removed as manager of the station and assigned to the position of electronics teacher in the vocational technical school. His removal and transfer did not affect his salary or his tenured status.[92]

According to Lemons, he had broadcast certain editorials in which he objected to rules proposed by school officials for prior restraint and censorship of broadcasts, and in which he commented on matters discussed in school board meetings (which he attended). Because of the board's disagreements with his editorials, he said, defendants

---

89. *Id.* at 1328-29.
90. 629 F.2d 1389 (8th Cir. 1980).
91. *Id.* at 1390.
92. Id.

"demoted him in retaliation for" his exercise of his "constitutionally protected right of free speech. . . ." [93]

Lemons was unsuccessful in contesting the validity of his removal and transfer before the district court. In the court's view, the complaint failed to state a complaint upon which relief could be granted. The district court was of the opinion that Lemons' complaint did not allege facts that would permit recovery under a procedural due process theory.[94]

Citing *Mt. Healthy City School District Board of Education v. Doyle*,[95] *Perry v. Sindermann*,[96] and other cases as controlling, the Eighth Circuit saw Lemons' allegations as sufficient to state a bona fide, substantive due process claim, in violation of his first and fourteenth amendment guarantees.[97] Lemons' complaint, said the court, had also alleged a "liberty violation," that he suffered severe damage to his reputational interest as a result of his demotion, an allegation rejected by the district court but one which the Eighth Circuit said his attorneys did not develop until too late in the court procedure. It should also be pointed out that Lemons had conceded at trial that he had no "property interest" in his positions as station manager and teacher of broadcast technology.[98]

Making its ruling on a procedural issue, and not on the merits of Lemons' charges, the Eighth Circuit reversed the district court's decision and remanded the case back for further proceedings. In the opinion of the appellate court, Lemons' cause of action should not be dismissed simply because he failed to establish the particular legal theory he

---

93. *Id.*
94. *Id.* at 1390-91.
95. *Supra* note 12.
96. *Supra* note 3.
97. *Lemons, supra* note 90, at 1390.
98. *Id.* at 1391 n.3.

advanced in his complaint. The entire complaint should be examined by the lower court.[99] It is interesting to note that each side bore its own costs for the appeal.

(C) FREEDOM TO SPEAK IN THE CLASSROOM.

As the above subsection illustrates, teachers have become involved in § 1983 litigation as a result of their public comments about school matters appearing in the news media. So too have teachers' exercises of speech within their classrooms culminated in numerous civil rights complaints.

As emphasized at the beginning of this Chapter, the Supreme Court in *Tinker* extended first amendment guarantees to public school teachers in school, as well as to students. However, the Court did caution that these guarantees may be limited because of the unique nature of the school.[100] The Supreme Court did not equate speech in the public school classroom with speech on the "public street corner." In other words, a difference remained between the teacher speaking as teacher and the teacher speaking as citizen.

Generally, and within the bounds of state law and school board policy, classroom teachers can determine what specific subject matter will be incorporated into their class syllabi. Also, state law and school board policy do not tell a teacher "how to teach" his subject. The appropriateness of the subject matter, the ways in which it is presented, and the age and maturity of the students present in the class have, however, been sources of § 1983 court action.

In a 1970 case, *Robins v. Board of Education,*[101] a former probationary teacher brought unsuccessfully a civil rights

---

99. *Id.* at 1391.
100. *Tinker, supra* note 1, at 509.
101. 313 F. Supp. 642 (N.D. Ill. 1970).

action on the ground that she had not been rehired because of her civil rights activities. Claiming denials of her first amendment guarantees to speech, assembly and petition, and violations of her fourteenth amendment rights to both due process and equal protection, she sought remedy under § 1983.

In response, the school board claimed that plaintiff had not been rehired because of chronic tardiness, leaving her class unattended on numerous occasions, failure to assume corridor duty, poor judgment in discussing in class a school board disciplinary action taken against another teacher for growing a beard, and her use of sexual references in class.[102] The latter two charges represented the crux of the board's defense.

At the outset of its opinion, the district court referenced both § 1983 and *Pickering*,[103] and made it clear that

> [a]n individual does not relinquish his First or Fourteenth Amendment rights when he becomes a public school teacher . . ., and if his teaching contract is not renewed because of the exercise of these rights, the Civil Rights Act provides remedy.[104]

At trial, in addition to showing evidence to substantiate the other charges, the school board demonstrated that plaintiff had devoted forty minutes of one class session and fifteen minutes in another to a discussion, initiated by students, of the actions of the school board to relieve a coach of his duties because he had grown a beard. She was also charged for mentioning that the swim team might boycott future swim meets as one possible cause of action. Other evidence was presented that plaintiff's superintendent had

---

102. *Id.* at 642-43.
103. *Pickering, supra* note 16.
104. *Robins, supra* note 101, at 643.

formally criticized her for making "two sexual references . . . when discussing literature in class." [105]

Plaintiff was thus denied relief for failure to satisfy the burden of proof that she was terminated solely because of her civil rights activities. The board was able to show by evidence presented that it would have reached the same decision not to rehire plaintiff, absent her civil rights activities.

Knarr v. Board of School Trustees [106] offers another example of a similar case from 1970, wherein a United States district court dismissed on the merits a § 1983 action taken by a social studies teacher in Indiana. In his complaint, the teacher complained that he was nonrenewed (causing him to be denied continuing contract status) because of his exercise of his first amendment rights to speech and association. Specifically, he claimed his nonrenewal was caused by the school board's disapproval of his union activities.

As did the court in the previous case, this court cited *Pickering.* The court made it clear that "[t]he decision of a school board not to renew a teacher's contract is impermissible if it deprives a teacher of constitutionally protected rights." [107]

The school board was able to show the court through evidence presented, however, that its decision not to renew the plaintiff's contract was predicated partially on his tardiness in arriving at school on more than one occasion, his tendency toward insubordination and neglect of duty, his obvious lack of concern for parents, his causing dissention and divisiveness among fellow teachers, and his

---

105. *Id.* at 644.
106. 317 F. Supp. 832 (N.D. Ind. 1970).
107. *Id.* at 833.

significant difference in philosophy from that desired by the school board.[108]

The school board's main argument for nonrenewal dealt with plaintiff's use of class time. Substantial evidence was presented to support the board's conclusion that plaintiff "abused his teaching position by using his classroom 'as his personal forum to promote union activities, to sanction polygamy, to attack marriage, to criticize other teachers and to sway and influence the minds of young people without a full and proper explanation of both sides of the issue.' " [109]

Inappropriate use of classroom time was also an issue in a 1971 decision from a federal court in Arkansas. In *Cooley v. Board of Education*,[110] a teacher with eleven years of service in a school system was discharged for using his classroom time to conduct organizational meetings with outside adult citizens and representatives of community agencies. The board was able to demonstrate that said activities "continuously interfered with normal classroom activities." [111]

The plaintiff, who was a civil rights activist, had his complaint dismissed for failure to sustain the burden of proof that his services as a classroom teacher were terminated solely on racial considerations. Remedy under § 1983 was thus denied.[112]

---

108. *Id.* at 834.

109. *Id.* at 836. For a more recent civil rights case wherein a teacher was dismissed for using his classroom for disseminating his political convictions, see Burns v. Rovaldi, 477 F. Supp. 270 (D. Conn. 1979).

110. 327 F. Supp. 454 (E.D. Ark. 1971).

111. *Id.* at 455-56.

112. *Id.* at 458-59. For a recent case wherein a dismissed teacher alleged that the board's actions were actually motivated by racial prejudice see, Jones v. Jefferson Parish School Boards, 533 F. Supp. 816 (E.D. La. 1982).

Two years later, in a Florida case, a tenth grade biology teacher in a public school took his school board and other school officials into federal court claiming that he was denied continuing contract status (he was not rehired for a fourth year) in violation of his first and fourteenth amendment rights.[113] Seeking remedy under § 1983 (permanent injunction, compensatory damages, costs and attorney's fees), plaintiff alleged that his nonrenewal was caused by his making statements in his classroom critical of the school system, school board, and superintendent; his relating to his class some personal experiences he had with prostitutes; and, his discussion of other topics not related to biology.[114]

According to plaintiff, he was offered a fourth contract on condition that he refrain from discussing such matters with future classes. This required condition, he said, was intended to penalize him for protected utterances and statements and to chill and inhibit the exercise by other teachers of their right to engage fully in constitutionally protected forms of speech.[115]

In denying plaintiff's request for relief, the district court focused upon his use of classroom time and the age and maturity level of his students. In the court's opinion there was no question that a teacher is free to criticize his employers. However, "that exercise may not invade the classroom occupied by fifteen-year-olds and must be balanced against the need for meaningful school administration." [116] Tenth grade students, said the court, "have a right and freedom not to listen and as a captive audience should

---

113. Moore v. School Board, 364 F. Supp. 355 (N.D. Fla. 1973). Plaintiff was joined in this suit by his wife in an amended complaint.

114. *Id.* at 356-57.

115. *Id.* at 357.

116. *Id.* at 360.

109

be able to expect protection from improper classroom activities." [117]

On the subject of covering controversial issues in the classroom, the court differentiated between "straight criticism" by a teacher and presenting ideas with "commentary reflecting two sides of an issue. . . ." Students should be left with a "preference" as to that issue.[118] The court also saw as an abuse of teacher-classroom authority plaintiff's digressions about his experiences with Japanese prostitutes.

In the court's view, the board's setting the condition that plaintiff either refrain from such discussions with future classes or not get a fourth contract was a reasonable exercise of authority. Thus, plaintiff's request for a permanent injunction enjoining the denial of his continuing contract in the school system, and his requests for compensatory damages, costs and attorney's fees were all denied.

At the appellate level, both the Seventh Circuit and the Tenth Circuit have been faced with § 1983 actions involving teacher first amendment rights in the classroom. Both cases involved non-tenured teachers.

Out of the Seventh Circuit, *Brubaker v. Board of Education*[119] involved three non-tenured elementary school teachers who had their contracts nonrenewed. At the heart of the matter were some incidents involving a brochure containing a poem entitled "Getting Together," acquired at

---

117. *Id.*

118. *Id.* at 361. Brought out at trial were the following statements made in class by plaintiff: "You'd better tell your parents to get off their ass and elect a new school board." "You can't call yourself a Christian if you vote for Mr. Craig (the Superintendent)." Also brought out at trial was evidence of lengthy class discussions of the inadequacy of teacher salaries. *Id.*

119. 502 F.2d 973 (7th Cir. 1974).

a local theater where one plaintiff and another teacher attended the movie "Woodstock." One plaintiff, a French teacher, placed some of the brochures in the teachers' lounges, and gave copies to her husband and to another teacher for use in their classes. These teachers distributed the brochures to students. Plaintiff did not, however, distribute the brochures to her students, but did place in her classroom a poster for the brochure. Some of the brochures were taken home by the students.[120]

Not long after the brochures reached some homes, parents began to complain to the school administration, especially about the poem "Getting Together." They complained about what they deemed was the obscene, suggestive and harmful nature of the poem's content. Soon after that the school board met and resolved that the three teachers involved be terminated from employment for violating school board policy dealing with the distribution of such material in the schools.[121]

A district court had entered summary judgment for the board and the Seventh Circuit affirmed that decision. To the high court the board's termination decision was not unconstitutionally motivated. Said the court:

> We do not believe that however much the reach of the First Amendment has been extended and however eager today's courts have been to protect the many varieties of claims to civil rights, the appellee school board had to put up with the described conduct of appellants.[122]

Thus, the teachers' claim of violation of their first amendment guaranteed academic freedom was defeated. Citing

---

120. *Id.* at 975-76.
121. *Id.* at 976.
122. *Id.* at 983-84.

both *Keefe v. Geanakos* [123] and *Mailloux v. Kiley,* [124] the Seventh Circuit emphasized that academic freedom does not give approval to conduct which can reasonably be deemed both offensive and necessary to the accomplishment of educational objectives. Also, material used in classrooms must be judged by such factors as the age and sophistication of the students, relevance of the educational purpose, and context and manner of presentation. [125] The plaintiffs' requests for job, back pay, and attorney's fees were defeated.

In a civil rights action taken under § 1983 and 28 U.S.C. §§ 1331 and 1343, the decision of the Tenth Circuit also involved three non-tenured teachers, only one of whom had more than one year's teaching experience. In *Adams v. Campbell County,* [126] plaintiffs alleged that they had been nonrenewed due primarily to an incident involving the publication of a student underground newspaper, to their each wearing long hair, to their having discussions in the classrooms about long hair and flag burning, to the threat they presented to administrative authority, and other such exercises of protected conduct. A United States district court had ruled against plaintiffs, finding that the aforementioned incidents did not enter into the board's decision to nonrenew the teachers' contracts. [127] On appeal, the

---

123. 418 F.2d 359 (1st Cir. 1969).

124. 448 F.2d 1242 (1st Cir. 1971).

125. *Brubaker, supra* note 119 at 984-85. For another excellent case from that same year, see Birdwell v. Hazelwood School District, 491 F.2d 490 (8th Cir. 1974) wherein a probationary high school algebra teacher unsuccessfully sued for reinstatement, back pay, injunctive relief and, in the alternative, money damages for loss of reputation and breach of contract in the amount of $100,000. School officials were able to show a direct connection between the teacher's use of his classroom as a forum (urging students to employ violent measures as a demonstrative device) and actual disruption in the school.

126. 511 F.2d 1242 (10th Cir. 1975).

127. *Id.* at 1244-45.

Tenth Circuit placed the burden of proof on appellant teachers to show that the alleged first amendment exercises caused their terminations.

On the board side, the evidence showed that the school principal had recommended that the teachers not be rehired. He based his decision on grounds that he could get better teachers and, among other things, on such specifics as lack of classroom discipline, causing disharmony among other teachers, insubordinate acts to the principal, as well as the underground newspaper incident and the time spent on inappropriate classroom discussions already mentioned.[128]

On the teachers' speech claim the appellate court said,

> Plaintiffs also argue that teachers have a First Amendment right to discuss controversial subjects and use controversial materials in the classroom. Undoubtedly they have some freedom in the techniques to be employed, but this does not say that they have unlimited liberty as to structure and content of courses, at least at the secondary level. . . . We have found no law which allows a high school teacher to have the broad latitude which appellants seek.[129]

Additionally, said the court, even though experts may have testified that the teaching methods of plaintiffs had educational value, "this is not equivalent to saying that they had a constitutional right absolute in character to employ their methods in preference to more standard or orthodox ones."[130]

The Tenth Circuit found that the trial court's findings were supported by the evidence. Plaintiffs' request for remedy under § 1983 failed, since they could not prove that

---

128. *Id.* at 1243-44.
129. *Id.* at 1247.
130. *Id.*

they were terminated for exercising protected constitutional conduct.[131]

Kingsville Independent School District v. Cooper is a more recent case in point. Decided by the United States Court of Appeals for the Fifth Circuit on February 15, 1980, the *Cooper* case involved a suit brought by a public school district in Texas for a judgment declaring that it did not violate the constitutional rights of an untenured high school teacher when it decided not to renew her contract.[132] A federal district court below had found for the teacher (who sought equitable relief, including reinstatement). In addition to ordering reinstatement, the district court awarded her $15,000 in damages, plus $4,500 for attorneys' fees. The damages were intended to be approximately the amount of her salary for the 1972-73 and 1973-74 school years. The school district appealed that order.

At trial, the following facts were presented.[133] Cooper was hired in 1967 as an American history teacher. Even though the school district had received some complaints about her teaching (the number of complaints received was about average among all teachers), Cooper's contract was renewed each year until 1972. It should be pointed out that the school district had no formal tenure system, and that Cooper and all other teachers were employed on annual contracts. Also, over the five year period no parent complaint about Cooper was ever investigated.[134]

In the fall of 1971, Cooper employed a technique known as "sunshine simulation" to teach her classes about the post-Civil War Reconstruction period. The simulation technique involved students in role-playing situations to

---

131. *Id.* at 1248.

132. Kingsville Independent School District v. Cooper, 611 F.2d 1190 (5th Cir. 1980).

133. *Id.* at 1111.

134. *Id.*

recreate the period of history. The process helped to bring out student feelings on racial issues.

Following her use of the "sunshine simulation" technique, parental complaints increased significantly. As a result, Cooper was called twice before her principal to discuss the technique. At the second meeting the district's director of personnel was present, and he told Cooper "not to discuss Blacks in American history," and that "nothing controversial should be discussed in the classroom." [135] The record shows that she did not follow that advice.

In 1972-73, however, both the principal and superintendent recommended that Cooper's contract be renewed. The school board disagreed and voted not to renew her contract. Board members testified at trial and by deposition "that they disapproved of the Sunshine project and that the volume of complaints received diminished Cooper's effectiveness as a teacher." [136] Board members could not remember other complaints about Cooper's teaching, only those associated with "sunshine simulation." Thus, the district court found that the nonrenewal was precipitated only by Cooper's use of the controversial technique.

According to the school district, the district court's finding that the sunshine project precipitated the nonrenewal is clearly erroneous. Also, the board asserted that Cooper's conduct was an unprotected activity (the board saw it as an exercise of private expression). Finally, said the school board, the federal district court failed to determine, as required under *Mt. Healthy City School District Board of Education v. Doyle*,[137] whether the board would have made the decision on Cooper's contract without considering the sunshine project.[138]

---

135. *Id.*
136. *Id.*
137. *Mt. Healthy, supra* note 12.
138. *Id.* at 1113.

On appeal, the Fifth Circuit concluded, on the basis of the evidence considered by the district court, that the findings demonstrated that the sunshine project precipitated the nonrenewal and that other complaints about Cooper were minimal. Also, the appellate court saw as important the fact that both the principal and the superintendent (to whom Cooper was directly responsible, and who were best able to observe her performance as a teacher), recommended that her contract be renewed. In fact, in his final evaluation of her, the principal rated her as "thoroughly satisfactory" on each category of her teaching performance.[139]

The school district's argument that the "sunshine technique" was unprotected by the first amendment, because it was private expression, also failed. Citing as controlling, the United States Supreme Court's recent decision in *Givhan v. Western Line Consolidated School District*,[140] the appellate court held that private expression by a public employee is protected speech. Also, in keeping with decisions from the First and Sixth Circuits,[141] the Fifth Circuit held that "classroom discussion is protected activity." It follows, said the court, "that Cooper's discharge for discussions conducted in the classroom cannot be upheld unless the discussions 'clearly ... overbalance [her] usefulness as an instructor.' "[142]

Finally, the Fifth Circuit stated that the district court's findings of fact adequately support the inference that

---

139. *Id.*

140. *Givhan, supra* note 29.

141. Cited by the Court were: *Keefe, supra* note 123; and Minarcini v. Strongsville City School District, 541 F.2d 577 (6th Cir. 1976).

142. *Kingsville, supra* note 132, at 1113. *See* Dean v. Timpson Independent School District, 486 F. Supp. 302 (E.D. Tex. 1979) wherein a teacher was wrongfully discharged for using a survey of male sexual identity and female perceptions of such identity which the board of education said "was against community views."

"Cooper would have been rehired but for the Sunshine project." The district court decision was therefore affirmed. The award of $15,000 for damages and the award of $4,500 for attorney's fees were both vacated in order that the district court below could enter a fresh award.[143]

(d) DRESS AS EXPRESSION.

Over the years the notion of people expressing themselves (speaking out) through their mode of dress and attire (including hair style) has developed, mainly through the process of incorporation, into an acceptable concept of constitutional law. As such, the right to dress as one desires has been placed within the purview of the first amendment as an extension of the right to speak.

In the past decade the violation of public school system grooming regulations has been a cause for teacher litigation. As one source in school law reports,

> The early 1970's witnessed considerable controversy relative to regulation of the personal appearance of members of the teaching staff. The courts were torn between the authority of boards of education to adopt reasonable rules concerning the operation of schools and the right of self-expression guaranteed, or at least implied, in the Constitution. The decisions often attempted to distinguish between those aspects of appearance (dress) which could be applied to the schoolroom only and which would leave teachers free to appear as they desired at other times, and those aspects of appearance which must necessarily be the same in school and out, such as haircuts and beards. However, this distinction appeared superficial in consideration of constitutional guarantees.[144]

---

143. Kingsville, *supra* note 132, at 1114.
144. L. J. PETERSON, R. A. ROSMILLER, M. M. VOLZ. THE LAW AND PUBLIC SCHOOL OPERATION (2d ed. New York, NY.: Harper and Row, Publishers, Inc., 1978), at 454.

In more recent years, state the authors, the issue of teacher appearance has settled down.[145]

As with student appearance cases, teacher matters fall into two distinct types or categories. While some § 1983 cases involve teachers wearing or not wearing certain items or styles of clothing, other cases involve matters of hair (*e.g.*, style, length, beards, mustaches, and the like).

Lucia v. Duggan [146] is an example of an early civil rights action on point. Decided in 1969 by a United States district court in Massachusetts, this case developed when a nontenured teacher grew a beard.

Plaintiff (Lucia) was in his third year of employment in the school system when the school committee decided to terminate him. From the time he was originally hired (1967) until the time of his dismissal (January, 1969) he was clean-shaven, with one exception — during the winter school vacation (1968-69) he grew a beard. He returned to school with a beard when classes resumed on January 2, 1969. From that date until January 17, he performed his teaching duties with "no disruption of his classroom or the learning situation caused by his wearing a beard." [147]

During the first week of January the superintendent spoke to Lucia and told him that it was an unwritten policy of the school committee that teachers should be "clean shaven on the job." [148] Also, on January 8, because of some

---

145. *Id.*

146. 303 F. Supp. 112 (D. Mass. 1969).

147. *Id.* at 114. It should be noted that throughout his employment in the Monson public school system Lucia was consistently rated good or excellent in all facets of his performance as a teacher. The sole exception was his rating for grooming, assigned him after his suspension.

148. *Id.* It should also be noted that the Monson school system had no regulation or order prohibiting teachers from wearing beards. There was a student regulation stating that "mustaches and beards will not be tolerated."

questions and remarks from "a few citizens" of the community, the school committee directed that the superintendent write a letter to Lucia expressing its members' thoughts and those of the superintendent with respect to his wearing a beard "while in the performance of his personal duties." [149]

Between January 13 and January 28 the building principal, superintendent, and school committee (in several meetings) continued to pursue the matter of the beard with Mr. Lucia. At no time, however, did anyone "give plaintiff the choice between shaving his beard and having his employment terminated." [150] On January 16, however, the school committee met and voted to suspend Lucia for seven days, citing as its reasons both insubordination and his "improper example" as a teacher. [151]

On January 30 the school committee met again. When the meeting opened, the chairman immediately resigned and an acting chairman was appointed. Plaintiff then appeared before the committee and asked for a postponement because he was not yet able to get legal counsel. His request was denied. Next, a group of thirty or forty townspeople gathered at the meeting and, through a spokesman, asked questions of the committee "as to what charges were against plaintiff and why a good teacher . . . should be removed." [152] These questions were answered

---

149. *Id.*

150. *Id.* at 115-16. Plaintiff was, however, given a letter by the superintendent stating, among other things, that Lucia "not wear a mustache or beard while teaching."

151. *Id.* Plaintiff was not notified of the meeting and its purpose. Nor was he notified of another meeting, where in executive session, the school committee voted that "if plaintiff should appear at school with a beard on January 29, the superintendent should suspend him for an additional two days."

152. *Id.* at 116.

with either silence or the statement that "Mr. Lucia knows what the charges are." [153]

The committee went into executive session and voted unanimously to dismiss plaintiff and the superintendent was directed to notify him. Each member thereupon resigned from the school committee and left the meeting. The minutes of the meeting contain no reason for plaintiff's dismissal. It should be reiterated, as stated above, that at no time during the events of January did the committee "give plaintiff the choice between shaving his beard and having his employment terminated." [154]

In rendering its decision in this case, the district court made it clear at the outset that even though Lucia probably had a valid action against defendants under Massachusetts law "for breach of contract," this fact did not bar his action under § 1983. The court saw the federal remedy as supplementary to the state remedy, and the latter need not be first sought and refused before the federal one is invoked.[155]

Responding to Lucia's primary contention (that he has a constitutional right to wear a beard and that the action of the defendants in suspending and dismissing him operated to deny that right), the court made the point that plaintiff failed to present strong arguments to establish a "constitutional foundation" of such a right. However, on the other hand, defendants failed to show that plaintiff's

---

153. *Id.* According to stipulation of the parties, the reasons for Lucia's dismissal were: (1) the raising of a beard, (2) insubordination in refusing to comply with the order of the school committee to shave his beard, (3) bad attitude before the school committee at its January 15 meeting, and (4) improper dress before the school committee on January 15, 1969. Regarding the last two charges, Lucia went to that meeting directly from playing a recreation league basketball game.

154. *Id.* at 117.

155. *Id.* at 117.

wearing a beard would materially and substantially disrupt school work and discipline.[156] The court said:

> the resignation of all members of the school committee immediately after dismissing plaintiff and their prior refusal to answer the townspeople's questions about any charges against him suggest that they were imposing their own personal standards concerning beards.[157]

In the court's opinion, Lucia's freedom to wear a beard (whatever the basis of that claim), in combination with his "professional reputation as a school teacher, . . . may not be taken from him without due process of law." [158] The court said: "[p]laintiff's interest in wearing a beard and in his career as a teacher is not nullified by his having been employed less than the three years required to achieve tenure status." [159] Thus, defendant's argument, that Lucia had no constitutional right to work for the school system, was specifically rejected.

After weighing the evidence, the court found two major procedural faults in the actions of the school officials. First, Lucia was never told what the charges against him were and that his refusal to shave would result in his termination. Second, and prior to his dismissal, there was no written or announced policy "that male teachers should not wear beards in the classroom." [160] In the court's view, therefore, Lucia's procedural due process had been violated.

As remedy, the court said that Lucia was entitled to all benefits, including salary (stipulated at $1,575). Also, plaintiff was awarded $1,000 in compensatory damages for

---

156. *Id. See,* in particular, *id.* at 117, n.2.
157. *Id.*
158. *Id.* at 118.
159. *Id.*
160. *Id.*

pain and suffering. The court ordered that (1) the school committee's decisions to suspend and dismiss Lucia violated the due process clause of the fourteenth amendment and were null and void; (2) plaintiff is entitled to the benefits of his contract as a teacher, including the right to compensation without deduction for moneys otherwise earned throughout the remainder of his contract; (3) that judgment be entered for plaintiff against individual named defendants in the amount of $2,575 (specified above), plus costs of the action; and (4) the defendants be restrained and enjoined from giving any effect whatsoever to the orders of suspension and dismissal.[161]

In 1975, the Fifth Circuit heard the appeal of a junior college teacher who had been dismissed from his job because of a beard that he had grown over his summer vacation.[162] In *Handler v. San Jacinto Junior College,* Handler brought a civil rights action under § 1983 seeking reinstatement to his teaching position, backpay, and a permanent injunction against enforcement of a "faculty grooming regulation;" however, he did not claim either a violation of free expression or of privacy.[163]

In December of 1970, San Jacinto Junior College (a public junior college) promulgated a regulation governing faculty

---

161. *Id.* at 119. The district court made it clear that it left to be determined by the state law the question of whether or not Lucia now had tenure. Also made clear was the court's desire not to blur the distinction between the rights of nontenured and tenured teachers. It should be noted here that the district court made no award of damages for emotional distress, because of defendants' good faith reliance on state law regarding the rights of nontenured teachers.

162. Handler v. San Jacinto Junior College, 519 F.2d 273 (5th Cir. 1975).

163. *Id.*

appearances. According to the policy, "[f]aculty members and all of the male employees of San Jacinto Junior College are required to be clean shaven, wear reasonable hair styles and have no excessively long sideburns." [164] Handler wore a beard, which he had grown during the summer prior to the enactment of the aforementioned policy.

In January 1971, he was personally informed by the college's president that his beard violated the new policy. On the president's request, the Board of Regents conducted a hearing "to determine what action to take against him." [165] The Board gave Handler "four days in which to shave his beard or be discharged." [166] He refused, was immediately dismissed from his job, and was paid the remainder of his salary for the 1970-71 term.

Suing in federal district court, Handler claimed that the board's actions violated both his due process and equal protection guarantees under the fourteenth amendment. The grooming policy, he stated, "was designed to implement the personal tastes of the college administrators and as such bore no relation to their statutory authority to manage the college and that the grooming standard created an arbitrary classification." [167] The Junior College contended that "teachers in public institutions enjoy no constitutionally protected right to wear beards, that the eleventh amendment bars recovery of backpay and attorneys' fees, and that an award of attorneys' fees is inappropriate...." [168] The district court decided in his favor and granted him reinstatement, backpay and attorneys' fees (amounting to $5,112.50).

---

164. *Id.* at 275.
165. *Id.*
166. *Id.*
167. *Id.*
168. *Id.*

The Fifth Circuit affirmed the district court's order concerning reinstatement and backpay. The attorneys' fees award was reversed. Handler's discharge, said the court, did infringe upon his constitutional rights.[169] In the court's view,

> The plethora of public employee cases on which the college relies does not provide convincing precedent for this case. In the majority of cases in which federal courts have upheld dismissals in the face of constitutional challenges, the public employer has presented evidence of a compelling interest in enforcing the grooming regulation in question.[170]

It seems that the college tried to substantiate the need for the grooming regulations on two counts: first, the need for establishing discipline among its employees, and second, the need to maintain the public's confidence in those working at the college. Both contentions failed. To the Fifth Circuit, "[t]eachers, even at public institutions such as San Jacinto Junior College, simply do not have the exposure or community-wide impact of policemen and other employees who deal directly with the public. Nor is the need for 'discipline' as acute in the educational environment as in other types of public service."[171]

Similarly, the college's contention that the wearing of a beard might "diminish the respect which a teacher must have from his students," also failed. In the court's opinion,

> [s]chool authorities may regulate teachers' appearance and activities only when the regulation has some relevance to legitimate administrative or educational functions. . . . In this case, the college contends that the wearing of a beard diminishes the respect which a

---

169. *Id.* at 281.
170. *Id.* at 276.
171. *Id.* at 277.

teacher must have from his students and "the community" in order to properly perform his duties. The college, however, presented no evidence whatsoever to support this position. . . . The mere subjective belief in a particular idea by public employers is, however, an undeniably insufficient justification for the infringement of a constitutionally guaranteed right. . . . Furthermore, it is illogical to conclude that a teacher's bearded appearance would jeopardize his reputation or pedagogical effectiveness with college students, . . .[172]

In a concurring opinion written by Chief Judge Brown, he stated very clearly that he was happy that the federal courts are "out of the hair business as Mr. Justice Black long ago said we should be." At this point in our nation's history, he suggests, we find "thousands of entirely responsible adult members of the community wearing all sorts of hair and face trims. . . ." [173] In his opinion, the public "has come to its senses and does not see in such variations the seeds of violence and revolution." [174]

Two federal appellate level decisions out of the late 1970's offer examples of situations involving teachers and clothing, not beards, that found their way into court through application of § 1983. The first case, *Tardif v. Quinn*,[175] involved the appeal of a female, nontenured high school French teacher, while the second case, *East Hartford Education Association v. Board of Education*,[176] involved the appeal of a male, nontenured English teacher.

Ms. Tardif, in the spring of her third year of teaching French at the high school level, received notification that

172. *Id.*
173. *Id.* at 281.
174. *Id.* at 282.
175. 545 F.2d 761 (1st Cir. 1976).
176. 562 F.2d 838 (2d Cir. 1977).

her contract would not be renewed. In the nonrenewal letter four reasons were cited, each relating to her abilities and professional growth activities as a teacher. No comment in the letter referred to Tardif's appearance.[177]

In the fall of 1969, Ms. Tardif began to wear "shortened dresses." According to the record, her new dress style "was met with vigorous objection" on the part of her (female) department head, culminating, more than one year later, in a statement to Ms. Tardif by the department head that unless she "changed her mode of dress, she would no longer be in the school system." [178]

Ms. Tardif was asked to resign in March of 1971. She refused, and the nonrenewal action was taken by the board. At the time she was asked to resign no reasons were given for the request. Ms. Tardif filed suit in federal district court alleging that her constitutional rights were violated because the "real reason" for her nonrenewal was the "length of her dress."

At trial, the court found that plaintiff had been a superior teacher, and that the charges stated in the nonrenewal letter were contradicted by the "overwhelming weight of evidence," and that her "image was that of an energetic, imaginative and dedicated teacher." [179] The court did find, however, that she had "failed to meet her contractual requirements with respect to taking outside courses for

----

177. *Tardif, supra* note 175, at 762. The reasons stated were: (1) lack of interest in professional growth, (2) insufficient participation in school activities, (3) unwillingness to work with students after school, and (4) poor image.

178. *Id.* The case report shows that Ms. Tardif, who was then 25 years old, was told for over a year by her department head, who had been a teacher for 35 years, that the length of her skirts would affect her students. And, from time to time, their relationship was strained and "marked with frequent hostile exchanges."

179. *Id.*

credit." [180] After three days of trial, and on the basis of this last finding, the district court dismissed the action without reaching the question whether her termination because of her dress length violated her constitutional rights.

On appeal, the First Circuit did not treat the question of dress as a nonissue. Moreover, the appellate court assumed from the trial court's findings that plaintiff's dress length was within reasonable limits. The high court did say, however, that the trial court's independent judgment regarding the impact and propriety of Tardif's dress "does not amount to a finding that defendants' objections to the length were irrational in the context of school administration concerns." [181]

The First Circuit considered Ms. Tardif's matter of "choice" in personal appearance as "an aspect of the Fourteenth Amendment's 'commodious concept of liberty, embracing freedoms great and small.' " [182] The court placed this entitlement within a contractual context (between employee and employer) and said, "[w]hatever constitutional aspect there may be to one's choice of apparel generally, it is hardly a matter which falls totally beyond the scope of the demands which an employer, public or private, can legitimately make upon its employees." [183] Additionally, said the court, just because teacher appearance or choice of dress is an issue does not automatically signify that a constitutional issue is present. [184]

---

180. *Id.*

181. *Id.* at 763.

182. *Id.*

183. *Id.*

184. *Id. See* Miller v. School District, 495 F.2d 658 (7th Cir. 1974), *rehearing denied,* 500 F.2d 711 (7th Cir. 1974), wherein it was held that "even if the individual interest in one's appearance may be characterized as an interest in liberty, the denial of public employment because the

Citing *Bishop v. Wood* [185] as controlling, the appellate court emphasized that it was not in the business of reviewing the day-to-day judgments of public school administrators. Since the case did not show an invasion of Ms. Tardif's constitutional right "so irrational as to demonstrate lack of good faith . . .," the decision of the district court dismissing Tardif's action was affirmed. In the opinion of the First Circuit,

> Whether the conclusion that plaintiff's dress had a distruptive effect was correct or not, we could not say it was not "motivated by a legitimate school concern." [186]

In 1977 the Second Circuit decided *East Hartford Education Association v. Board of Education,* a teacher "dress code" case.[187] The case involved the appeal of a male, nontenured English teacher (he also taught filmmaking) in the East Hartford Public Schools. He was joined in this case by his local and state teachers' unions.

Originally, suit was brought in federal district court under §§ 1983 and 1988 asking for both a declaratory judgment and an injunction against the enforcement of a "teachers' dress code" (also referred to as a "tie code" for male teachers). At trial the school system won a summary judgment and an appeal was taken.[188]

On appeal, the Second Circuit saw an individual's interest in his appearance as "a general liberty interest" that became stronger (under the purview of the first amendment) when placed within the context of teaching in a public school. In the court's opinion, "[t]he academic context has

---

employer considers the applicant's appearance inappropriate for the position in question, does not in and of itself represent a deprivation that is forbidden by the Due Process Clause." *Id.* at 668.

185. *Bishop, supra* note 4.

186. *Tardif, supra* note 175, at 764.

187. *East Hartford, supra* note 176.

188. *Id.* at 839.

long been given special constitutional protection in our country, because the educational needs of a free people are of utmost importance. . . ." [189] Additionally, said the court, a teacher's appearance is within an "inseparable complex of speech, conduct and character known as teacher." [190] As such, a teacher's appearance "should be protected from needless regulation by the State." [191]

The Second Circuit seemed to place a teacher's choice of appearance into a category with "methods of teaching." In the court's view, school officials may have complete authority to regulate course content (and a teacher must not subvert that content); but a "teacher's freedom to choose teaching methods is entitled to be weighed in the constitutional scales." [192] Thus, in judging the appropriateness of a teacher's appearance (i.e., dress, style of clothing, etc.), a court must look to see if the teacher's mode of attire is, in fact, subverting community values, and at such other issues as neatness, cleanliness and morality.[193]

The Second Circuit placed the burden on the school officials to establish its countervailing interests in infringing upon the appellant's first amendment entitlement. As reasons for the dress code the school board listed (1) the establishment of a professional image for teachers, (2) the promotion of good grooming habits among students, and (3) the maintenance of respect for teachers and of decorum in the classroom.[194]

---

189. *Id.* at 842.
190. *Id.*
191. *Id.*
192. *Id.* at 843-44. The teacher claimed that he believed that his "informal attire" was a teaching method making him more effective with his classes.
193. *Id.* at 844.
194. *Id.*

The court's analysis of the dress code focused upon the specific mandate at issue, the wearing of a necktie by male teachers. In the court's opinion the term "professional image" is "almost meaningless" as applied to "neckties for men." The court cited as its rationale the informality present in other professions (*e.g.*, medicine, law, dentistry, and engineering) as well as in teaching — especially among younger practitioners. Thus, the board's reason for its policy was given "little weight." Similarly, the court saw no causal connection between a necktie on male teachers and good grooming of students.[195]

Of the reasons advanced by the board for the necktie rule, the maintenance of respect, discipline and decorum in the classroom seemed the most valid exercise of its authority. Yet, no connection could be established between the wearing of neckties by men teachers and the furtherance of respect, discipline and classroom decorum.[196]

In reversing the district court, and remanding the case for a rehearing on the merits, the Second Circuit concluded its opinion with the statement that "a school board may make regulations that help to promote the effective and efficient education of children. It may not, however, make regulations that infringe on constitutional interests while not realistically and significantly furthering the board's proper purposes." In this case the teacher's interest far outweighed the board's countervailing interests.[197]

(e) FREEDOM FROM RETALIATORY ACTION.

As emphasized early in this chapter, the Supreme Court made it clear in *Pickering* that teachers should be free to speak in school and out of school "without fear of retaliatory

---

195. *Id.* at 845.
196. *Id.*
197. *Id.* at 846.

dismissal." [198] A common thread emerging from those cases subsequent to *Pickering* reviewed above illustrates a further development and refinement of this "freedom from retaliatory dismissal" mandate. In two other somewhat different decisions (one from 1977 and one from 1981), the federal courts hearing the matters were faced squarely with the claim of *retaliatory dismissals.*

Johnson v. Butler [199] was decided in 1977 by a federal district court in Virginia, and grew out of a situation which began when a nontenured elementary school teacher complained to her principal about her working conditions. The teacher, who worked as a "floating" teacher (*i.e.,* she served as a junior high school teacher of mathematics and science, but had no permanent classroom assignment), was in her third year of employment when her contract was not renewed.

Ms. Johnson instituted her action in federal court under § 1983, challenging the Roanoke City School Board's decision to terminate her services. She charged that the sole reason for the board's decision was her complaint to her principal, which she subsequently filed as a formal grievance through the state grievance procedure. [200] The school officials denied her allegations, and responded that their decision was based upon Johnson's insubordinate conduct and on her display of a poor attitude. [201]

Tried before a seven-member advisory jury, testimony revealed that Ms. Johnson had received satisfactory evalua-

---

198. *Pickering, supra* note 16.

199. 433 F. Supp. 531 (W.D. Va. 1977).

200. *Id.* at 533. Jurisdiction was alleged pursuant to 28 U.S.C. § 1343 and the first and fourteenth amendments to the Constitution.

201. *Id.* at 534. Specifically, they cited incidents of leaving a class unattended, leaving school prior to the end of a contract day, being late for a class, and being insubordinate to the principal.

tions during her first two years of teaching and that she was given outstanding ratings in several categories (ratings were particularly high for her ability to cooperate with other people). In fact, her principal had stated (in an evaluation written at the end of her second year) that "Miss Johnson is a satisfactory teacher and works hard at her teaching." [202]

Ms. Johnson did not complain about her floating teacher status until June of 1975. That month, she was notified by her principal that she would not be given a permanent classroom assignment. According to testimony given at trial, the principal told her that there was nothing that he could do about the situation and that he "didn't want to hear any more about it." Dissatisfied with that, Ms. Johnson wrote a letter to her superintendent and complained about her situation.[203]

In August, the superintendent wrote to Ms. Johnson and advised her to comply with the established grievance procedure by first attempting to reconcile the problem with her principal. She met with her principal, at which time she told him that she felt very strongly that her status as a floating teacher adversely affected her as a teacher. She later placed her complaint in writing, but received no response from the principal.[204]

---

202. *Id.* at 533.

203. *Id.* A significant point in the case is the fact that prior to her complaining to her principal, Ms. Johnson received consistently favorable ratings as a teacher. After she began to complain, her ratings changed to unfavorable. Also, had her contract been renewed for the fourth year she would have received, under Virginia law, a continuing contract.

204. *Id.* at 534.

In September, Ms. Johnson spoke to an assistant to the superintendent about her room assignment problem and decided, at that time, to withdraw her grievance and to proceed informally. The assistant advised her to apply for a transfer if she were unable to secure a satisfactory teaching assignment.[205]

During the month of October, the principal evaluated Ms. Johnson's performance as a teacher. At no time did he criticize her attitude or her ability. The following March, however, he informed Ms. Johnson that he would recommend that her contract not be renewed for the 1976-77 school year. At the end of that month, Ms. Johnson received a letter from the superintendent advising her that, based upon the principal's recommendations, he too would recommend to the board that her contract not be renewed. In April, the board met and voted three to two to uphold the superintendent's recommendation. No reasons were given at that time for her termination and Ms. Johnson was not allowed to be present when the principal testified before the board.[206]

At the outset of his opinion in this case, District Judge Williams relied on *Tinker v. Des Moines, Johnson v. Branch, Pickering v. Board of Education, Perry v. Sindermann,* and other cases on point to establish the importance of protecting the personal, associational and academic liberty of public school teachers. "Scholarship," stated Judge Williams, "cannot flourish in an atmosphere of suspicion and distrust. It is essential that teachers be able to speak out freely without fear of retaliatory dismissal." Thus, he continued, "a teacher may not be dismissed from

---

205. *Id.*

206. *Id.* at 534-35. Prior to the meeting of the board, the principal and superintendent met privately to discuss Ms. Johnson's nonrenewal.

employment for exercising his or her legitimate First Amendment right to protest conditions existing within the school system." [207]

Employing the *Mt. Healthy City School District Board of Education v. Doyle* causation standard, Judge Williams submitted two questions in special verdict form to the advisory jury. These questions were: (1) Has Ms. Johnson established, by a preponderance of evidence, that her making a complaint to the school principal was a substantial and motivating factor in the board's decision not to renew her contract? (2) If the answer to question one is yes, has the school board shown, by a preponderance of evidence, that it would have reached the same decision not to rehire Johnson in the absence of her complaint? [208]

The jury answered question one in the affirmative, but also found that the board would not have reached the same decision, absent Johnson's complaint. Even though the court was in no way bound by the jury's verdict, the court decided, after an independent review of the evidence, that Ms. Johnson's contract was nonrenewed solely because of her exercise of speech. In Judge Williams' opinion, "it is not important whether her complaint was valid or not, the sole question is whether the complaint was the root cause of her nonrenewal." [209]

The court found no evidence of insubordination, disrespectfulness, or dereliction of duty on Ms. Johnson's part. What is more, the court was of the opinion that "the minor infractions advanced as reasons for dismissing a teacher of Ms. Johnson's caliber are neither individually nor collectively such as to justify nonrenewal of her

---

207. *Id.* at 535.
208. *Id.*
209. *Id.* at 536.

contract." [210] Thus, the charges against her were a "mere pretext" to obtain a dismissal. Final judgment was entered granting Ms. Johnson reinstatement with tenure, back pay from the time of her termination of her contract until reinstatement (less any sums earned or received from unemployment compensation). [211]

More recently at the appellate level, the Fifth Circuit heard the case of a nontenured teacher who claimed that his contract was not renewed solely in retaliation for his exercise of speech. [212] It seems that he had made both *private* (to his superiors) and *public* (at a faculty meeting) comments regarding internal matters of the school system and criticized its internal functioning. [213]

Plaintiff Brown brought suit in federal district court under § 1983 against the school district and its trustees (officially and individually) for both monetary damages and equitable relief. He also named as defendants his superintendent and supervising principal. Unlike the previous case, punitive damages were an issue in this case.

After a jury trial at defendants' request, Brown was awarded $17,500 in lost wages, $5,000 in attorney's fees, and mandatory reinstatement. However, punitive damages were not assessed against defendants. Defendants appealed, insisting that the entire award should be set aside because Brown's exercise of speech "was not protected by the First Amendment and that the record will not support a judgment premised upon an unconstitutional retaliation." [214]

---

210. *Id.* at 537.

211. *Id.*

212. Brown v. Bullard Independent School District, 640 F.2d 651 (5th Cir. 1981).

213. *Id.* at 653.

214. *Id.* at 652-53.

Brown filed a cross-appeal asking that the Fifth Circuit affirm the entire award of the district court, and asking that the matter be remanded back to the trial court to reconsider the punitive damage claim and the attorney's fee award, which sum he claimed was inadequate.[215]

The appellate court could not find the district court in error and affirmed the denial of a directed verdict for defendants. Also, the high court could find no error in the jury's finding, in response to interrogatories, that the school board members and school administrators were not entitled to a "good faith immunity defense." [216]

Regarding the issue of punitive damages, the court could find no evidence that Brown had been subjected to "systematic oppression or a continuous course of harrassment." Nor could the court find "evidence of the type of malevolent, outrageous or abusive conduct which justified more than compensatory damages." [217]

The Fifth Circuit did, however, remand the case for reconsideration of attorney's fees. Since the district court failed both to explain how it arrived at the figure awarded and to make any references to guidelines for figuring attorney's fees set forth by the Fifth Circuit in an earlier case, the adequacy of the $5,000 figure must be reconsidered.[218]

---

215. *Id.*

216. *Id.* at 653.

217. *Id.* at 654. The Fifth Circuit cites the Supreme Court's decision in Carey v. Piphus, 435 U.S. 247 (1978). Punitive damages bear no relationship to plaintiff's injuries. They are awarded by the court in an effort to set an example to deter similar conduct from others. Thus, they must be large enough sums to act effectively as a deterrent.

218. *Id.* at 654.

§ 3.4. Freedom of Association.

Americans have long cherished the right to gather together and assemble with others in whom they find a common bond. Yet, like several others, this basic entitlement or "freedom of association" is not explicitly included in the United States Constitution. It is, however, implied in two clauses of the first amendment: assembly and petition.

Over the years, courts of law have extended constitutional protection to the freedom of association of teachers, protecting their entitlement from unwarranted invasions by both the federal and state governments. In the several cases on point of the past three decades, the common two-part question facing the courts has been: For what reasons and to what extent (if any) may school officials set conditions on and regulate a teacher's freedom of association? A corollary question has also been faced in many of these same cases: May school officials take disciplinary action (including nonrenewal and dismissal) against a teacher solely because of his or her personal and professional associations and affiliations?

A leading § 1983 case from the 1960's is *Johnson v. Branch*,[219] in which a black teacher with twelve years experience in her job, who was very active in civil rights in a North Carolina community experiencing racial tensions, was not rehired. She took an action in federal district court charging that she was not rehired as a teacher solely because of her civil rights activities.[220]

---

219. Johnson v. Branch, 364 F.2d 177 (4th Cir. 1966).

220. *Id.* at 178. The record disclosed that defendants conceded that appellant was "a well qualified, conscientious, and competent teacher. . . ."

The school board denied the allegations and asserted that the plaintiff was not rehired because she was incompetent. According to the board, she was dismissed for such things as being fifteen minutes late in supervising an athletic contest, arriving a few minutes late to school, failing to stand outside her door in supervising students as classes changed, and failing to see that cabinets in her room were clean and hazard free.[221]

A United States district court granted defendant's motion to dismiss.[222] Appeal was taken to the Fourth Circuit.

The appellate court found error in the district court's methods in determining its findings. In the high court's opinion,

> It is apparent on this record that absent the racial question, the issue would not have arisen. The only reasonable inference which may be drawn from the failure to renew Mrs. Johnson's contract in the face of her splendid record of twelve years on such trivial charges was the Board members' objections to her racial activity.[223]

The Fourth Circuit's weighing of the school board's "trivial charges" against Mrs. Johnson's "splendid record of twelve years" seemed to be the pivotal point of the decision.

The order of the district court was reversed and the case was remanded with instructions to enter an order directing the school board to renew Mrs. Johnson's contract. Also to be determined were any damages.

---

221. *Id.* at 178-79.

222. *Id.* at 179-81. The district court was convinced that personnel decisions in the North Carolina Public Schools are within the wide discretion of the local school board. The court was also convinced that plaintiff's civil rights activities consumed so much of her time and interest that they interfered with her extracurricular activities at school and they had caused some dissention between her and the school principal.

223. *Id.* at 182.

Teacher union activity has also been a source of civil rights tort litigation. An early case on point is *McLaughlin v. Tilendis,* decided by the Seventh Circuit in 1968.[224]

In *McLaughlin,* two male probationary teachers in Illinois took an action under § 1983 seeking $100,000 in damages from their superintendent and members of the school board. One teacher was not offered a second year contract and the other teacher was dismissed before the end of his second year. Each plaintiff alleged that his employment was terminated solely because of his association with Local 1663 of the AFT, AFL-CIO.[225]

The district court granted defendants' motion and dismissed plaintiffs' complaint. To the district court, since plaintiffs had no first amendment rights to join or form a labor union, there was no jurisdiction in this case.[226]

On appeal, the Seventh Circuit reversed the district court. "It is settled," said the appellate court, "that teachers have the right to free association, and unjustified interference with teachers' associational freedom violates the Due Process Clause of the Fourteenth Amendment." [227]

Next, the high court placed the right to form and join a union within the purview of the first amendment. The court said to dismiss a teacher solely for asserting this right will not be acceptable. Unless there is some illegal intent on the part of a teacher to form or join a union, or unless a teacher's union activities impede the "proper performance of . . . daily

---

224. 398 F.2d 287 (7th Cir. 1968).
225. *Id.* at 288.
226. *Id.*
227. *Id.*

duties in the classroom . . .," termination of employment will not be considered proper.[228]

Citing *Johnson v. Branch*[229] and other similar cases, the Seventh Circuit declared that appellants' not being tenured did not deprive them of remedy under § 1983. The court held, on the record, that the complaint sufficiently stated a justifiable claim under § 1983.[230]

Regarding any possible immunity claims made by defendants, the Seventh Circuit extended only a qualified immunity, and that immunity was dependent on good faith action. To hold defendants absolutely immune from this type of suit "would frustrate the very purpose of Section 1983. . . ."[231] The district court decision was reversed and the case was remanded for a new trial.

Six years later, in a more publicized § 1983 decision out of the Fourth Circuit, a teacher in Montgomery County, Maryland claimed that school officials wrongfully transferred him to a nonteaching position when they discovered that he was a homosexual. In *Acanfora v. Board of Education*,[232] the United States district court had denied relief because of plaintiff's subsequent press and television interviews. He appealed to the Fourth Circuit.

Even though the appellate court held that Acanfora's public statements were protected by the first amendment,

---

228. *Id.* On this last point the court cited Pickering v. Board of Education, *supra* note 16. *See* O'Connor v. Mazzulo, 536 F. Supp. 641 (S.D.N.Y. 1982).

229. *Johnson, supra* note 219.

230. *McLaughlin, supra* note 224, at 289.

231. *Id.* at 290. Recently, the Fifth Circuit held that a good-faith immunity cannot be asserted by officials whose actions clearly violate established state law. William v. Treer, 50 U.S.L.W. 2590 (April 13, 1982).

232. 491 F.2d 498 (4th Cir. 1974), *cert. denied,* 419 U.S. 836 (1974).

that court also denied relief, but for different reasons.[233] In that court's opinion, where a teacher had intentionally withheld from his employment application information concerning his homosexuality, he was subject to school board sanctions for his action. The court said:

> Acanfora purposely misled the school officials so he could circumvent, not challenge, what he considers to be their unconstitutional employment practices. He cannot now invoke the process of the court to obtain a ruling on an issue that he practiced deception to avoid.[234]

The fact that he made public statements regarding his homosexuality did not protect him from warranted board action concerning his employment application.

A Sixth Circuit case, *Hickman v. Valley Local School District Board* involved a female, certified, nontenured elementary school teacher in an Ohio public school system. Having taught for a total of nine years, Ms. Hickman was midway through her fourth year of teaching in the Valley Local School District when the school board decided not to renew her contract for the next year. Under Ohio law, had her contract been renewed, she would have achieved tenure in the school system.[235]

Hickman filed suit in federal district court, "alleging that her contract had not been renewed because of her union activities." Named as defendants in the suit were the school board, individual school board members, the school superintendent and her principal (both of whom were sued in their individual and official capacities).[236]

---

233. *Id.* at 501. It should be pointed out that the Fourth Circuit was assured that publicity of his admitted homosexuality did not disrupt nor impair the educational process of the school.

234. *Id.* at 504.

235. Hickman v. Valley Local School District Board, 619 F.2d 606 (6th Cir. 1980).

236. *Id.* at 607.

At trial the following facts were presented. Ms. Hickman was active in the local teachers union. In her first year in the school system she served as a representative on the union's negotiating team. In her second year she served as vice president of the local, and in her third year she was elected president of the local. Also, throughout the three years, she published the union's newsletter.

According to Hickman, a number of her other activities irritated her superintendent and principal. For example, she had taken a complaint about an "outbreak of scabies" among students in her school directly to the school board, bypassing both her principal and the superintendent. In a related matter, she had removed a book of board policies from the principal's office and given it to the school nurse, to help her enlist the help of other school personnel to fight the scabies outbreak.

On another occasion Hickman reported that she sought and received P.T.A. support for a bill pending before the Ohio legislature that would give public employees a collective bargaining bill of rights. While that was going on, she helped a fellow teacher successfully process a salary grievance against the board.

At trial it was shown that Hickman was evaluated as a teacher by her principal during each of her three years. The principal used the accepted school system form (a rating scale of one to five, highest to lowest, was employed for each item) for each evaluation. For the first year her classroom teaching received an "excellent" rating, and her second year rating was the same. However, her ratings (over the two years) in both "intra-school relationships" and "professional ethics" plummeted from one to five, and three to five respectively.

Upon completion of her second year in the system, her principal recommended that Hickman's contract not be renewed. The superintendent did not agree with him and she was renewed. After the third year, however, both recommended that the board not renew Hickman's contract. Ultimately, three members of the board voted to accept the recommendation, one voted to renew her contract, and one abstained from voting. Thus by a vote of three to one her contract was not renewed.[237]

In the final list of reasons cited for Hickman's nonrenewal were the following: improper playground supervision, personally calling in and involving a county supervisor as a part of settling a teacher's salary dispute; and unauthorized removal of the principal's school board policy book. Also presented to the court were documented recommendations made by the principal, during Ms. Hickman's third year, that she (1) do less talking to other teachers in the halls during class time, (2) show more cooperation with the administration, (3) do less "tearing down" and more "building up" of the school system, (4) personally reevaluate her own philosophy and purpose for doing her job, (5) stop intimidating other teachers who refuse to join the teachers association, and (6) stop trying to be teacher, principal and union president all at the same time.

The principal testified that he based his recommendation of nonrenewal on Hickman's decline in classroom performance, poor teacher ratings in intraschool relationships and professional ethics, and on her assuming too many "outside the classroom" responsibilities. It is interesting to note that the record showed that the principal made the "unfavorable teaching" evaluation based upon one or two

---

237. *Id.* at 606-08.

fifteen-to-thirty minute classroom observations made over the three year period.[238]

The United States district court entered judgment in favor of defendants and Hickman appealed. The United States Court of Appeals for the Sixth Circuit reversed that judgment.

On appeal Ms. Hickman argued that the "personality con- flict" and "declining performance" evaluations cannot serve as reasons to justify her nonrenewal, because they are inextricably linked to the "antagonism generated by her union activities." Also, she urged the court to give closer examination to the bases for the principal's and superintendent's recommendations to the board, since the board placed sole reliance on them to reach its nonrenewal decision. The Sixth Circuit agreed with both of her points.[239]

The *Mt. Healthy* causation standard was applied by the appellate court. In that court's opinion, "the 'personality conflict' is a consequence of Hickman's protected con- duct. . . ." Also, the decline in her teaching performance was traceable to her union activities. "It is hardly surprising," said the court, "that the principal, with whom Hickman had done battle on numerous occasions as union representative, would grade her so poorly in these categories. . . . Therefore, the decline in her teaching evaluations is tainted by her supervisors' disapproval of her protected conduct. . . ."[240]

In finding the district court in error, the high court stated:

In our view, the facts compel the conclusion that Hickman would not have been dismissed but for her

---

238. *Id.* at 608-09.
239. *Id.* at 609.
240. *Id.*

union activities. The alleged personality conflict ... germinated from her union activities. To allow any rancorous feelings engendered in this manner to justify a dismissal would decimate constitutional protections. Moreover, there is no evidence, and the district court did not find, that Hickman's conduct had in any way impeded or disrupted the operation of the school.... Nor is there a question here of maintaining discipline by immediate supervisors or coworker harmony.... Many teachers signed petitions urging the reinstatement of Hickman.[241]

The appellate court did not go so far as to view the defendant's actions as "retaliatory"; rather, it concluded that defendants could not show that the nonrenewal would have occurred absent Hickman's exercise of protected conduct.[242]

On remand, the Sixth Circuit ordered the district court to cause defendants to: (1) offer reinstatement to Hickman (with continuing contract); (2) compensate her for lost earnings; and (3) consider the appropriateness of awarding attorney's fees. All appeal costs were to be paid by the defendants.

§ 3.5. Other Sources of § 1983 Case Law.

In addition to the source of teacher civil rights tort litigation presented above (basically claims of first amendment violations of speech, expression and association), such cases have developed from other alleged infractions by public school officials. The decisions reviewed below are illustrative of this point.

---

241. *Id.* For a similar case on point see Columbus Education Association v. Columbus City School District, 623 F.2d 1155 (6th Cir. 1980).

242. *Id.* at 610. Reheard on remand at 513 F. Supp. 659 (S.D. Ohio 1981). Hickman received $19,149 in back pay, $33,500 in attorney's fees, and an offer of reinstatement with a continuing contract.

(a) TEACHERS' PRIVATE LIVES.

Generally, a teacher's behavior in his or her private life is not, in and of itself, just cause for termination of employment. However, if a teacher's private outside school activities are proved by fact to have a detrimental impact on his or her functions as a professional inside school, or are disruptive of the educational process, or pose a threat of harm to students or other teachers, a board's termination decision will most likely be sustained if challenged in a court of law.

In an early § 1983 case, a male middle-aged, tenured, sixth grade teacher in Massachusetts was dismissed from his teaching position, which he had held for five years, for "engaging in public conduct unbecoming a teacher."[243] This charge stemmed from his having been seen "moving about his property . . . on many an evening with a dress mannequin and dressing and undressing that mannequin."[244]

Plaintiff Wishart brought suit in federal district court under § 1983, seeking declaratory and injunctive relief, as well as monetary damages. Named as defendants in his suit were his school superintendent and the members of the school committee (all defendants were sued individually and in their official capacities).[245]

Wishart did not deny the charges, but argued that his public conduct with the mannequin in no way damaged his ability to function as a teacher. Since he was rated as an above-average to excellent teacher, to terminate his employment for unrelated conduct was impermissible.[246]

---

243. Wishart v. McDonald, 367 F. Supp. 530, 531 (D. Mass. 1973).

244. *Id.*

245. *Id.* at 532. Wishart sought, among other things, reinstatement to a full-time teaching position, and both compensatory and exemplary damages totalling $200,000.

246. *Id.* at 534. Written evidence was introduced through his school principal that showed Wishart's above-average to excellent teacher ratings.

Defendants sought to have the action dismissed on the ground that Wishart had not exhausted state remedies before going into federal court. This motion was denied. In the court's view, even though plaintiff may be required to exhaust state administrative remedies, he was not required to exhaust state judicial remedies. The district court said: "[t]o exact such a requirement from a plaintiff in a [§] 1983 action would be to ignore the policy behind the statute of providing a federal cause of action for alleged deprivations of civil rights." [247]

At the completion of the trial, the district court denied Wishart's requests for remedy under § 1983. The court seemed impressed by the "public notoriety" of Wishart's conduct. To the court there was a basis for the superintendent's belief that "the conduct had, or certainly would in the future, gain a degree of notoriety which would damage plaintiff's effectiveness as a teacher in the school system and his working relationship within the educational process." [248] Thus, by following the recommendation of its superintendent, the school committee was not acting arbitrarily or capriciously. Nor was there was any evidence that these school officials acted intentionally or maliciously to intrude unconstitutionally into Wishart's right of privacy.[249] In conclusion, the court held that "the evidence in this case is ample that on various occasions the conduct was public in nature or at least was carried on with such reckless disregard of whether or not he was observed that it lost whatever private character it might have had." [250]

At the federal appellate level that same year, the Eighth Circuit was faced with a similar case. The case involved a

---

247. *Id.* at 533.
248. *Id.* at 535.
249. *Id.*
250. *Id.*

female Nebraska teacher who had lost her job for "unbecoming conduct" in her private life. In *Fisher v. Snyder*,[251] a high school teacher in a rural county school district was dismissed at the close of the 1972 school year.

A middle-aged divorcee who lived alone in a one-bedroom apartment, Ms. Fisher had allowed guests (her twenty-six year old son's friends — married couples, young ladies, and young men) to stay with her in her apartment, since hotel accommodations were generally sparse or not available. Some guests would stay overnight. One such guest was a twenty-six year old male who visited town frequently. In fact on one occasion he stayed one week so that he could visit classes to meet one of his college requirements.[252]

Ms. Fisher made all the class visitation arrangements with school officials, and his visits were even reported in the local newspaper. It was following the young man's week-long visitation that the board notified Ms. Fisher that her contract would not be renewed.[253]

Ms. Fisher brought suit in district court under § 1983. The court ordered reinstatement and the board appealed.

The Eighth Circuit affirmed the lower court's judgment to reinstate Ms. Fisher. In that court's opinion, the board's action to terminate was arbitrary and capricious. The court said:

> the presence of these guests in her home provides no inkling beyond subtle implication and innuendo which would impugn Mrs. Fisher's morality. Idle speculation certainly does not provide a basis in fact for the board's

---

251. 476 F.2d 375 (8th Cir. 1973).

252. *Id.* at 376.

253. *Id.* It should be noted that the board never accused Ms. Fisher of "immoral conduct." They actually charged her with "social misbehavior" that was not conducive to the maintenance and integrity of the school system.

conclusory inference that "there was strong potential of sexual misconduct" and that, therefore, Mrs. Fisher's activity was "social misbehavior" that is not conducive to the maintenance of the integrity of the public school system.[254]

The court also said there was no evidence presented of either adverse community reaction or that Mrs. Fisher could no longer maintain classroom discipline because of her having overnight house guests.[255]

Six years later, the Tenth Circuit decided a Wyoming case involving a nontenured elementary school teacher who had been denied renewal of her contract for what school officials claimed were teaching deficiencies.[256] Annabel Stoddard instituted an action in federal district court alleging that her former employers failed to renew her contract for reasons violating the first and fourteenth amendments and § 1983. As defendants she named the school district, the school board, the school superintendent and principal (in their official capacities), two specific board members (in their individual capacities), and the principal (in his individual capacity).[257]

Events leading up to the court action were the following. In 1973 Ms. Stoddard was hired to teach the third grade. Unable to find housing, she and her four children moved into a mobile home in a trailer court.

As a teacher during the 1973-74 and 1974-75 school years, her performance was rated as generally satisfactory. During the 1974-75 school year, however, there was some concern about her lack of discipline in her classes, but this was excused since she was about to undergo surgery.[258]

---

254. *Id.* at 377.
255. *Id.* at 378.
256. Stoddard v. School District, 590 F.2d 829 (10th Cir. 1979).
257. *Id.* at 831.
258. *Id.* at 832-33.

In February 1975, the principal handed Ms. Stoddard a letter advising her that he would not recommend contract renewal for the next school year. However, since Ms. Stoddard had majored in physical education, and since the school needed a physical education teacher, the principal invited her to submit a proposal for that position. She prepared and submitted the proposal.[259]

When one of the defendant board members heard of the possibility that Ms. Stoddard might be employed as a physical education teacher, he immediately telephoned the other defendant board member. In their conversation the first board member told the other that he was "definitely opposed" to reemploying Ms. Stoddard.[260]

Approximately one week later the school principal, after reviewing Ms. Stoddard's physical education proposal, advised her that he would not recommend her renewal in any capacity. In a letter to her he stated that her physical education program was impressive on paper, but was too "idealistic" and would not work. He also stated he believed that Stoddard would not perform satisfactorily as a teacher because: (1) her elementary classroom had been disorderly; (2) there was reason to believe that she would not maintain the physical education equipment properly; (3) there was real doubt that she could maintain discipline in physical education classes; and (4) she lacked dynamics in motivating students.[261]

At a meeting between Ms. Stoddard and her principal, he said that the reasons stated in his letter were not the "real" reasons for her nonrenewal. According to him, the "real" reasons were: (1) recurring rumors that she was having an affair with another resident of the trailer park; (2)

---

259. *Id.*
260. *Id.*
261. *Id.*

dissatisfaction in the community that she played cards and that she did not attend church regularly; (3) she did not have an attractive appearance which was required of all physical education teachers; and (4) her "lack of dynamics" was due to her obesity. At the same meeting the principal told Ms. Stoddard that he had received a telephone call advising him that if he recommended contract renewal for Ms. Stoddard there would be "hell to pay." Finally, the principal also told her that if she resigned, he would give her a good recommendation for another job.[262]

At the completion of a jury trial, the jury by its general verdict found in favor of Ms. Stoddard. Judgment was entered against defendants in the sum of $33,000 as compensatory damages, $5,000 as punitive damages, and $5,800 as attorney's fees.[263] Both the punitive damages and attorney's fees were later disallowed by the trial court on the ground that the defendants acted without malice.

On appeal the Tenth Circuit found no error in the trial court's judgment that would necessitate reversal. In the appellate court's opinion there was direct evidence that the school principal was motivated by constitutionally impermissible reasons to recommend nonrenewal. Also, there was circumstantial evidence of pressure on the principal by certain board members not to recommend renewal.[264]

Citing the Supreme Court's decision in *Monell*,[265] the Tenth Circuit made it clear that the school district was a "person" within the meaning of § 1983, and the district

---

262. *Id.* at 833-34. Ms. Stoddard refused to resign. She stated that to do so would be the same as admitting that the rumors were true.

263. *Id.*

264. *Id.* The appellate court saw as significant the fact that Ms. Stoddard's satisfactory teaching record should have warranted renewal.

265. *Monell, supra* note 69.

could be held liable for the actions of its board. The only way a district can act, said the court, is by and through its board.[266]

The Tenth Circuit, as did the trial court, rejected defendant's claim of eleventh amendment immunity. In the high court's view the school district in this case was "more like a city or county than it is like an arm of the state." [267] Also undisturbed was the trial court's rejection of punitive damages, since the Tenth Circuit found no evidence of malicious conduct.

Regarding attorney's fees, the Tenth Circuit was of the opinion that on remand plaintiff should be allowed to file a motion for attorney's fees under 42 U.S.C. § 1988. Such a claim, said the Court, should therefore be "adjudicated on its merits in accordance with appropriate judicial discretion." [268] The *Stoddard* case was thus remanded to the trial court. Direction was given that a judgment be entered for plaintiff in the amount of $33,000 in compensatory damages.[269]

Thompson v. Southwest School District [270] is a 1980 case on point. In *Thompson* a female teacher with eleven years experience (the last four years of which she served as a teacher of children in the second grade) was suspended from her job in a Missouri public school system for allegedly engaging in immoral conduct. The conduct in question involved her living with a man to whom she was not married.

---

266. *Stoddard, supra* note 256, at 834-35.

267. *Id.* at 835. On this point, in addition to other cases, the court cited *Mt. Healthy, supra* note 12.

268. *Id.* It seems that the original claim for attorney's fees was treated as a "common law" matter and was not statutorily based.

269. *Id.*

270. 483 F. Supp. 1170 (W.D. Mo. 1980).

In December of 1979, Ms. Thompson took action in federal district court pursuant to § 1983. She alleged in her complaint that on November 14, 1979, she was asked to sign a statement on her performance evaluation indicating that she was living with a man to whom she was not married; but, that she did plan on marrying him in the near future. On November 15, 1979, she was informed by school officials that she could resign, in which case she would be given a favorable recommendation for employment. If she did not resign, said the officials, she would be fired and her credentials as a teacher would be taken away.[271]

On November 19, she married the man with whom she had been living and on that day also notified the school board of her marriage. On November 20, she was sent a letter informing her that she was suspended with pay "because of the charge of immorality brought against her by the school board and that she had a right to a hearing."[272] A termination hearing was held on December 20.

On December 21, 1979, the district court issued a temporary restraining order enjoining defendants from enforcing certain sections of the Missouri Revised Statutes until 6:00 p.m., on January 4, 1980. A hearing on a preliminary injunction was held on January 4, 1980. At that hearing both parties agreed to extend the temporary restraining order until January 18, 1980, in order to have time to prepare and submit briefs.[273]

---

271. *Id.* at 1173. Named as defendants in the suit were the school district, the school board, individual school board members, the school superintendent, and the school principal.

272. *Id.* Evidence presented showed that after her suspension Ms. Thompson attended a Christmas performance at her elementary school and was told to leave or a sheriff would be called.

273. *Id.* The Missouri statutes were those related to cause for teacher dismissal and those related to determining professional competence.

At trial the court was sufficiently convinced that even though Ms. Thompson's employment had not yet been terminated, there was an actual case or controversy between plaintiff and defendants, and that the plaintiff teacher was in immediate danger of sustaining a direct injury as the result of the actions of school officials.[274] Also, the district court stated that even though plaintiff did not exhaust administrative remedies available to her, her case was not taken prematurely.

The district court next addressed the issue of whether or not the Missouri Statutes were in fact vague in their specific references to types of conduct sufficient as causes of teacher dismissal (*e.g.*, immoral conduct, physical or mental condition making him unfit to instruct or associate with children, incompetency, inefficiency, insubordination, etc.). In the court's view, the intent of the legislature was to state causes capable of precise definition and application. It was intended that each cause, as applied in each case, could be supported by evidence showing a connection between the teacher's conduct and some adverse effect on the teacher's professional performance.[275]

Regarding Ms. Thompson, the court saw no evidence presented indicating that her conduct had rendered her unfit to teach. In fact, the board itself admitted that Thompson's teaching ability was never an issue and was not disputed.[276]

The district court then turned directly to Ms. Thompson's complaint that the board had acted arbitrarily and capriciously, violating her right to substantive due process.

---

274. *Id.* at 1177.

275. *Id.* at 1180-83.

276. *Id.* at 1182. Ms. Thompson's performance evaluations as a teacher had always been good. She had experienced no disciplinary problems in her classroom, and there was no evidence presented that she had lost her students' respect.

Citing *Fisher v. Snyder,*[277] the court placed the initial burden of proof on the plaintiff to prove

> that each of the stated reasons [underlying his dismissal] is trivial, or is unrelated to the educational process or to working relationships within the educational institution, or is wholly unsupported by a basis in fact.[278]

In this case, the court was sufficiently convinced that plaintiff had established serious questions regarding the merits of the board's case against her. In addition, the district court was convinced that the balance of hardships (even if Ms. Thompson would prevail in this case) was tipped decidedly in plaintiff's favor.[279]

Thus, the district court ordered that the defendants were restrained from suspending Ms. Thompson or from terminating her employment on the basis of the immoral conduct charge, until further order of the court. The court gave the parties thirty days from the date of the order to present any further evidence on the matter of whether the injunction was to be made permanent.[280]

A similar case, *McGhee v. Draper,* was first heard by a United States District Court for the Northern District of Oklahoma, where a directed verdict was granted defendant school officials. The case was then appealed by the plaintiff teacher to the Tenth Circuit in 1977, where that court affirmed in part and reversed in part the district court and

---

277. *Fisher, supra* note 251.

278. Quoted directly from *Fisher* (at page 377). *Thompson, supra* note 270, at 1183.

279. *Thompson, supra* note 270, at 1184. The court saw Ms. Thompson's chances of future employment would most likely be hampered. The court saw no undue hardships accruing on the side of the school officials.

280. *Id.* at 1185.

remanded the case for further proceedings.[281] In January of 1981, the matter was once again before the Tenth Circuit.[282]

McGhee involved a discharged female, nontenured teacher who alleged that "as a result of unfounded rumors and gossip in the community of immorality her teaching contract was not renewed for the 1974-75 year." [283] She alleged further, "that the board acted because of 'community turmoil,' that she was the victim of community gossip and rumors concerning her morality and private life, that she was never allowed to confront her accusers or afforded a due process hearing to clear her good name, and that as a direct consequence she has been unable to secure another teaching position and is unemployed." [284]

Originally brought into federal court as a civil rights action under § 1983 (claiming violations of both property and liberty without due process), the plaintiff sought an injunctive order for reinstatement, and in addition, she sought back pay, damages and attorney's fees. Named as defendants were the school district board of education, the board members and the school superintendent.

On appeal for the first time in 1977, the Tenth Circuit was convinced that the district court's directed verdict was proper, insofar as it denied recovery of damages against the defendants since, at the time, the qualified immunity defense was clearly established and school officials were acting in good faith to comply with state law.[285] However,

---

281. McGhee v. Draper, 564 F.2d 902 (10th Cir. 1977).
282. McGhee v. Draper, 639 F.2d 639 (10th Cir. 1981).
283. *McGhee, supra* note 281, at 904.
284. *Id.* at 906.
285. *Id.* at 915.

the court reversed the lower court's rejection of considering possible equitable relief on the liberty claim and the case was remanded for further proceedings on that issue.[286] The appellate court was convinced that sufficient evidence was produced showing that the actions of school officials imposed a stigma or disability foreclosing the freedom of the teacher to take advantage of other employment possibilities. Thus, with a liberty interest implicated, as a matter of law the school board should have provided the teacher a sufficient hearing.

A second appeal was taken by plaintiff teacher in 1981 challenging the district court's rejection of certain claimed remedies. In particular, plaintiff wanted a review of her claims for back pay and compensatory damages in light of the Supreme Court's decision in *Owen v. City of Independence.*

On appeal, the school officials argued that because the school district itself had earlier been dismissed from the case, and that dismissal had not been a part of the first appeal, then there were no members of the board now before the court in their official capacities in this appeal. In its opinion, the court treated the remedies issues as mooted, since a request for equitable relief "requires an official-capacity party."[287] The defendants also said the plaintiff-teacher had not alleged that "her deprivation was the result of the execution of the School District's policy, rule or custom...."[288] Such a deficiency, said school officials, would remove the basis for a § 1983 suit against the district or the individual officials in their official capacities.

---

286. *Id.* at 916.
287. *McGhee, supra* note 282, at 642.
288. *Id.*

Regarding defendants' first argument, the Tenth Circuit opined that defendants were clearly considered to have been sued in their official, as well as individual, capacities. The named board members, said the court, "are before us in their official capacities." [289] Regarding the latter argument, in the opinion of the court, "*Owen v. City of Independence* . . . disposes of defendants' argument that no board 'policy, rule or custom' is here involved." [290] In the instant case, as in *Owen* " 'it is the local government itself that is responsible for the constitutional deprivation.' " [291] Hence, said the court, "it is perfectly reasonable to distribute the loss to the public as a cost of the administration of government, rather than to let the entire burden fall on the injured individual." [292]

The appellate court then scrutinized the teacher's liberty interest claim. The court placed an initial burden on the plaintiff to show that the official conduct about which she complained "stigmatized or otherwise damaged her reputation." [293] However, in a § 1983 claim, said the court, this stigmatization or reputational damage alone is not enough to support such a claim. In the court's opinion:

> In order to justify relief under liberty clause of the 14th amendment via § 1983, plaintiff's alleged reputational damage must be entangled with some other "tangible interests such as employment. . . ." Plaintiff must be allowed to attempt to convince the trier of fact that these elements are present . . . . Thus, if plaintiff can show to the trier of fact that the non-renewal caused or enhanced her alleged reputational damage, she will

---

289. *Id.*
290. *Id.*
291. *Id.*
292. *Id.*
293. *Id.* at 642-43. "Such damage," said the Tenth Circuit, "is properly vindicated through state tort actions."

have shown that she was entitled to a hearing or other reasonable opportunity to clear her name. . . . Once it is determined that a hearing right was triggered because of an infringement upon plaintiff's liberty, the constitutional sufficiency of a purported hearing is a legal issue to be determined by the courts.[294]

Given these requirements, the Tenth Circuit was convinced that the teacher was not afforded a "constitutionally adequate hearing. . . ." [295] This alone was enough to establish a violation of procedural due process. The truth or falsity of the charges against her, said the court, "is relevant only in fashioning the appropriate remedy." [296] In this case, since a violation of due process was established (failure to provide an adequate hearing), "[a]n appropriate remedy must then be fashioned." [297]

Interpreting *Owen,* the Tenth Circuit voiced the opinion that local government officials in their official capacities are liable for compensatory damages regardless of good faith. The court said, "[t]he broad remedial and deterrent purposes of § 1983 outweigh any deleterious impact on the public treasury . . . . Defendant school board members in their official capacity therefore may not escape liability for any actual damages traceable to the denial of procedural due process unless protected by the Eleventh Amendment." [298] However, the burden falls upon the plaintiff to

---

294. *Id.* at 643.

295. *Id.*

296. *Id.*

297. *Id.* at 644. Citing Carey v. Piphus, 435 U.S. 247 (1978), the court suggested as available appropriate remedy (1) nominal damages (even if charges prove to be truthful), (2) a post-termination hearing (if requested), and (3) compensatory or equitable relief (if the disseminated charges are determined as either improper or false).

298. *Id.* On this point the court is not clear, since in other cases cited Oklahoma school boards have been held as "not the state," but "merely a sueable political subdivision of the state." On this same point of law

prove the causal connections. Damages are not presumed, said the court. In the court's words, "[t]he burden remains on the plaintiff to prove the link between the due process violation and any particular consequence that would support an award of damages." [299]

In her arguments to the court, plaintiff insisted that since she had no pre-termination hearing, "only reinstatement can make her whole." [300] The appellate court did not agree with her argument. However, said the court, if plaintiff could prove that she would have been retained had "full procedural due process" been afforded her, she may be reinstated.[301] However, this theory of recovery, said the court, "requires a purely factual determination of the consequences of the due process violation." [302]

In response to plaintiff's claim of back pay, the court first clarified (quoting from another case) that such an award "is an integral part of the equitable remedy of reinstatement and is not comparable to damages in a common law action." [303] As such, and because of precedent on point, "the good faith of school board members does not preclude an

---

(addressed in another state), see Holladay v. Montana, 506 F. Supp. 1317 (D. Mont. 1981), wherein a federal district court declared that it lacked jurisdiction over the State of Montana and the State Department of Institutions. In that court's view, "(a) a state is not a citizen for purposes of diversity jurisdiction, (b) the state of Montana cannot be sued by a private citizen under the 11th Amendment prohibition against such suits, and (c) the State of Montana is not a 'person' under 42 U.S.C. 1983 . . . ."

299. *Id.* at 645.

300. *Id.*

301. *Id.* at 646.

302. *Id.* The success of this, said the court, seemed remote. *Mt. Healthy, supra* note 12, and *Givhan, supra* note 29, are cited on this point.

303. *Id.*

equitable award of backpay. As with reinstatement, backpay is therefore an appropriate remedy in this case if plaintiff is able to prove a direct causal link between her denial of procedural due process and her termination." [304]

Thus, the Tenth Circuit remanded the case back to the district court with instructions that plaintiff must be given an opportunity to prove that she was entitled to a hearing in connection with her nonrenewal of employment. The court said, if this can be shown, "plaintiff should be awarded nominal damages and any other relief which, consistent with this opinion, she can show is warranted." [305]

Not every § 1983 case developing out of teachers' private lives has come from some charge of immoral or unfitting conduct. A good example is a matter recently litigated in a federal district court in New Jersey. In *Niederhuber v. Camden County Vocational and Technical School District Board of Education,*[306] a nontenured teacher (whose duties involved teaching handicapped children) was discharged from his job for what the school board said were his unauthorized absences from school.[307] Plaintiff-teacher took a civil rights action challenging his dismissal on grounds that his termination deprived him of both his first amendment right to free exercise of his religion and his due process rights under the fourteenth amendment. Plaintiff Niederhuber, as a member of the Worldwide Church of God, had absented himself from school to observe his religion's holy days.[308]

Upon hearing the evidence, the trial court concluded that the school board had dismissed Niederhuber for absences

---

304. *Id.*
305. *Id.*
306. 495 F. Supp. 273 (D. N.J. 1980).
307. *Id.* at 276.
308. *Id.* at 274-75.

taken to celebrate his religion's holy days. However, the court had not discerned any evidence of "discriminatory intent" on the part of the school board.[309] The critical inquiry, said the court, "is the coercive effect of governmental action as it operates against an individual in the practice of his or her religion." [310]

A major contention of the board was that allowing plaintiff's religious absences would be detrimental to the students, especially handicapped students, by depriving them of a "stable and structured learning environment." [311] No evidence was presented to support this assertion. The board also contended that to honor plaintiff's numerous requests for leave would obligate them to honor the many requests received from other teachers. This obligation, said the board, "would strain the management and the budget of the school system...." [312] No evidence was presented to support this assertion. In the court's opinion, "the Board of Education has failed to demonstrate sufficiently compelling reasons to justify plaintiff's dismissal, or, that accommodation of his religious convictions would result in undue hardship." [313] The school district may be "inconvenienced" to some extent, said the court, but their inconvenience is "outweighed by the hardship on the plaintiff if the accommodation is not made." [314]

As a result of his unlawful discharge, the court found that plaintiff Niederhuber was entitled to back pay (computed from day of discharge to date of court judgment). The board

---

309. *Id.* at 275.
310. *Id.* at 278.
311. *Id.* at 280.
312. *Id.*
313. *Id.*
314. *Id.*

was ordered to reinstate Niederhuber to his former position as a full-time teacher under the same or better terms as his former contract provided.[315]

Niederhuber's claim of damages for mental and emotional distress failed. His request for punitive damages was also defeated. The court found no evidence of "malicious and wanton" conduct on the part of the school officials.[316]

As to the matter of attorney's fees, the court held that plaintiff was entitled to such recovery. However, the court ordered that these fees be calculated in accordance with standards set by the Third Circuit in previous cases, and that the following guidelines be considered: "(1) the number of hours spent in various legal activities by the individual attorneys; (2) the reasonable hourly rate for the individual attorneys; (3) the contingent nature of success; and (4) the quality of the attorneys' work."[317] The court gave the parties time to agree on the fee; and, if no fee was agreed upon, time was allotted for the parties to file motions regarding their determinations of what is reasonable. Thus, the district court's final judgment in this case was delayed pending a determination of a reasonable fee for plaintiff's attorneys.

(b) RACIAL DISCRIMINATION.

Beginning in the 1970's, several civil rights actions were taken in federal court challenging alleged racial discrimination in public school system employment practices. The impact and primary effect of these cases were to force school boards and school officials to remove arbitrary and irrational practices from their processes of personnel deci-

---

315. *Id.* at 281.
316. *Id.*
317. *Id.* at 282.

sion-making. Section 1983 and a host of subsequent federal laws and regulations offered civil rights lawyers the legal leverage necessary to force equal employment opportunity into action, and to attempt to bring an end to racial discrimination in employment.

One of the earliest § 1983 cases out of the early 1970's was *Porcelli v. Titus*,[318] a New Jersey case decided by the Third Circuit. Action was originally brought in federal district court by Victor Porcelli and some other white teachers employed by the Newark Board of Education. In their suit these plaintiffs claimed that the defendant superintendent of schools, acting under color of state law for the Newark school system, discriminated against them because of their race in appointing non-white elementary school principals and vice-principals. This discrimination against eligible whites was allegedly accomplished by the abolition of a promotional list which had been in existence since 1953. At the time of the abolition of the promotional list, plaintiff Porcelli's and the other plaintiffs' names were on the list as eligible for such jobs.[319]

At trial, Superintendent Titus admitted that race was a prime factor, but not the only factor that motivated the decision on the promotional list. The procurring of "qualified individuals" was the real objective.[320] Since there was such a racial imbalance in the principal and vice-principal positions, the superintendent felt that adding a qualified Negro would help make the Newark School Sys-

---

318. 431 F.2d 1254 (3d Cir. 1970), *cert. denied*, 402 U.S. 944 (1970). *See* Gay v. Wheeler, 363 F. Supp. 764 (S.D. Tex. 1973) wherein a federal district court held that "race per se" cannot be a factor in hiring, firing or not rehiring.

319. *Porcelli, supra* note 318, at 1255-56.

320. *Id.* at 1256.

tem faculty more integrated. The district court ruled against plaintiffs and they appealed.[321]

The Third Circuit affirmed the lower court's decision. Boards of education, said the appellate court, "have an affirmative duty to integrate school faculties and to permit a great imbalance in faculties . . . would be in negation of the Fourteenth Amendment to the Constitution and the line of cases which have followed *Brown v. Board of Education* . . . ."[322]

Stating that faculty selection must remain the prerogative of the school board and its administrative officers, the court focused its attention on the *objective* of the defendant's actions. In the court's opinion, "[s]tate action based partly on considerations of color, when color is not used *per se,* and in furtherance of a proper governmental objective, is not necessarily a violation of the Fourteenth Amendment."[323]

In 1977, the Ninth Circuit heard the appeal of an Arizona teacher who brought suit in federal district court against her school district and school principal for alleged denial of employment on the basis of her national origin. The case, *Chavez v. Tempe Union High School District,*[324] involved a teacher in a public school district who had applied for but was not selected as foreign language department chairperson at a newly opened high school within that district. Upon being denied the position, plaintiff Chavez filed a complaint with the Equal Employment Opportunity Com-

---

321. *Id.* For another case involving a school system's departure from an existing seniority list and good faith attempts to achieve racial balance in the professional work force, see Bacica v. Board of Education, 451 F. Supp. 882 (W.D. Pa. 1978).

322. *Id.* at 1257-58.

323. *Id.* at 1257.

324. 565 F.2d 1087 (9th Cir. 1977).

mission, which issued her a letter to sue, whereupon she brought suit in federal court under both Title 7 (C.R.A. 1964, as amended) and 42 U.S.C. § 1983.[325]

Following a jury trial, the district court concluded as a matter of law that Ms. Chavez' civil rights had not been violated. The court also rejected her claim of overt discrimination, finding that she was not denied the chairperson's position because of her national origin; rather, she was denied the job because at the time of her application the position was already filled. Finally, the court held that the school district's employment practices were nondiscriminatory and "the district was under no obligation to institute any different hiring practice."[326]

In the opinion of the Ninth Circuit, the complainant in a suit under Title VII is required to carry the burden of proving a prima facie case of discrimination. Among the factors necessary to prove such a case, "the failure to prove the existence of a job opening is a fatal defect in a prima facie case of overt discrimination."[327] After examining the evidence presented, the appellate court held that "Chavez failed to prove that the position was available and thus failed to establish a prima facie case of overt discrimination under Title VII."[328]

Regarding the § 1983 claim, the court focused upon Chavez' failure to show discriminatory purpose on the part of school officials. To the Ninth Circuit, § 1983 requires plaintiff to prove a discriminatory motive, not simply discriminatory impact, in school officials' refusal to appoint her as chairperson. In this case, Chavez could not prove the existence of such an impermissible motive.[329]

---

325. *Id.* at 1089-90.
326. *Id.* at 1090.
327. *Id.* at 1091.
328. *Id.* at 1092.
329. *Id.* at 1095.

In affirming the district court's decision, the appellate court also held that the district court judge did not abuse his discretion in awarding costs to the school district and the school principal. In this case, said the high court, the principal and the school district "were the prevailing parties." [330]

Adams v. Jefferson Davis Parish School Board [331] offers an example of a class civil rights action taken in federal district court under both § 1981 and § 1983. Title VII, C.R.A. 1964 was also invoked by plaintiffs. In *Adams,* plaintiffs asserted that they represented "the class of all employees or potential employees or defendants who have been or will be discriminated against because of their race." [332] Named as defendants in the suit were the school district and seven members of the school board.

The claimed discrimination alleged refusal to hire certain black applicants as well as refusal to elevate various faculty members — clerical employees, members of coaching staffs and others — to higher positions in the school system "solely because they are black." [333] Plaintiffs also alleged that the "defendants ... have followed a policy that discourages blacks from applying for employment or advancement." [334]

The defendants moved for the court to dismiss and strike the class action suit claiming that the plaintiffs did not represent a class as defined by Rule 23 (Federal Rules of Civil Procedure).[335] The district court granted conditional

---

330. *Id.*

331. 450 F. Supp. 1141 (W.D. La. 1978). *See also* United States v. Richardson Independent School District, 483 F. Supp. 80 (N.D. Tex. 1979).

332. *Adams, supra* note 331, at 1142.

333. *Id.*

334. *Id.* at 1143.

335. *Id.*

class certification. The defendants next filed a motion for summary judgment claiming that the plaintiffs had filed their complaint beyond the statutes of limitation. The district court thus had to decide finally on the class certification question as well as the motion for summary judgment.[336]

Thus, the crucial issue in this case was whether the appropriate statutes of limitation had been exceeded. To decide this important question the court separated Title VII from §§ 1981 and 1983. Regarding Title VII claims, the court held that plaintiffs had exceeded the time limitation for filing charges, thus they were barred from recovery (for example, they could not claim back wages under Title VII).[337]

Speaking of §§ 1981 and 1983, the court held that since these sections do not delineate the prescriptive period, "[t]he controlling period should therefore be the most appropriate one provided by state law." [338] In Louisiana, where this case arose, the period of limitation was set at one year for the type of matter represented in this case. Thus, the district court said: "acts allegedly perpetrated by defendants more than one year prior to the filing of the case at bar ... may not be urged by plaintiffs as the basis for their complaints under §§ 1981 and 1983." [339]

Based upon the above rationale, the district court made no ruling as to which plaintiffs, if any, were thereby

---

336. *Id.*

337. *Id.* at 1143-44. On this point the court said: "We therefore hold that with regard to claims for back wages under Title VII a two-year statute of limitations is to be applied and the plaintiffs may assert such claims if they arose within two years of the filing of complaints with the EEOC."

338. *Id.* at 1144.

339. *Id.* at 1144-45.

prevented from representing the class which allegedly had been wronged. The court also declined to rule on defendant's motion for reconsideration of the conditional certification of class, until all parties had a chance to present further briefs and oral arguments on the issue.[340]

In 1981, the Fifth Circuit heard the appeal of an Alabama public school board in a case involving the termination of a black principal allegedly because of his race. In rendering a decision in *Lee v. Monroe County Board of Education,*[341] a federal district court held that the principal's termination was racially motivated and he was awarded back pay. It was the back pay award that prompted the school board appeal.

Prior to 1969, the Monroe County School System had a long history of *de jure* segregation. The plaintiff had served in the school system since 1954. He had served seven years as a teacher and nine years as a principal in all-black schools. In 1968-69, while serving as principal of an all-black junior high school, his school was phased out and closed by court order. Three principalships were open for the 1969-70 school year — all in traditionally white schools. The plaintiff was given an opportunity to apply for one of the vacancies, but he never showed up for his interview.[342]

All three new positions were ultimately filled by whites. The board created another new position (assistant principal of one of the largest, traditionally black elementary schools)

---

340. *Id.* at 1145.

341. 640 F.2d 755 (5th Cir. 1981).

342. *Id.* at 756. The board had no criteria for determining what to do with the faculty and staffs of the schools that were closed by court order. Also, there was no evaluation of the qualifications of faculty members for the purposes of selecting those to fill the vacancies. Finally, the 1967 court order provided that no staff vacancy will be filled through the recruitment from outside the system unless no such displaced staff member is qualified to fill the vacancy.

and offered it to plaintiff. The plaintiff wrote a letter to the board expressing dissatisfaction with the offer and requested a hearing. A hearing was held. However, because of a problem with not receiving notification of the hearing until late, when the plaintiff arrived the meeting had just ended. That same day the board wrote the plaintiff and told him that his letter was interpreted as "a refusal to accept the assignment" and the board voted to terminate his contract.[343] He asked for another hearing but none was granted.

In affirming the decision of the district court, the appellate court agreed that there was ample evidence that the plaintiff did not refuse a new position, and that he had not removed himself voluntarily from the system.[344]

The board had also asserted that it had no duty to retain plaintiff in its employ because his position had been abolished. To this contention the Fifth Circuit responded: "[t]his overlooks the fact that it made no effort to compare qualifications of persons in the system to see who should be retained and had no criteria for dealing with a situation like that presented except policies of leaving principals where they were and assigning black principals to black schools." [345]

The crucial point of the case was the board's creation of a "racially identifiable job" for plaintiff. In the appellate court's opinion, this act further contributed to a dual school system and, as such, was not a substitute for failing to honor plaintiff's "constitutional right not to be discriminated against on account of race." [346] Thus, the district court's

---

343. *Id.* at 757.
344. *Id.* at 758.
345. *Id.*
346. *Id.*

award of back pay to plaintiff was affirmed by the Fifth Circuit.[347]

(c) SENIORITY.

The principle of "last-hired, first-fired" has become an issue in public education as more and more school systems face the necessity of reducing their professional staffs in the face of shrinking enrollments and austerity budgets. Better known as the "seniority system," employees are classified solely on the basis of their length of service for purposes of determining the order in which employees will be laid off when that action is necessary.

Currently, the seniority system in public school employment remains intact. Also, seniority is generally recognized by school boards as an important factor to consider when making personnel decisions.

In recent years, however, seniority has been the subject of legal challenge. Most often in such cases the question before a court has been the following: Is seniority a system that perpetuates or renews the effects of past discrimination against some persons, under the guise of respecting the long years and devotion of senior employees?

Corrigan v. Donilon, offers an excellent and recent example of a § 1983 case wherein seniority was challenged.[348] In *Corrigan*, two of the original sixteen plaintiffs appealed a decision of a federal district court ordering that the Providence, Rhode Island School Committee provide hearings, within ninety days, at which they may contest the commit-

---

347. *Id.* at 758-59. It should be noted here that the Fifth Circuit emphasized that the requirement that one mitigate (reduce the amount) his damages does not override the Constitution. For another recent case involving a black principal who was displaced from his position because of the dismantling of a formerly dual school system, see Cousin v. Board of Trustees, 648 F.2d 293 (5th Cir. 1981).

348. 639 F.2d 834 (1st Cir. 1981).

171

tee's action in dismissing them from their teaching positions. The two teachers challenged the court's order as "inadequately remedying the School Committee's violation both of their right under the fourteenth amendment not to be deprived of their property interests in employment without due process of law, and of their right under Rhode Island law, as tenured teachers, not to be discharged without 'good and just cause.' " [349]

The teachers (Mullins and Pezza) were two of 156 in Providence whose employment was terminated or suspended at the end of the 1976-77 school year. The reason given to Mullins and Pezza was that a teacher with greater seniority, for whom they had served as long-term substitutes, would be returning to employment. Meetings were held following receipt of these letters, at which administrators were available to explain such letters, but neither Mullins nor Pezza attended.[350]

On February 18, 1977, each of the two teachers received another letter. This letter advised them that, pursuant to a resolution of the school committee, their employment as "long-term substitutes" would terminate as of the last day of the second semester of the school year. Mullins and Pezza, along with other teachers, requested a hearing. However, at the time that this suit was taken a hearing had not been held.[351]

After trial, the district court, finding that both teachers were "tenured teachers" under Rhode Island law, concluded that they were owed a meaningful statement of cause for dismissal. Thus, the court ordered that appellants be granted a hearing within ninety days.[352]

---

349. *Id.* at 834-35.
350. *Id.* at 835.
351. *Id.*
352. *Id.*

On appeal, the First Circuit agreed with Mullins and Pezza that the district court should have ruled that they had been improperly discharged. The only reason given for their dismissal was "they were being replaced by senior teachers." [353] This reason alone, said the court, "plainly did not amount to 'good and just cause'," under Rhode Island law.[354]

At this point in the opinion, the First Circuit addressed the issue of state law providing procedures for adjudicating this matter versus the fact that plaintiffs were seeking remedy under § 1983. In the opinion of the court, had appellants been afforded a prompt hearing before the school board, they would have had no occasion to invoke federal jurisdiction for lack of procedural due process. The state procedures, said the court, "would have fully met, indeed, would have exceeded, constitutional due process standards. But timely procedures were not afforded.... Over three years have now elapsed without hearings." [355]

In reaching its decision to vacate and remand the case for further proceedings the court made the following summary statement:

> Appellants ... appear before us both as persons whose constitutional rights to due process were violated and as teachers who, by stipulation of the School Board itself, were not long-term substitutes and hence could not be properly discharged under state law other than for cause, of which none appears. Under such circumstances it would be unjust to make appellants relitigate their employment claim before the very School Committee which has been so careless in its attention to their rights both under state law and the federal Constitution.... To permit the Committee to

---

353. *Id.* at 836.
354. *Id.*
355. *Id.* at 837.

rule on appellants' employment status now would be to
permit it to repudiate the very facts on which it has so
far proceeded and would result in both judicial inefficiency and on undeserved burden on appellants.[356]

In addition to the court's attitude that in this case
seniority was not a sufficient cause for termination, it
should be noted that the court saw § 1983 as the vehicle for
remedy, since the available state procedures would place an
undue burden on the teacher plaintiffs.

Since, in the court's opinion, Mullins and Pezza had
prevailed, they were entitled also to request the district
court for attorneys' fees, pursuant to 43 U.S.C. § 1988.

(d) HANDICAP.

Over the past decade great strides have been made
legally to ensure the rights of disabled persons, children and
adults. Brought about mainly through court decree, all
forms of discrimination against the disabled have been
greatly diminished, especially those that may have existed
in public school systems.

In addition to statutes passed by the various state legisla-
tures, new federal laws have also been enacted in recent
years intended to bring this nation's disabled children and
adults into the mainstream of both education and employment. Of several statutory steps taken by Congress, the two
most influential federal statutes passed were the Rehabilitation Act of 1973 (§ 504) [357] and the Education for All
Handicapped Children Act.[358]

Section 504 of the Rehabilitation Act mandates that "no

---

356. *Id.* at 837-38.

357. P.L. 93-112, 29 U.S.C. § 794 (1973).

358. P.L. 94-142, Revision of Part B, Education for All Handicapped
Act (1975).

otherwise qualified handicapped individual . . . shall, solely by reason of his handicap, be excluded from participation in, be denied the benefits of, or be subjected to discrimination under any program or activity receiving federal financial assistance." Better known as Public Law 94-142, the Education for All Handicapped Children Act mandates that states provide a free, appropriate education for all handicapped children. Coupled together, these two statutes are intended to cause public school systems and public institutions of higher education to take immediate steps to remove and eliminate all forms of exclusion and discrimination (including physical barriers) involving disabled persons (*i.e.,* employees, students, visitors, etc.).

So far, the courts have been reluctant to declare that a private action for remedy is implied in matters involving Public Law 94-142. However, the courts have not expressed such an attitude with § 504 matters. A civil rights tort action taken under 42 U.S.C. § 1983 may represent an alternative course of action for advocates of disabled persons. Arguing from either a statutory base (violation of § 504, for example) or from a constitutional base (equal protection, for example), plaintiffs in such cases will most likely seek remedy (*i.e.,* equitable relief and damages) alleging that they were either denied employment, or a promotion, or lost their job "solely because of their disability (*i.e.,* handicap). Two recent § 1983 cases offer excellent examples.

Gurmankin v. Costanzo,[359] combines both the element of employee handicap with that of employee seniority (discussed in the previous subsection of this Chapter). Judith Gurmankin is a blind person holding a Professional

---

359. 556 F.2d 184 (3d Cir. 1977).

Certificate as a Teacher of Comprehensive English in the Pennsylvania Public Schools.

In 1969 she attempted to obtain a teaching position in the Philadelphia Public School System. At the time of her application the school system's medical and personnel policy "excluded blind teachers from teaching sighted students in the public schools." [360] In 1974, Ms. Gurmankin took and passed the Philadelphia Teachers Examination and her name was placed on an "eligibility list."

Subsequent to her name being added to the eligibility list, Ms. Gurmankin was offered several positions in the school system, but she did not accept any of the offers. Her decisions were based upon the fact that she would not have been afforded seniority "as of the time she should properly have been admitted to the examination." [361]

Ultimately, Ms. Gurmankin brought a civil rights action against officials of the school district and the district itself alleging that she had been discriminated against because she was a blind person. The federal district court hearing the matter entered a judgment in favor of plaintiff Gurmankin. The court ordered the defendants to offer her employment "as a secondary school English teacher, with seniority rights and all other rights accruing to a secondary school English teacher commencing employment in September 1970." [362] The district court did not award her tenure. Also, the district court did not certify the case as a class action.

---

360. *Id.* at 185. The case report shows that applicants who were certified as having a "chronic or acute physical defect," including blindness, were prevented from taking the Philadelphia Teachers Examination.

361. *Id.*

362. *Id.*

Ten months after the court's decision, Gurmankin still was not employed by the school district as an English teacher. Several offers had been made, but she rejected each "as not reflecting the seniority awarded her by the court." [363] In January 1977, Ms. Gurmankin filed a motion to amend the order, arguing "that the District had offered her only the least attractive school in the system, while teachers with less seniority were placed in more attractive schools." [364] The court found in her favor and amended the injunction to state that defendants had thirty days to provide Ms. Gurmankin with a position as an English teacher at one of the six schools designated by her, or at some other school acceptable to her.[365]

When the case reached the Third Circuit, Ms. Gurmankin argued in defense of the injunction that in addition to the constitutional grounds on which the district court relied (the school district's policy of refusing to allow blind persons to take the Philadelphia Teachers Examination violated her due process), the original injunction could be defended on equal protection grounds and on a statutory supremacy ground (here she cited § 504, Rehabilitation Act of 1973). Regarding this last point, however, since the law did not become effective until December 1973, Ms. Gurmankin conceded "that it would not apply to pre-1974 injuries." [366]

---

363. *Id.* at 186. It should be pointed out, however, that the mere fact that a professional may be disappointed with an assignment does not entitle that professional to seek relief in federal court. On this point of law see Gordon v. Anker, 444 F. Supp. 49 (S.D.N.Y. 1977).

364. *Id.*

365. *Id.*

366. *Id.* On this point, the appellate court therefore did not determine whether § 504 conferred "affirmative rights enforceable in private law suits." For a recent handicapped teacher employment case wherein a federal district court held that provisions of the Rehabilitation Act of 1973 do not create a private cause of action, see Myerson v. Arizona, 507 F. Supp. 859 (D. Ariz. 1981).

Thus, the appellate court considered the validity of the district court's holding on constitutional grounds.

In the opinion of the Third Circuit, Ms. Gurmankin's complaint did not address the requirement that Philadelphia teachers pass a qualifying examination, but rather the denial of the opportunity to demonstrate her competence. The refusals by the school system to permit her to take the examination violated her due process "by subjecting Ms. Gurmankin to an irrebutable presumption that her blindness made her incompetent to teach sighted students." [367] She was, said the court, by virtue of the irrebutable presumption of incompetency, deprived of the opportunity to take the examination between 1970 and 1974.

In response to the school board's contention that the award of seniority was beyond the equitable powers of the district court, the appellate court said: "[t]here is no distinction in the law of equitable remedies between suits brought under Title VII and suits brought in reliance on 42 U.S.C. § 1983, or directly on the fourteenth amendment." [368] The equitable relief of an award of a retroactive seniority date, said the court, on the record presented was "entirely appropriate." [369] The court went one step further by holding that the district court had the discretion to grant plaintiff "competitive seniority" even if such an order would have required "bumping" a currently employed teacher.[370] Finally, the court agreed that Ms. Gurmankin was entitled to an award of backpay beginning from the date that the

---

367. *Id.* at 187. Cited by the court as controlling on this point was Cleveland Board of Education v. LaFleur, 414 U.S. 632 (1974).

368. *Id.* at 188.

369. *Id.*

370. *Id.* at 188-89. The appellate court also affirmed the trial court's finding that awarding tenure to Gurmankin would be premature since the school district was entitled to an opportunity to evaluate her performance as a teacher.

trial court had previously found she would have been offered employment absent discrimination.

In 1980, another aspect of the *Gurmankin* litigation was appealed to the Third Circuit.[371] The purpose of this appeal was to review the district court's refusal to certify the matter as a class action (involving a class of visually handicapped individuals qualified to teach in the public schools of Philadelphia). The Third Circuit found no reason to overturn the federal district court's decision. The district court's judgment was vacated and remanded, however, for consideration of the need for effective remedial relief, if any, in an effort to "insure not only the elimination of the unlawful discrimination but the adequate publication of the new policy." [372]

Section 504 of the Rehabilitation Act of 1973 did play an important part in another § 1983 case decided by a federal district court in California in 1979. The case, *Upshur v. Love*,[373] involved a suit filed by a tenured, blind teacher who charged that discriminatory policies and practices of the school system prevented him from obtaining an administrative position in the school district. He further alleged that he was qualified to be an administrator yet he was denied placement on a list of those eligible for administrative jobs because of his blindness.[374]

---

371. Gurmankin v. Costanzo, 626 F.2d 1132 (3d Cir. 1980).

372. *Id.* at 1136-37. Commenting on the import of this case, U.S. Law Week carried the following statements in the July 15, 1980, edition: "Employees who prosecute successful actions under Title VII of the 1964 Civil Rights Act have for some time enjoyed the presumption that they are entitled to an award of back pay. Now, the U.S. Court of Appeals for the Third Circuit comes within whisker of importing that presumption into employment discrimination cases brought under 42 U.S.C. § 1983." 49 U.S.L.W. 1011.

373. 474 F. Supp. 332 (N.D. Cal. 1979).

374. *Id.* at 333.

Taken under both the Rehabilitation Act and § 1983 (claiming denials of both equal protection and due process), Upshur named as defendants the Superintendent of Schools of the Oakland Unified School District, members of the Oakland School Board, the school district itself, and various other school officials. The plaintiff's arguments focused almost exclusively on federal claims.[375]

Regarding plaintiff's § 1983 claim (the equal protection allegation in particular), the district court had to decide two interrelated matters. First, should visually handicapped persons be considered as members of a "suspect class"? If the answer to this question were "yes," then should the plaintiff's claim be evaluated under the strict scrutiny standard, rather than the rational basis standard?[376] The district court answered "no" to the first question, thus the rational basis standard was the applicable standard. The court said:

> Under that test, the defendants clearly did not violate Upshur's rights under the Equal Protection Clause. The Court assumes that a visually handicapped individual can become a successful school administrator and that a rule denying all blind persons the opportunity to be considered for school administration positions would be unreasonable and would perhaps constitute a denial of equal protection under the rational basis test. However, no such blanket exclusion occurred in this case.[377]

Evidence had shown that, wholly apart from his visual impairment, Upshur was not qualified to serve as a school administrator. Upshur's blindness "was not the determinative factor" denying him placement on the admin-

---

375. *Id.*
376. *Id.* at 336.
377. *Id.* at 337.

istrative eligibility list. Using *Mt. Healthy City School District Board of Education v. Doyle* as its benchmark, the court concluded that the preponderance of evidence showed that the school system would have reached the same conclusion on Upshur if he had not been blind.[378]

It should be noted, however, that the district court did not rule that a violation of § 504 could give rise to an action under § 1983. What the district court did say, however, was that even if exhaustion of administrative remedies generally would be required in suits brought under § 504, that requirement would not preclude consideration of a claim taken under § 1983.

Based upon the evidence presented, the court found no violations of § 504 of the Rehabilitation Act of 1973, nor did it find any violations of the federal or state constitutions. Thus, an order was entered in favor of the defendants.[379]

§ 3.6. Summary.

The Supreme Court made it clear in *Bishop v. Wood,* that the posture of the federal judiciary should be one of noninterference with the day-to-day administration of public school systems. In the Court's opinion, the United States Constitution cannot be construed to require judicial review of every administrative error, especially errors in judgment. However, said the high court, where school officials have acted or are acting with intent to curtail employee exercises of federally protected civil rights, or to penalize and retaliate against an employee for his or her exercise of such rights, federal judges have a duty to fashion appropriate relief.

---

378. *Id.*
379. *Id.* at 344.

The cases reviewed in this chapter demonstrate that beginning in the early 1970's, and especially since 1976, teachers and other professional employees in public school systems have successfully used § 1983 to get their complaints of civil rights violations before the federal bench. Moreover, as the case law shows (especially through such cases as *Mt. Healthy* and *Givhan),* their status for seeking remedy in federal court (in the form of equitable and legal relief) is not contingent upon their holding tenured or continuing contract positions in their school system. All that is necessary is for an employee to establish at the prima facie level that a civil rights violation, either statutorily or constitutionally based, is in fact present, and that that violation played a substantial part in the decision of school officials to nonrenew, dismiss, or in some other way punish him or her. Once this has been successfully done, and the case goes forward, the burden of proof then shifts to school officials to convince that trier of fact through the presentation of hard evidence that neither their intent nor motive was to violate the employee's civil rights; rather, their action was motivated by a legitimate school concern (for example, to remove an incompetent teacher or administrator, to quell a disruptive situation, to eliminate a dangerous situation for the safety and welfare of the children, or to remedy past forms of discrimination, or others.)

In both Chapters 1 and 2, the Supreme Court's landmark decision in *Wood v. Strickland* was highlighted, especially the Court's statement that school officials may be held liable for damages under § 1983 if they knew or reasonably should have known that their actions violate an individual's federally protected rights. The cases reviewed in this chapter help to bring meaning to and expand the Court's words. For example, when the high court uses the words "if

182

they knew," the authors believe that they are implying the presence of *intent.* The cases reviewed show that the federal courts have consistently held school boards, school board members, and other school officials liable if their intent (through either direct action or through conspiracy) was to violate an employee's civil rights, or to punish otherwise that employee for his or her exercise of a civil right. Similarly, when the Court uses the phrase "reasonably should have known," the authors also believe that they are referring to certain "red flag" elements that trigger heightened scrutiny of judges in civil rights litigation (for example, the first amendment guarantees of speech [expression] and association, as well as being handicapped or of a certain race). The cases reviewed clearly demonstrate that where such elements are present, public school officials cannot avail themselves of ignorance or the affirmative defense of good faith, and must be overly careful to convince the trier of fact that they would have taken the same action with that employee absent that protected element, or that school officials' reasons for acting were so compelling that they overbalanced the employee's right.

Clearly, where school officials are held liable under § 1983, the possibilities for remedy are broad. As the cases demonstrate, injunctive relief, reinstatement (with tenure where appropriate), back pay, lost benefits, expungement of personnel records, removal of letters of reprimand from personnel files, monetary damages (compensatory and punitive), attorney's fees, and the payment of other costs are all possible forms of remedy available in § 1983 cases. What makes these remedies even more significant is that they do not necessarily preclude but are supplementary to any available state remedies. However, the exhaustion of state judicial remedies is not a fixed requirement for seeking available federal remedies under § 1983.

Regarding monetary damages, the case law reviewed in this chapter reveals that as a general rule compensatory damages (to compensate plaintiff for actual injuries suffered) are commonly awarded in public school employment cases where plaintiff parties are able to demonstrate that they suffered a measureable loss. Punitive damage awards (to deter such possible future conduct), however, are made only if the plaintiff employee can establish beyond a reasonable doubt that a school official or group of officials acted with either malicious or wanton intent to violate his or her civil rights, or that a school official or group of officials acted with the vindictive intent of punishing plaintiff (*e.g.,* continuous harassment or abuse) for his or her exercise of a basic civil right. Also, when punitive damage awards are made, they will be made against individual officers who committed the act and not against school boards, and they will be limited to amounts large enough to deter such possible future conduct by school officials.

Until very recently, it was a case hardened tenet of school law that public school boards and their administrative officers are presumed to be acting in good faith when carrying out their legal prerogatives. Very simply put, good faith indicates that a school official always acts with honest lawful intent and with proper motives. Also, a school board official acts only in performance of legal duties, abstaining from taking advantage of anyone and without malice toward anyone. The affirmative defense of good faith became the major claim of defendants in § 1983 suits; plaintiff parties carried the burden of proof to show that the board or its officers acted otherwise.

As is illustrated in this chapter (see, for example, *McGhee v. Draper, supra)* the doctrine granting public school boards immunity for discretionary functions may no longer be as strong a basis for claiming a good faith defense in § 1983 cases, especially since the Supreme Court's decision in *Owen*. It seems plausible to predict that future courts may hold public school boards and individual officials (in both their official and individual capacities) liable for compensatory damages for actual injuries suffered by a plaintiff employee regardless of good faith. In future § 1983 cases, the burden will likely fall squarely on the plaintiff employee to show a link between the civil rights violation by school officials and consequences that support an award of damages.

In future § 1983 cases, the blame and liability, once established by plaintiff, will come to rest with the school board and its members. The primary exception to this principle will be in the realm of punitive relief, where the acts of an administrative officer or officers intentionally violate an employee's civil rights and were clearly done without board sanction, or where such acts were exercised outside or beyond the scope of school board policy or outside the bounds of that administrator's authority sanctioned by the board. Boards of education will not be held vicariously liable or on a respondeat superior theory for such acts, unless in some actual way they participated in or approved such acts.

185

CHAPTER 4

STUDENTS AND § 1983

§ 4.0. Introduction.

The previous chapter indicated that the 1960's and the 1970's were a period in which the rights of teachers were increasingly litigated in the courts. Those two decades also corresponded to an increase in student litigation. It began in 1961 with the pronouncement that students were entitled to rights of procedural due process under the fourteenth amendment in suspensions,[1] and proceeded to cover a number of landmark decisions on a variety of topics. Within the Supreme Court of the United States the justices handed down some noteworthy decisions affecting the civil rights of young people. For example, they held in 1967 that due process applied to students in juvenile court proceedings.[2] Two years later they held that student expression was protected by the first amendment.[3]

---

1. Dixon v. Alabama State Board of Education, 294 F.2d 150 (5th Cir. 1961), *cert. denied,* 368 U.S. 930 (1961).

2. In re Gault, 387 U.S. 1 (1967). *See* Goldstein v. Spears, 536 F.Supp. 606 (N.D. Ill. 1982).

3. Tinker v. Des Moines Independent Community School District, 393 U.S. 503 (1969).

187

In the mid-1970's the Court handed down two landmark decisions. It extended *Gault* to the school setting and held that in short-term suspensions, students were entitled to some elements of procedural due process.[4] During the same term it ruled for the first time that § 1983 protected students as well as teachers and, for a denial of a protected right, students could sue school board members.[5]

The focus of this chapter is on the areas of student freedom that have been litigated on § 1983, the degree to which students have been successful in their litigation, and the kinds of damage awards given students. Ten such areas have been identified and have been organized by sections. As an introduction to each section, a brief statement of the current holding of law is given prior to the application of § 1983 to that issue.

§ 4.1. Assignment to School.

Law governing the assignment of a student to a given school functions at three different levels: federal, state, and local. The entitlement of a student to attend a school is grounded in our federal Constitution under the equal protection clause.[6] Clearly, it is now well established that a school district cannot discriminate against a student in assignment to a school solely on the basis of race.[7] Further,

---

4. Goss v. Lopez, 419 U.S. 565 (1975).

5. Wood v. Strickland, 420 U.S. 308 (1975).

6. *Goss, supra* note 4, in which the Supreme Court held that a student has no constitutional right to education at public expense. The Court held that a student has a "legitimate claim of entitlement to a public education." Note that the Supreme Court held in San Antonio Independent School District v. Rodriguez, 411 U.S. 1 (1973) that education is not a fundamental right under the equal protection clause of the Federal Constitution.

7. 29 U.S.C. § 794 (1973), popularly referred to as § 504 of the Rehabilitation Act of 1973.

it may not discriminate against a student either on the basis of a handicap or on the basis of exceptionality.[8]

State law determines who is eligible to attend school. A legislature sets minimum age limits as to who is entitled to a free, public education. It also sets other conditions, such as requiring vaccination before one can enroll. It will determine whether parents may educate their children at home or whether education is required in a more formalized setting. Finally, a state will determine the kind and nature of penalties for noncompliance with compulsory attendance requirements.

Local school board policies govern pupil assignment and attendance. A local school board establishes specific attendance zones within a school district from which pupils are assigned to designated schools. Exceptions to this assignment plan must be approved by the board of education, as for example, in achieving some racial balance through busing of students or pairing of schools. The local board of education may also determine when a student becomes ineligible to attend school for such reasons as misbehavior or membership in a forbidden society. Expulsion is the remedy often used by the board as punishment for violators.

Courts are frequently called upon to resolve disputes between students and school authorities over the interpretation of assignment and attendance laws and policies as they apply to a specific situation. To date, these challenges have been grounded, for the most part, on claims other than on § 1983.

In a case out of Maine, a parent challenged the legality of a state statute that required a child to be six years old by

---

8. 20 U.S.C. § 1401 *et. seq.* (1976), often referred to as P.L. 94-142, the Education for All Handicapped Children Act.

October 15 before being admitted to the first grade.[9] The child, who missed the deadline by 65 days, charged that the minimum age requirement was a violation of equal protection and due process. The school district's defense was that the federal courts had no jurisdiction over the matter since education is not a right guaranteed by the Constitution. The court agreed with the defendant's defense, but added that a federal court can claim jurisdiction over an essentially state question where a plaintiff asserts a violation of equal protection or due process. The court rejected a second argument by the defense that a federal court should not entertain a case until a state court has ruled on the matter.

The parents claimed that their child was sufficiently mature and intelligent to enroll in grade one and should be allowed to take a readiness test. They charged that age was an insufficient reason for rejecting his admission. In response, the court held that there is no fundamental right involved in that assertion. The issue was then reduced to the question of whether there was a reasonable basis for the classification. The court accepted the findings of studies which showed that age six is an appropriate age for a child to begin school.

> [T]he challenged statute sets an objective and inexpensive standard which yields results reasonably approximating those that would be rendered by individual determinations. The use of such a standard is rationally related to the legitimate State purpose of providing public education at reasonable cost.[10]

In a second case, this one from Alabama, five students reassigned to a school sued the local board of education and

---

9. Hammond v. Marx, 406 F. Supp. 853 (D. Me. 1975).
10. *Id.* at 858.

the superintendent.[11] They objected to a change from a non-graded curriculum to one with a traditional graded system. The transfer involved approximately fifty students, both black and white. As in the previous case, the court rejected the plaintiffs' § 1983 claims for relief.

The transfer grew out of a court-ordered racial desegregation plan in which the local board of education was required to verify the residence of all students in the system and to see that they were actually enrolled in the system designated for them under the court-approved plan. The board complied with this order and, in the middle of the year, sought to transfer students not properly enrolled in their zone. The five plaintiffs challenged their transfer, including the testing that was an integral part of assignment and placement.

The court saw no racial bias in the testing. Instead, it saw the placement tests as an acceptable method of placing students in instructional groups. The tests were seen as aids in helping students to utilize a property right — a right to a public education.

A third case involved the question of a student being required to pay tuition.[12] During his freshman and sophomore years the student had lived in a district with his aunt. He claimed that he had been allowed to attend school the first two years on a tuition-free basis but that he had been dropped after the second year. The student claimed that his being dropped from the rolls without a hearing constituted a denial of procedural due process. Since there was no claim of malice on the part of school officials,

---

11. Smith v. Dallas County Board of Education, 480 F. Supp. 1324 (S.D. Ala. 1979).

12. Kraut v. Rachford, 51 Ill. App. 3d 206, 366 N.E.2d 497 (1977).

punitive damages were not sought. However, the plaintiff did seek compensatory damages on the basis that school officials had clearly disregarded the plaintiff's rights to the point that their actions could not be characterized as being in good faith.

The court held that, since the boy had been allowed to attend school for two years on a tuition-free basis, he had an objective expectation of continuing on the same basis for his junior and senior years. With respect to the specific due process to which he was entitled, the court recognized that the student was not barred from attending a school within the district of his parents, also on a tuition-free basis. Since this case involved no charges of misconduct, the student was not entitled to the same due process as if it were a suspension or expulsion case. In sum, the court ruled in favor of the defendants.

§ 4.2. Educational Program.

All taxpayers share in the education of children of a state. This arrangement has grown out of the belief that it is in the interest of the state that all children be educated, for the state benefits from a well-informed, literate citizenry. In fulfilling its obligation to educate young people, a state may determine what elements contribute to a basic education. More specifically, it may prescribe that certain courses be offered, such as language and mathematics, and it may forbid the teaching of certain subjects such as religion.

The state's responsibility for educating young people is not without limits. In fact, parents share in this partnership and may raise objections about their children taking certain courses, about the methodology used, and about materials offered. This interplay between school authority and parental interest has resulted in a number of court cases on the subject. Where a state requires a course, the rights of parents are less evident than where a school board offers an elective course. Similarly, where a state forbids the teaching of a course, parents may be successful in charging that the state's or the school board's action is in violation of their freedom of liberty under the fourteenth amendment. This occurred in Nebraska when the state legislature forbade the teaching of foreign language to elementary school children, ostensibly as a negative reaction to the feeling growing out of post-World War I. The Supreme Court struck down the law as interfering both with the teacher's right to teach and the student's right to learn.[13]

Historically, courts have invalidated laws that forbade the teaching of evolution.[14] The recent thinking of courts ruling on this issue has been that to restrict such teaching would constitute, in effect, an establishment of religion.

At the onset of the 1980's a number of individuals and organized groups have sought either to restrict the teaching of designated ideas that are at variance with their religious beliefs or have demanded that specified ideas be included in the school's curriculum. Among the most visible of these groups is the "Moral Majority," an amalgam of several smaller, diverse groups and individuals who seek, among other things, to reinstate prayer and Bible reading in the school, to eliminate the teaching of sex education, and to give balanced treatment to the teaching of evolution by relating the Biblical version when scientific evolution is taught.

---

13. Meyer v. Nebraska, 262 U.S. 39 (1923).

14. Scopes v. Tennessee, 154 Tenn. 105, 289 S.W. 363 (1927); Epperson v. Arkansas, 393 U.S. 97 (1968); Smith v. State, 242 So. 2d 692 (Miss. 1970); Wright v. Houston Independent School District, 486 F.2d 137 (5th Cir. 1973).

The pressures from individual citizens and organized groups on curriculum offerings extend also to selection of materials. Unquestionably, local boards of education have considerable authority in determining what instructional materials will be used, for it is they who financially approve the purchase of them.[15]

A topic that has generated as much controversy as the treating of evolution is that of sex education. Some states forbid the teaching of it, other states allow or encourage the teaching of it. The objection of individuals and groups to its being offered centers around two major points — it is in violation of one's rights under the first amendment, and school boards exceed their authority in prescribing it. Where the subject has a direct relationship to the course in which it is taught, courts have upheld its teaching.[16] Where parents have the option of their children attending classes in sex education, courts have also upheld the teaching of it.[17]

Against that general backdrop of court holdings on the teaching of controversies in the public schools, § 1983 has been used as a vehicle for parental challenge to curriculum materials. More specifically, the challenge has involved, for the most part, removal of books from the school library

---

15. This notion was reaffirmed in Williams v. Board of Education, 388 F. Supp. 93 (S.D.W. Va. 1975) where parents in Kanawha County, West Virginia, had sought to remove a number of books, alleging that the content was in conflict with Christian principles and good citizenship. Although recognizing that some of the materials may be offensive to one's religious beliefs, the court held that the school board had properly exercised its authority in the selection of materials.

16. State v. Board of School Directors, 14 Wis. 2d 243, 111 N.W.2d 198 (1961).

17. Mederios v. Kijosaki, 478 P.2d 314 (Haw. 1970); Valent v. New Jersey State Board of Education, 274 A.2d 832 (N.J. 1971).

194

because of their contents. These challenges are reflected in four cases decided in the second half of the 1970's. *Minarcini* is the lead case on this issue.[18] It involved a suburban school district of Cleveland which was sued along with board members and the superintendent for removing certain books from the library as well as for refusing to approve certain books for the school's use. The student plaintiffs alleged a violation of their first and fourteenth amendment rights.

The school board ordered two books, *Cat's Cradle* and *Catch 22,* to be removed from the library; it forbade their use as supplementary reading and prohibited teacher and student discussion of them. The board also refused to approve the use of two books, *Catch 22* and *God Bless You, Mr. Rosewater,* as texts or as library books.

The Sixth Circuit agreed with the district court that the school board's action did not violate any of the plaintiffs' constitutional rights.

> Clearly, discretion as to the selection of textbooks must be lodged somewhere and we can find no federal constitutional prohibition which prevents its being lodged in school board officials who are elected representatives of the people.[19]

The court recognized that the school board is neither required to provide a library nor to select given books for it. Having established a library, a school board was under no constitutional compunction to establish conditions for its use; those conditions emanate from other than constitutional bases. The court added:

> A library is a storehouse of knowledge. When created for a public school it is an important privilege created

---

18. Minarcini v. Strongsville City School District, 541 F.2d 577 (6th Cir. 1976). In contrast, note Sheck v. Baileyville School Committee, 530 F. Supp. 679 (D. Me. 1982).

19. *Id.* at 579.

by the state for the benefit of the students in the school.
That privilege is not subject to being withdrawn by
succeeding school boards whose members might desire
to "winnow" the library for books the content of which
occasioned their displeasure or disapproval.[20]

Just as the students lost their § 1983 claim in *Minarcini,*
so did parents in *Pico* at the district court, but the second
circuit overturned.[21] *Pico* involved a challenge to the
removal of eleven books from the school library.[22] Following
parental complaints about some books and materials, the
school board took the advice of its appointed book review
committee and had the books removed. The district court
saw the action as being proper. It went further in asserting
that a book does not acquire "tenure," for if it were so, "[a]
constitutionally required 'book tenure' principle would
infringe upon an elected school board's discretion in
determining what community values were to be
transmitted." [23]

On reversal, the court of appeals ruled on first amendment grounds. It held that the plaintiffs had made a *prima
facie* case of first amendment violation; the defendants had
thus not been entitled to the summary judgment of the
district court. The circuit court expressed several concerns.
It was concerned that the intervention in the school library
was by people not routinely concerned with such matters. It
was concerned that the criteria used in removing books

---

20. *Id.* at 581.

21. Pico v. Board of Education, 638 F.2d 404 (2d Cir. 1980), *aff'd,* 102
S. Ct. 2799 (1982).

22. The books in question were *Slaughterhouse Five, The Naked Ape,
Down These Mean Streets, Best Short Stories by Negro Writers, Go Ask
Alice, Laughing Boy, Black Boy, A Hero Ain't Nothing But a Sandwich,
Soul on Ice, A Reader for Writers,* and *The Fixer.*

23. Pico v. Board of Education, 474 F. Supp. 387, 396 (E.D.N.Y. 1979).

were vague. For example, it was not clear what was meant by the word "filth." The court was also concerned that the books had been removed before any school official had had the opportunity to read them after the complaints had been lodged and that their removal had been on the basis of mimeographed quotations by anonymous readers. On June 25, 1982, the Supreme Court ruled in *Pico* that students could bring suit against school boards in situations where the board had removed books from the school library.

The same circuit court held that there was no constitutional violation in removing two books from a school library. Here, the basis for the removal was vulgarity and indecency of language.[24] This action was challenged by students, parents and a librarian.

At the district court, the judges indicated that they did not necessarily agree with the wisdom of the board's action, but the board had not acted inconsistent with any constitutional provisions. Rather, they saw the selection of library books as being a curriculum matter over which the board members exercised considerable control.[25]

The court also refuted the notion that a book acquires tenure on a shelf.

> The life and utility of a library are severely impaired whenever works can be removed merely because they are offensive to the personal, political or social tastes of individual citizens, whether or not those citizens represent the majority of opinion in a community. ... Nevertheless, we cannot agree with plaintiffs' legal

---

24. Bicknell v. Vergennes Union High School Board of School Directors, 638 F.2d 438 (2d Cir. 1980). The two books were *The Wanderers* and *Dog Day Afternoon*.

25. *See* President's Council, District 25 v. Community School Board No. 25, 457 F.2d 289 (2d Cir.), *cert. denied,* 409 U.S. 998 (1972).

conclusions; what is desirable as a matter of policy is not necessarily commanded as a matter of constitutional law: . . .[26]

The court of appeals affirmed.[27] In addition to refuting the notion that a violation of the first amendment had occurred, it also held that the plaintiffs were not entitled to a due process hearing before the books were removed.

The court also distinguished this case from *Pico.* It held that the removal of the books in *Pico* were under circumstances that created a risk of a suppression of ideas. In the latter case, the books were removed for their language, not because of their ideas.

Zykan,[28] the fourth of these cases, raised a number of issues, the removal of books being only one of them. The following specific charges were filed: (1) removal of a textbook, *Values Clarification,* without proper consultation with teachers, parents or students; (2) ordering a teacher to return to the publisher one book she had planned to use in her course and not to use three others; [29] (3) requiring a teacher to excise certain portions of *Student Critic,* a book used for a number of years in the high school; (4) ordering the permanent removal of the book, *Go Ask Alice* from the school library; and (5) eliminating seven courses from the high school curriculum.

Plaintiffs charged that the school board took these actions, not so much because of the lack of educational value of the materials, but rather because the materials offended

---

26. Bicknell v. Vergennes Union High School, 475 F. Supp. 615, 619 (D. Vt. 1979).

27. Bicknell v. Vergennes Union High School Board of School Directors, 638 F.2d 438 (2d Cir. 1980).

28. Zykan v. Warsaw Community School Corp., 631 F.2d 1300 (7th Cir. 1980).

29. The book ordered returned was *Growing Up Female in America.* The teacher was ordered not to use in class *Go Ask Alice, The Bell Jar,* and *The Stepford Wives.*

their political, social and moral values. In response, the court asserted that student academic freedom is limited to the secondary school level. A student's right to and need for such freedom is bound by the level of his or her intellectual development. In the second place, "the importance of secondary schools in the development of intellectual faculties is only one part of a broad formative role encompassing the encouragement and nurturing of those fundamental social, political, and moral values that will permit a student to take his place in the community. . . . As a result, the community has a legitimate, even a vital and compelling interest in 'the choice [of] and adherence to a suitable curriculum for the benefit of our young citizens.' " [30]

That local school boards have considerable authority as well as discretion in selecting materials for use in the local schools was underscored by the court.

> Educational decisions necessarily involve choices regarding what students should read and hear, and particularly in light of the formative purpose of secondary school education, local discretion thus means the freedom to form an opinion regarding the instructional content that will best transmit the basic values of the community. As a result, it is in general permissible and appropriate for local boards to make educational decisions based upon their personal social, political and moral views.[31]

To date, with the four above cases as illustrative, the courts have refrained from extending § 1983 protection to students who have alleged a denial of constitutional rights by the action of school boards in selecting materials as well as in removing books from the curriculum and the school library.

---

30. *Zykan, supra* at 1304.
31. *Id.* at 1305.

Litigation under § 1983 has also been premised on a number of other issues related to the curriculum, among them being challenges by students over program areas of the curriculum, over specific courses in the curriculum, and over the amount of time devoted to curriculum offerings. Each of these areas will be examined in turn.

Challenges to program areas of the curriculum have grown out of religious and ethnic objections. On the religious issue, parents of children brought a § 1983 suit against school authorities who required their exposure to audiovisual materials.[32] The plaintiffs, members of the Apostolic Lutheran Faith, comprised approximately twenty percent of the school's population. Their religious tenets hold that it is sinful to watch or listen to movies, television, or other audiovisual materials, to engage in playacting, or to sing or dance to worldly music. Until 1971, the school board had respected the thinking of these people and had accommodated their beliefs by excusing them from the room when objectionable activities were held. However, as a result of increasing disciplinary problems, the school board revoked its policy and required the children to remain in the room. Parents of two children then removed their offspring from school and subjected themselves to a possible violation of the compulsory attendance statutes. In their suit that followed, the parents sought two kinds of relief: their children's excusal from the classroom during the objectionable activities, and a court order enjoining the school district from enforcing the mandatory attendance rule at music classes and in a prospective health class.

The court rejected both parents' requests. It saw that excusing the children from class every time audiovisual materials were used in educating the children and the children's interest in being educated outweighed the interests

---

32. *In re* Davis, 318 A.2d 151 (N.H. 1974).

of the parents. The religious rights asserted here were primarily those of the parents, not those of the children.

On the second point, the court found that the parents' objections to the health course were based on personal and philosophical grounds rather than on religious convictions.

In another § 1983 action, a group of migrant children initiated court proceedings, charging the local school board with a number of violations.[33] They alleged that the school district policies denied them of their right to a meaningful education. Since they had been late in enrolling in school because of harvesting schedules, the children asserted that they were given neither the opportunity nor the programs to make up their work. They charged also that they were unable to transfer credits from other schools. The school district denied all the allegations.

The court held that the fourteenth amendment does not prohibit all discrimination; rather it prevents arbitrary and invidious discrimination aimed at any individual or group by state action. "However, state action which affects a greater proportion of one group more than another, standing alone, is not invalid under the Equal Protection Clause. . . . There must be a showing that the facially neutral legislation or policy has the purpose and intent to invidiously discriminate against the disproportionally affected group." [34]

The court saw that these children were not entitled by law to any additional or alternative programs. Otherwise, the school district's attendance policy had a rational purpose in providing for an education for the children of the state.

---

33. Valadez v. Graham, 474 F. Supp. 149 (M.D. Fla. 1979).
34. *Id.* at 155.

Challenges to specific courses in the curriculum under § 1983 occurred in the last half-decade of the 1970's. Two cases involved objections to required courses; the third, a challenge to a student's dismissal from an activity.

For refusing to attend and participate in physical education classes, a girl was excluded from school.[35] In turn, she sought compensatory and punitive damages of $120,000. The course was required of all seventh grade students. The only reason given for the girl's nonparticipation was that she "should have every right to do only what she wanted to."[36] No reasons were advanced in terms of health, religion, discrimination or expression. Later, the girl's father added two reasons for his child's nonparticipation. He said that she had insufficient time to dress and change classes and a lack of private shower facilities.

The court rejected the father's claims, including those for damages. It stated that:

> While there is a legal entitlement to a public education provided by the State, free from impairment of protected liberties, there is no right under the paramount law to receive a public education on special terms and conditions designed by the student.[37]

For refusing to take a required ROTC course, a student was suspended from school.[38] He claimed a violation of freedom of religion and speech and sought declaratory and injunctive relief plus attorneys' fees.

Sapp, the student, objected to ROTC because he claimed that he objected to being taught to kill. He indicated that these objections were grounded in his religious beliefs. The

---

35. Ouimette v. Babbie, 405 F. Supp. 525 (D. Vt. 1975).

36. *Id.* at 527.

37. *Id.* at 530.

38. Sapp v. Renfroe, 511 F.2d 172 (5th Cir. 1975).

board responded that, although students are given marksmanship training, they are not taught to kill; neither is an ROTC student required to enter the armed forces.

The court of appeals upheld the district court ruling that Sapp could not claim a violation of his religion. The court did not treat the merits of Sapp's claim to a violation of his speech. His claim to attorneys' fees was rejected since he was not the prevailing party, and his claim to damages was rejected on the basis that there was no evidence that the school board had acted maliciously.

In the third case, a girl dismissed from her school's drill team charged racial discrimination.[39] She sought damages, otherwise unspecified. The court of appeals reversed the district court's decision of a summary judgment for the defendant and remanded for further proceedings.

The history of the case showed that the school had no black cheerleaders or drum majorettes. The plaintiff, a black girl, tried out for the drill team which had been organized at the suggestion of the NAACP to give opportunities to minority girls. She was accepted as a member of the team. When practices began during the summer, they were scheduled at a time when the plaintiff had a part-time job. Consequently, she missed a number of drill sessions. She was able, however, to attend a two-week band camp held during the day but missed an evening practice session while working. Initially dismissed from the drill team, she was later reinstated. When school opened in the fall and the drill team met during activities period, the girl was excluded from it.

There were two basic issues before the court of appeals: (1) the decision of the state's Human Relations Commission

---

39. Boykins v. Ambridge Area School District, 621 F.2d 75 (3d Cir. 1980).

refuted the charge of racial discrimination; and (2) the complaint lacked specificity required for a civil rights action case.

On the first issue, the court could not actually determine what the Human Relations Commission had decided. The problem was compounded when the court of appeals noted that the state's supreme court had ruled that the Commission lacked jurisdiction to award compensatory damages, the relief sought here.

On the second issue, the court ruled that the case met the test of specificity for a civil rights suit since it had alleged a racial motive for the expulsion from the drill team. The complaint had also noted the times and the places complained of and the persons responsible.

Another § 1983 challenge involved the length of time a child spends at school under teacher supervision.[40] As a result of financial problems and teacher strikes, the board of education of New York City voted to a reduction of teacher preparation periods, resulting in a union agreement leading to early student dismissal on Monday and Friday afternoons.

Parents objected to this plan.[41] They claimed irreparable injury to their children so as to warrant injunctive relief. The court overruled them. It recognized that education is not a fundamental right under the federal Constitution. Although a student spent one and one-half hours less class time per week under teacher supervision, it did not neces-

---

40. Zoll v. Anker, 414 F. Supp. 1024 (S.D.N.Y. 1976).

41. Parents had earlier challenged this action as denying them their rights under the fifth and fourteenth amendments. These contentions were rejected in New York City School Boards Ass'n v. Board of Education, 39 N.Y.2d 111, 347 N.E.2d 568, 383 N.Y.S.2d 208 (1976) and were reframed in a § 1983 suit.

sarily mean that one has been deprived of educational opportunity. The shortened school day was seen as being a rational solution to the severe financial and labor problems of the city. The court added that: "Common sense alone indicates that 'the right to enjoy a full education' is defined by contours more broad than the number of minutes in a school day." [42]

In the final case in this section, the Fifth Circuit rejected a girl's complaint that she was denied the right to enroll in certain courses of study.[43] She charged that, in disregarding the requests, the school district placed her in courses not suited to her goals. This condition would prevent her from continuing in higher education in a specialized field.

The court of appeals affirmed the dismissal for failure to state a cause of action. The complaint failed to state any independent source of entitlement that would create for her a special course of study. Absent any such entitlement, the plaintiff's preferences for given curricular choices did not constitute a property interest under the fourteenth amendment.

When one examines the number of cases treated in this section and realizes the number of decisions that have gone against the student plaintiffs, it is clear that, to date, individuals have been very unsuccessful in altering the considerable school board authority in determining curriculum and materials used in teaching it.

§ 4.3. Participation in Athletics.

In terms of law, participation in interscholastic athletics is not viewed as being a protected right under the federal

---

42. *Id.* at 1028.

43. Arundar v. DeKalb County School District, 620 F.2d 493 (5th Cir. 1980).

Constitution. As a consequence, whenever an individual elects to engage in such competition, he is subject to a variety of rules — the policies and regulations of one's local school district, laws and policies at the state level, and federal regulations such as Title IX. In addition, many schools are affiliated with an interscholastic association of athletics which has its own constitution and by-laws regulating participation.

As a general rule, restrictions on athletic competition must pass a "rational relationship" test. That is, if the rule has some reasonable or rational relationship to the desired end sought by the enactment of the rule, it will likely be upheld.

Challenges on the basis of § 1983 have taken several different forms. They include the legality of a one-year residency transfer requirement, participation in summer and post-season competition, and discrimination on the basis of gender. These three topics will be treated in this section.

A typical rule among the various state athletic associations is to require a one-year residency for transfer of students from another school system.[44] This rule grew out of the belief that unethical recruiting practices for able athletes would be minimized. The legality of such a rule has been challenged on § 1983 grounds. Plaintiffs have sought to overturn it on the twin bases that one has a constitutional right to participate in interscholastic

---

44. *See, generally,* MOHLER & BOLMEIER, THE LAW OF EXTRACURRICULAR ACTIVITIES IN SECONDARY SCHOOLS (Cincinnati: W. H. Anderson Company 1968) and Chapter Four of Harvey, Legal Aspects Governing the Organization and Control of the Pennsylvania Interscholastic Athletic Association in Its Role with Pennsylvania's Public and Private Schools (unpublished doctoral dissertation, Temple University 1975).

athletics and that participation involves a property interest under the fourteenth amendment. To date, courts have not succumbed to these two arguments. Judges have seen the greater good accrue the school system and the athletic association by minimizing harmful recruiting of promising young athletes than by waiving the eligibility requirement.

The one-year eligibility requirement was challenged in Pennsylvania in 1975, and the federal district court upheld it.[45] In transferring to a nearby school district, a boy became ineligible for athletic competition for one year. He sought to raise the issue of eligibility to a constitutionally protected standard, but the court refused to accept his argument. The court saw the right-privilege dichotomy as being irrelevant when it said: "It is irrelevant indeed whether the instant plaintiff's participation in interscholastic athletics is either a right or a privilege." [46] The court stated: "The only right reasonably at issue in the instant case is the right to be free from a deprivation of life, liberty or property interest without due process called for in the 14th Amendment." [47]

The court recognized that once a state transforms a privilege into a property interest, no matter what its weight, due process attaches.

> It seems to us that the property interest in education created by the state is participation in the entire process. The myriad activities which combine to form that educational process cannot be dissected to create hundreds of separate property rights, each cognizable under the Constitution. Otherwise, removal from a particular class, dismissal from an athletic team, a club or any extracurricular activity, would each require ultimate satisfaction of procedural due process.[48]

---

45. Dallum v. Cumberland Valley School District, 391 F. Supp. 358 (M.D. Pa. 1975).

46. *Id.* at 360.

47. *Id.* at 361.

48. *Id.*

In sum, the court held that there is no constitutionally protected property interest in competing for a place on a secondary school athletic team.

In Louisiana, parents sought to overturn a student transfer rule.[49] This case had an added dimension to the one above in that, in addition to asserting a denial of due process and equal protection, the parents also claimed a violation of free exercise of religion. The state association rule provided that, upon graduation from an elementary or a junior high school, a student would be eligible to participate immediately in athletic competition within his home district. These home districts are geographical areas designated by the local boards of education as the attendance zones for the public high schools. The home district of a nonpublic school is the geographical attendance zone of the public high school in which the nonpublic school is situated. If a student enrolls in a high school outside his home district after completing elementary or junior high school, he must sit out one year before competing in interscholastic athletics.

The facts showed that in greater New Orleans there were seven elementary or junior high schools and one high school operated by the Lutheran Church Missouri Synod. None of the lower schools was located within the high school's home district. When the plaintiffs graduated from elementary schools, they each became ineligible for one year.

On the charge that the application of the rule constituted a violation of their first amendment right to free exercise of religion, the court disagreed.

> A regulation that is neutral on its face and is motivated by legitimate secular concerns may, in its application, offend the first amendment requirement of govern-

---

49. Walsh v. Louisiana High School Athletic Ass'n, 616 F.2d 152 (5th Cir. 1980).

mental neutrality if it unduly burdens the free exercise of religion. . . . To pass constitutional muster, the application of such a regulation either (1) must not interfere with, burden, or deny the free exercise of a legitimate religious belief or (2) must be justified by a state interest of sufficient magnitude to override the interest claiming protection under the free exercise clause.[50]

The court held that any incidental burden on the plaintiffs' free exercise was incidental, for the parents could still practice their faith, enroll their child in the parochial school, and obtain a religious education for that child. Further, although the child could not participate in interscholastic athletics for one year, he could engage in intramural competition.

On the issue of the parents' claim of an entitlement to an education as a property interest which extended to all parts of the educational program, the court disagreed.

The due process clause of the fourteenth amendment extends constitutional protection to those fundamental aspects of life, liberty, and property that rise to the level of a "legitimate claim of entitlement" but does not protect lesser interests or "mere expectations." . . . A student's interest in participating in a single year of interscholastic athletics amounts to a mere expectation rather than a constitutionally protected claim of entitlement. . . . [I]t falls "outside the protection of due process." [51]

On the third issue, a charge of denial of equal protection, the plaintiffs raised two complaints: (1) the transfer rule creates two classes of students and it treats these classes differently; and (2) the transfer rule creates two classes of schools. The courts held that the classification of students is reasonably related to the state's valid interest in deterring

---

50. *Id.* at 157.
51. *Id.* at 159.

or eliminating excessive recruitment of students. It saw no reasonable alternative to the regulation. The court saw the classification of schools as being rationally related to a valid state interest.

In a brief opinion, the eighth circuit upheld a student's request to be eligible for participation on the school's football team during his senior year.[52] The memorandum order of the district court and its circuit court's ruling reveal very limited facts. The primary issue at the circuit court was whether the student was entitled to attorneys' fees since he had prevailed on a nonconstitutional ground. The court held that he was entitled to attorneys' fees of $200.

In addition to the issue over the legality of the one-year eligibility rule, a suit was filed also on the authority of a state high school athletic association to prevent a boy from participating in a summer basketball program.[53] This program involved a camp in which participants had the opportunity to compete against very able players under the supervision of professional athletes and able coaches. The plaintiff, a rising senior, was 6'11" tall and considered to be a much sought after recruit by colleges. The Texas University sity Interscholastic League prohibited this kind of play.

The court limited its ruling to this one student only. It held that a school's interests in an athlete are greatly diminished during the summer "where the conduct . . . has no relationship to the school's legitimate interest in creating an orderly learning environment."[54] The court saw no rational relationship between the rule and the object to be achieved by the enforcement of the rule. It saw that

---

52. Kimbrough v. Arkansas Activities Ass'n, 574 F.2d 423 (8th Cir. 1978).

53. Kite v. Marshall, 454 F. Supp. 1347 (S.D. Tex. 1978).

54. *Id.* at 1349.

the student would suffer more harm than the defendants if the rule were enforced. No damages were awarded; the only relief sought was the right to participate in the camp without forfeiture of eligibility.

In the same year the third circuit decided a case brought by a high school junior whose basketball team was declared ineligible for post-season competition because it was under suspension for prior violation of league rules.[55] The school had used players who were ineligible because of absenteeism. The following punishment was assessed: (1) forfeiture of all games which were played during the years the violations occurred; (2) censure of the school board, high school principal, and the football and basketball coaches; and (3) holding as ineligible the high school football and basketball teams for post-season competition for the next two years.

Moreland, an above average basketball player, saw post-season competition as being important in terms of his being recruited for college play. He claimed that he was treated differently from other members of the basketball teams in tournament play in the state. He also claimed unequal treatment in that teams other than the football and basketball teams from his school did not lose their eligibility for post-season play. He did not claim that participating in basketball is a federally protected right.

In deciding the case, the court rejected the test of "strict scrutiny" and instead applied the "rational basis" test. Based on the latter standard, it concluded that a rule regulating class attendance is an expression of the league's legitimate interest in educational values and thus meets the "rational basis" test. The rule relating to the suspension

---

55. Moreland v. Western Pennsylvania Interscholastic Athletic League, 572 F.2d 121 (3d Cir. 1978).

of the athletic teams also bears a rational relationship to a school's purpose — the stigma of suspension may serve as a deterrent to future violations. The court reminded the plaintiff that, at the time he entered high school, the school was on probation. The court acknowledged that the application of the rule had caused the student to suffer, but it recognized that it is not unusual for innocent people to suffer in the sports world.

This section treats, finally, two § 1983 suits premised on discrimination in girls' athletics. Most of the cases involving gender discrimination in athletics have been grounded on Title IX and not on § 1983. However, two cases, one decided in 1977 and the other a year later, tested the applicability of § 1983 to this issue.

In the first case, a girl challenged several of the rules that applied uniquely to girls' basketball: (1) one requiring each player to play only half court; (2) one requiring each player to play only guard or forward; and (3) one requiring six instead of five players.[56] She sought a modification of the above rules to be more aligned to those of boys' basketball. She also sought damages for a deprivation of equal protection.

The court recognized that the actions of the high school athletic association are under color of state law. However, "the decision in *Brown v. Board of Education of Topeka,* ... cannot and must not be stretched to such lengths as to require every program, every rule, every facility, and every policy in every school to be the same. In Oklahoma, girls are treated on a par with boys insofar as a program for interscholastic basketball is concerned." [57]

---

56. Jones v. Oklahoma Secondary School Activities Ass'n, 453 F. Supp. 150 (W.D. Okla. 1977).

57. *Id.* at 154.

The court offered the girl a pragmatic solution, for her to change her position from guard to forward if it would enhance her chances for further play. But her allegations of reduced opportunity to participate in basketball beyond high school did not give rise to an equal protection argument. "There are, or should be, sensible limits to the extent courts will go in characterizing as real and substantial deprivations of constitutional rights the myriad of asserted complaints and grievances being sought before them." [58]

The final case involved a charge by female high school students that the Interscholastic Athletic Association of Wisconsin deprived them of equal protection by limiting boys and girls from competing against each other.[59] Girls were not allowed to try out with boys for the varsity baseball team, and the school in question offered no separate team for females for interscholastic competition. Girls were also denied permission to compete with boys on the swimming and tennis teams; the school sponsored a girls' swim team but had no tennis team for girls.

The athletic association later amended its constitution to conform to Title IX. The case then reduced itself to two issues: (1) the right of a girl to qualify for a boys' athletic team involving contact when no comparable team is available to girls; and (2) the right of a girl to qualify for a boys' team when the latter engages in a higher level of competition than the girls' team.

Addressing the first issue, the court ruled that if a school elects to sponsor interscholastic competition, it must make that activity available to all on equal terms. "Although plaintiffs do not have a constitutional right to compete on

---

58. *Id.* at 156.

59. Leffel v. Wisconsin Interscholastic Athletic Ass'n, 444 F. Supp. 1117 (E.D. Wis. 1978).

boys teams in contact or noncontact sports, the defendants may not afford an educational opportunity to boys that is denied girls." [60]

On the second question, the court saw that differences in the level of athletic competition arose from the ability of team members and not as a result of gender differences. Since there was no indication of intentional discrimination, the court saw that equal protection was not involved. Consequently, the court did not require that girls be allowed to qualify for positions on boys' varsity teams when the latter had a higher level of competition than the girls' team.

§ 4.4. Corporal Punishment.

Ever since citizens have banded together to organize a school, those entrusted with administering and supervising the educational program have had to assume responsibility for the discipline of students. This discipline is an integral part of an educational program, for without it, teachers cannot teach, and students cannot learn.[61] A desirable discipline program provides a proper climate which leads toward student self-direction and maturity. As a function of the responsibility entrusted to them, teachers and administrators are expected not only to correct students for misbehavior, but also to prevent undesirable behavior. They possess the authority to promulgate rules and regulations and see that they are enforced.

---

60. *Id.* at 1122.

61. The *Thirteenth Annual Gallup Poll of the Public Attitudes Toward the Public Schools* listed lack of discipline as being the biggest problem which the public schools must deal with. For many years discipline has led the list of the most severe problems of the schools. Reported in PHI DELTA KAPPAN 63 (September 1981), p. 33 *et seq.*

The responsibility of school personnel for holding students accountable for their behavior extends to four main foci: (1) from the time students leave home until they arrive at school, (2) during the time the students are at school; (3) from the time the students leave school until they arrive home (assuming of course, that they go directly home); and (4) at school-sponsored activities after school hours, whether they be held at school or at some other site. There is also a fifth dimension whereby students may be held accountable to school authorities for their actions, and that is for misbehavior outside school which has a direct and deleterious effect on a student's relationship to school personnel.

School personnel possess two major remedies for disciplining students whose behavior is not otherwise easily remediable. These remedies are corporal punishment and exclusion. The former will be considered in this section of this chapter; the latter in the next section.

Law on corporal punishment has not changed significantly through the years. Fewer than six states have outlawed it through legislation, and both federal and state courts have consistently upheld its use, provided it is administered reasonably.[62]

The Supreme Court of the United States ruled for the first time in the 1970's on the legality of corporal punishment, and in two instances upheld its practice. In *Baker v. Carr* the Court affirmed without comment that, even though parents had objected, a teacher could administer corporal

---

62. For guidelines on administering corporal punishment, see H.C. HUDGINS, JR. & RICHARD S. VACCA, LAW AND EDUCATION: CONTEMPORARY ISSUES AND COURT DECISIONS (Charlottesville: The Michie Company, 1979), p. 229-33.

punishment.[63] However, for a teacher to be upheld in spanking a child, four guidelines must be observed: (1) a student must be warned in advance of the kinds of misbehavior that could result in corporal punishment; (2) it must not be used as a first-line of punishment; (3) a second school official must be present to witness the spanking; and (4) parents, on request, must be furnished a written statement about the spanking, including the reasons for it and the witnesses. In its decision, the Court made it clear that this decision had only limited application, that being to North Carolina, the state in which the incident occurred.

In a more substantive decision than in *Baker,* the Supreme Court ruled that corporal punishment is not a violation of the eighth amendment's prohibition against cruel and unusual punishment.[64] The Court held that this amendment did not apply to noncriminal matters and the children involved had other recourse, such as a civil suit.

The facts of the case showed that two junior high school students were paddled for misbehaving; one suffered from hematomas and the other lost partial use of one arm for several days. The Court held, however, that the apparently excessive punishment was not in violation of the eighth amendment.

The most definitive ruling on the application of § 1983 to corporal punishment is from the fourth circuit in a 1980 decision.[65] The court held that, in some instances, a student can recover damages under § 1983. Unlike the above case which, in addition to the question of the legality of corporal

---

63. Baker v. Owen, 395 F. Supp. 294 (M.D.N.C.), *aff'd,* 423 U.S. 907 (1975).

64. Ingraham v. Wright, 430 U.S. 651 (1977).

65. Hall v. Tawney, 621 F.2d 607 (4th Cir. 1980).

punishment, involved procedural due process (the right to a hearing prior to being spanked), *Hall* treated substantive due process (in this case, the right to ultimate bodily security) and the court ruled that it applies to corporal punishment. "The existence of this right to ultimate bodily security — the most fundamental aspect of personal privacy — is unmistakably established in our constitutional decisions as an attribute of the ordered liberty that is the concern of substantive due process." [66]

The plaintiffs charged that a male teacher spanked their daughter with a homemade rubber paddle and, in an ensuing struggle, he shoved her against a desk, twisted her arm, and pushed her in the presence of the school's principal who granted permission for the teacher to spank her. The teacher then spanked the girl again. As a result of the spanking, the girl was treated in a hospital for ten days for injuries to the hips, thighs, and buttocks.

The district court dismissed the action against the defendants in light of the *Ingraham* decision. The plaintiffs appealed, and the circuit court ruled that corporal punishment does not *per se* violate a child's substantive due process rights. However, if the force used is so great as to cause severe injury which is disproportionate to the need to maintain order and is so inspired by malice or sadism that it amounts to brutal and inhumane use of official power literally shocking the conscience, then a violation of substantive due process may be found. The court added that not every violation of state tort law or criminal assault law will amount to a violation of this constitutional right. The court finally concluded that the student could not prove the claim which would entitle her to relief.

---

66. *Id.* at 613.

In a second case, a secondary school student brought a § 1983 suit for his school's imposition of two penalties for an illegal absence: suspension for three days and corporal punishment.[67] Although the eighteen-year-old boy had not actually been spanked, the court addressed the issue, since, under the school's regulations, a spanking was part of the penalty for an unexcused absence. The penalties had been well publicized so that the youth was aware of them, and he had been warned prior to a previous unexcused absence. The paddle to be used was 23 and $\frac{3}{4}$ inches long, 2 and $\frac{5}{8}$ inches wide, $\frac{1}{2}$ inch thick, and weighed 7 and $\frac{3}{4}$ ounces. The spanking was to be witnessed by another teacher as well as be administered in the presence of one or more of the boy's parents.

The court rejected the allegation that the child had been denied due process. Further, the parents' knowledge of and assent to their child's absence was subordinate to the rule and the interest of school authorities in enforcing the attendance law. In citing *Ingraham,* the court held that paddling a child does not subject him to a grievous loss for which the fourteenth amendment due process standards should be applied. No damages were awarded.

One other case, of lesser significance than those above, also treated the question of liability under § 1983. It is of lesser significance because of the lack of clarity of the application of § 1983 to student discipline matters at the time of the court's decision in 1969.

In this case, a student underwent injuries resulting from a confrontation with a teacher.[68] The teacher allegedly jerked a chair from the student, causing him to fall to the

---

67. Coffman v. Kuehler, 409 F. Supp. 546 (N.D. Tex. 1976).
68. Patton v. Bennett, 304 F. Supp. 297 (E.D. Tenn. 1969).

floor, resulting in physical injuries, embarrassment and humiliation in the presence of his peers. He claimed a violation of the fourth, eighth, and fourteenth amendments. He charged the school board with being liable in that it had employed the teacher and assigned him to duties likely to result in a situation such as this. He sought to remove the teacher from any employment in which this kind of behavior might be repeated.

The court rejected the student's claim and dismissed the complaint. Since this was a pre-*Owen* case, the court held that the school board was not a person under § 1983. However, it ruled that the members of the board as well as the teacher could be liable, a determination that was to be made later.

§ 4.5. Exclusion from School.

It is well established in law that school authorities have a right to exclude from school students whose conduct interferes with the normal operation of the school program. Exclusion may take either of two actions — suspension or expulsion. The differences in the two actions lie in who does the exclusion and the length of it. Suspension is characteristically a function of a school administrator for a short period of time. Expulsion is characteristically a function of the local board of education for a longer period of time. Law has not yet defined what exact periods of time constitute either of the two exclusionary measures. Thus, suspensions can vary from one or two days to two weeks or even longer. An expulsion is viewed as lasting possibly until the end of a semester, a school year, or even permanently.

Litigation in recent years has treated, not so much the right of school authorities to suspend or expel, but rather the right of students to procedural due process prior to suspension or explusion. This recent era of litigation entered a new phase in 1961 when the Fifth Circuit held in *Dixon* that, prior to being suspended from college, a student is entitled to at least two fundamental elements of procedural due process — notice of charges against him and the right to a hearing.[69] These precedents influenced a 1975 decision by the Supreme Court, *Goss v. Lopez* where the justices extended the *Dixon* holding to apply also to elementary and secondary school students.[70] In overturning an Ohio statute that allowed summary suspensions for up to ten days, the Court ruled that, in suspensions of ten days or less, a child is entitled to a notice of charges against him and the right to a hearing. If he denies the charges, the child must be informed of the evidence against him and be given the opportunity to present his side of the story.

In its ruling the Court observed that a child has a property right to an education, and this right is grounded in the fourteenth amendment. If this right is taken from a child, it can be only after adherence to minimum due process procedures.

In the last two decades courts have consistently recognized the necessity and importance of education.[71] To deny a young person the entitlement to such an education requires school officials to justify removing that student from school, and this can be done only by first offering the child an opportunity for a hearing. If the child requests the hearing, it should then be determined by a presentation of the evidence whether there is sufficient ground for suspension or expulsion.

---

69. Dixon v. Alabama State Board of Education, 294 F.2d 150 (5th Cir. 1961), *cert. denied,* 368 U.S. 930 (1961).

70. Goss v. Lopez, 419 U.S. 565 (1975).

71. This notion was clearly articulated in Brown v. Board of Education, 347 U.S. 483 (1954) and was reaffirmed in *Goss, supra* note 4.

The specific elements of a hearing are still in the process of clarification by the courts. The Supreme Court has spoken on what is required in short suspensions; it has not yet addressed the question of what due process is required in longer suspensions, although in *Goss* it did observe that more formal procedural steps may be required in an exclusion exceeding ten days. There has not been to date a definitive ruling on what due process is required in an explusion hearing. In one of the most comprehensive statements on this issue, Phay, in his book, recommends that the following elements of due process be observed:

1. *Notice* — A warning to the student of the types of misconduct that will lead to expulsion. Giving the student and his parents notice supporting the charges. Telling the student where and when the hearing will take place. Informing the student of his procedural rights prior to a hearing.
2. *Hearing* — Giving the student the opportunity to be heard in a fair and equitable manner within a setting that does not have to comport with the rules in a court of law.
3. *Counsel* — Phay indicates that courts are divided on whether a student may have counsel, but he views access to counsel as being desirable.
4. *Inspection of Evidence* — Allowing the student to inspect, prior to the hearing, any material that may be used against him at the hearing.
5. *Trier of Fact* — Assuring that the principal will conduct the hearing in an impartial manner, otherwise, having a third party to conduct the hearing.
6. *School Attorney* — Having the school attorney to play a secondary role at a hearing and instead, allowing the principal and the superintendent to present the case.

7. *Witnesses* — Allowing the student to confront and cross-examine witnesses.

8. *Evidence* — Allowing liberal use of evidence, including hearsay and character evidence.

9. *Self-incrimination* — Disallowing a student's claim that to testify against himself is a violation of the fifth amendment.

10. *Sufficiency of Evidence* — Using as a basis for determining a student's guilt the standard, "substantial evidence." That standard encompasses "such relevant evidence as a reasonable mind might accept as adequate to support a conclusion."

11. *Transcript* — Phay indicates that courts are divided on whether a student must be provided with a transcript of the proceedings.

12. *Appeal* — Recognizing that a student has a right to appeal to a higher authority.[72]

With respect to the procedural due process rights of students in exclusionary hearings, the courts have shown some reluctance to extend this right to be protected by § 1983. Several cases have been handed down in which students sought relief under § 1983, but for the most part, the courts have instead preferred to settle the matter only on the basis of a fourteenth amendment claim. This is in spite of the *Wood* and *Carey* decisions by the Supreme Court, which held that school authorities could be liable under the act.[73] Most of the cases were handed down after the mid-1970's or shortly after the *Goss* and *Wood* decisions.

In late 1975, a federal district court in Rhode Island ruled

---

72. PHAY, THE LAW OF PROCEDURE IN STUDENT SUSPENSIONS AND EXPULSIONS (Topeka: National Organization on Legal Problems of Education 1977).

73. *Wood, supra* note 5. Carey v. Piphus, 435 U. S. 247 (1978). These cases are treated comprehensively in Chapter Two.

primarily on jurisdictional and technical matters while affirming that, while a local school committee is not a "person" under § 1983, the court nonetheless assumed jurisdiction over the school committee, based on three grounds: (1) the student had alleged a constitutional deprivation; (2) the constitutional deprivation fell within the purview of rights covered by the statute in question; and (3) the claim for damages fell within the amount prescribed by the above statute.[74]

The student had been summarily suspended from school on two occasions, for five months and for one month. The court ruled that it was inappropriate to honor the defendant's motion for dismissal, in that the school committee was not immune from liability.

Succeeding cases have helped clarify the extent to which § 1983 applies to exclusion, more particularly with respect to the application of *Goss* and *Wood*. A district court in Louisiana held in 1978 that *Goss* does not require a formal hearing in the true adversary process prior to suspension;[75] to do otherwise would place too great a burden on the school administration. The court ruled further that the school board was not required to furnish counsel to the student.

The facts of the case revealed that the local school board had upheld the suspension of a student for becoming involved in an altercation with a coach. The boy's mother challenged the suspension on four procedural grounds: the son was not given a right to compulsory process of witnesses, confrontation and cross-examination, list of witnesses, and access to advanced written documentation.

The court recognized that the boy had been given notice of charges against him and had had three different opportunities to explain his version of the incident. Thus,

74. Panzarella v. Boyle, 406 F. Supp. 787 (D.R.I. 1975).
75. Whiteside v. Kay, 446 F. Supp. 716 (W.D. La. 1978).

the school had complied with the requirements of due process.

In *Coffman,* treated in the previous section on corporal punishment, the legality of a child's suspension was questioned since the suspension had preceded parental notification. In ruling on the legality of a suspension without first notifying the child's parents, the court held that the school's action did not negate its legality, for the methods used in solving the discipline problems the school was encountering outweighed any procedural due process rights the child may have had. Further, the child had advanced warning of the penalty for such an infraction.

Student suspension can take two forms. The most commonly used form is in restricting a child from attending school. More recently a different form has been used, and it allows a child to attend school but under a number of restrictions. These restrictions typically prevent a child from engaging in normal classroom activities, for he may be confined to a disciplinary center with specified academic assignments. This suspension is referred to as in-school suspension. Case law is very limited as to its use, and only one court decision to date has been handed down on its application to § 1983.

For making an obscene remark to a teacher, a student was suspended for the remaining eleven days of the school year.[76] The punishment was an in-school suspension. The following restrictions were placed on the student: (1) forbidding him to join in the senior class trip to Philadelphia; (2) requiring him to have a pink slip signed at the main office before going to any place in or out of the school building during the day; (3) requiring him to sit in the cafeteria with other students on restriction and not

---

76. Fenton v. Stear, 423 F. Supp. 769 (W.D. Pa. 1976).

being allowed to go outside; (4) forbidding him to speak to any other person in walking from class to class; and (5) forbidding him to participate in any school athletic or other extracurricular activities.

In beginning the suspension, the student had to sit in the same chair in a small classroom dubbed "the jail" for three days.

The court held that the child's punishment was not contrary to § 1983.

> The plaintiff's education was not materially infringed by the in-school discipline. Surely, his reputation could not have been seriously damaged by being kept in school with the restrictions imposed. Therefore, since it appears that plaintiff's constitutional rights to property and liberty were not violated and due process was accorded to him, § 1983 does not extend the right to relitigate in federal court evidentiary questions arising in high school disciplinary proceedings or the proper construction of high school regulations. Section 1983 was not intended to be a vehicle for federal court corrections of errors in the reasonable exercise of high school officials' discretion that does not rise to the level of specific constitutional guarantees. After all, trivial disciplinary sanctions imposed by high school officials are countless, and like those in this complaint sometimes give rise to hurt feelings and unwarranted desires to "get even" and challenge the responsible school authorities in a court.[77]

The court spoke out strongly for the necessity of school officials having some discretion in taking whatever action is deemed appropriate for maintaining proper discipline in the schools.

> We think there must be a degree of immunity if the work of the schools is to go forward; and, however

---

77. *Id.* at 772, 773.

worded, the immunity must be such that public school officials understand that action taken in the good-faith fulfillment of their responsibilities and within the bounds of reason under all the circumstances will not be punished and they need not exercise their discretion with undue timidity.[78]

Finally, the court likened the student's utterances to "fighting words" which the Supreme Court has held are not protected by the first amendment.[79]

In a case involving expulsion of eleven students charged with leading a riot, a federal district court in California rejected the students' claim that failure to follow the state statute constituted a violation of due process.[80]

Not every violation of state statute or a school board's procedural requirement is a denial of due process. . . . The defendant's failure to follow the procedure suggested by the plaintiffs would be a violation of state law only. Plaintiffs are not thereby deprived of any federal right. Title 42, U.S.C. § 1983 is not concerned with violations of state law unless such violations result in an infringement of a federally protected right.[81]

The court treated a second issue, that of bias of the school board in conducting the hearing. The plaintiffs contended that the board was not impartial in the hearing. They asserted that the members of the board had access to the students' files and that they had met with school officials prior to the hearing. The court responded:

Exposure to evidence presented in a nonadversary investigative procedure is insufficient in itself to impugn the fairness of the Board members at a later

---

78. *Id.* at 773, citing, *Wood, supra* note 5, at 321.
79. Whitney v. California, 274 U.S. 357 (1927).
80. Gonzales v. McEuen, 435 F. Supp. 460 (C.D. Cal. 1977).
81. *Id.* at 463.

adversary hearing. *Withrow v. Larkin,* 421 U. S. 35 . . .
(1975). Nor is a limited combination of investigatory
and adjudicatory functions in an administrative body
necessarily unfair, absent a showing of other circumstances such as malice or personal interest in the
outcome. *Withrow, supra,* at 47 . . . *Jones v. Board of
Educ.,* 279 F.Supp. 190, 200 (D.C., 1968). A school board
would be amiss in its duties if it did not make some
inquiry to know what was going on in the district for
which it is responsible. Some familiarity with the facts
of the case gained by an agency in the performance of
its statutory role does not disqualify a decisionmaker.
Hortonville Dist. v. Hortonville Ed. Assoc., 426 U.S.
482, 491 . . . (1976).[82]

The plaintiffs also argued that the superintendent was
biased because of the role he played in assisting the school
board in preparation for and in conducting the hearing. The
defense argued that the superintendent's role was minimal,
that he did not participate in the deliberations and did no
more than serve refreshments to the board members. The
court reacted:

Whether he did or did not participate, his presence to
some extent might operate as an inhibiting restraint
upon the freedom of action and expression of the Board.
Defendants argue that there is no evidence that Mr.
McEuen [superintendent] influenced or biased the
Board. Proof of subjective reasoning processes are incapable of corroboration or disapproval. Plaintiffs should
not be forced to rely upon the memory or sense of
fairness of Superintendent McEuen or the Board as to
what occurred there. Perhaps Mr. McEuen's physical
presence in deliberation becomes more offensive
because of the pre-hearing comments which showed
something less than impartiality.[83]

---

82. *Id.* at 464.
83. *Id.* at 465.

Since the court found a presumption of bias, it held that the plaintiffs were entitled to the court's review of the evidence according to a standard of "clear and convincing proof."

Finally, the court held that comment on the students' refusal to testify and the subsequent conclusion that guilt could be inferred from such a refusal was a violation of the students' rights under the fifth amendment.

A girl expelled from a private school in Delaware charged a deprivation of equal protection and due process.[84] The girl admitted to a charge of using marijuana in her room. The student handbook had no formal procedure for dealing with discipline problems, although all students had been reminded at the beginning of the year that the use of alcohol, marijuana and other drugs was forbidden, under penalty of expulsion.

The girl was expelled from the institution without a formal hearing. In addition to the equal protection and due process claims, she charged the institution with an impairment of contract. The court agreed that the student's relationship to the institution was a contractual one, but there had been no impairment here. The school had protected itself in three instances: (1) it had clearly proscribed in the handbook the use or possession of marijuana; (2) the school had provided each student with a copy of the handbook; and (3) the headmaster had repeated the rules at an assembly. The girl was not entitled to any relief, including damages.

§ 4.6. Search and Seizure.

For less than a decade and a half the issue of the right of school personnel to engage in search and seizure has been

---

84. Wisch v. Sanford School, Inc., 420 F. Supp. 1310 (D. Del. 1976).

litigated in the courts.[85] That issue has focused on the constitutional rights that students enjoy under the fourth amendment and the extent to which the amendment applies to school officials who undertake such searches.

The degree to which school officials are subject to the fourth amendment is still not fully resolved.[86] Initially, courts held that when school officials engaged in search and seizure, they acted *in loco parentis* and, as such, were not governed by the restrictions of that amendment.[87] More recently, courts have taken a closer look at this notion and have held that, under some circumstances, the amendment may not serve as a shield to school personnel.[88]

Two elements are critical with respect to the legality of a search of a student by school officials — the reason for the search and the way the search was conducted. With respect to the first element, courts are in considerable agreement that the fourth amendment's standard of "probable cause" as justification for a search does not apply; rather, a less exacting standard of "reasonable suspicion" is all that is

---

85. Prior to 1969 only two cases involving school personnel in search and seizure were heard in the courts, both of them in Tennessee. Phillips v. Johns, 12 Tenn. App. 354 (1930) and Marlar v. Bill, 181 Tenn. 100, 178 S.W.2d 634 (1944).

86. The fourth amendment provides:

The right of the people to be secure in their persons, houses, papers, and effects, against unreasonable searches and seizures, shall not be violated and no Warrants shall issue, but upon probable cause, supported by Oath or affirmation and particularly describing the place to be searched, and the persons or things to be seized.

87. *See, e.g.,* State v. Stein, 203 Kan. 638, 456 P.2d 1 (1969), *cert. denied,* 397 U.S. 947 (1970); In re Donaldson, 269 Cal. App. 2d 509, 75 Cal. Rptr. 220 (1969); People v. Overton, 301 N.Y.S.2d 479, 249 N.E.2d 366 (1969); Keene v. Rodgers, 316 F. Supp. 217 (D. Me. 1970).

88. *See* in particular State v. Mora, 307 So. 2d 317 (La. 1975) and 330 So. 2d 900 (La. 1976).

necessary for school personnel who undertake a search. "Reasonable suspicion" is not precisely defined, but it means essentially that one have sufficient information about the possession, dissemination or use of a harmful or illegal substance to warrant a search. When that standard does not exist, a school official will not be upheld, as for example, in *People v. D.*, where a teacher had observed a boy enter a restroom twice within an hour and stay for only five or ten seconds.[89] The student had been under suspicion for possible drug use and had been observed eating with another student, also under suspicion. The court held that these data did not constitute reasonable suspicion.

In contrast, the following set of circumstances did constitute reasonable suspicion.[90] An administrator had been informed that, earlier in the day, a student had sold drugs on campus. The administrator had observed bulges in the student's pockets and a pouch attached to his belt. The student had displayed money from his pouch but initially refused to show the contents of his pockets.

The second element governing the legality of a search is the way in which it is conducted. Courts have been consistent in upholding administrative searches of lockers and of cars, but have been in less than uniform agreement over the search of an individual. Some of the earlier cases upheld these searches, but students then became more secretive by hiding narcotics in their underclothing and school administrators became bolder by initiating strip searches. As a consequence, there has been more litigation over the search of a person than the search of lockers and cars. As a general rule, when an administrator requires a student to remove personal effects from his clothing, the courts will uphold the

---

89. People v. D., 34 N.Y.2d 483, 315 N.E.2d 466 (1974).
90. Nelson v. State, 319 So. 2d 154 (Fla. App. 1975).

search. This strategy is far more effective than an administrator or a teacher going into a student's clothing, for one could possibly be sued on an assault and battery charge. On the other hand, when an administrator requires that a student strip to his underclothing or undress completely, courts are likely not to uphold the search.[91] Such extreme measures are viewed as going beyond an educator's responsibility *in loco parentis*.

A more recent issue has involved the use of dogs as auxiliary agents in undertaking a search. Case law is just in the incubation period on this subject, and the legality of this practice is unclear. In a well-publicized case out of Indiana, the Seventh Circuit upheld the use of dogs in initiating a search but deplored the strip search by school officials which followed.[92] The appeals court said:

> It does not require a constitutional scholar to conclude that a nude search of a thirteen-year-old child is an invasion of constitutional rights of some magnitude. More than that: it is a violation of any known principle of human decency. Apart from any constitutional readings and rulings, simple common sense would indicate that the conduct of the school officials in permitting such a nude search was not only unlawful but outrageous under "settled indisputable principles of law." [93]

The courts were called upon to extend § 1983 to the search of students only four years after the 1969 locker

---

91. *See, e.g., People, supra* note 89; Doe v. Renfrow, 631 F.2d 91 (7th Cir. 1980), *cert. denied,* 49 U.S.L.W. 3880 (May 26, 1981); Bellnier v. Lund, 438 F. Supp. 47 (N.D.N.Y. 1977); M. M. v. Anker, 607 F.2d 588 (2d Cir. 1979); Bilbrey v. Brown, 481 F. Supp. 26 (D. Ore. 1979).

92. *Doe, supra* note 91.

93. *Id.* at 92.

search decisions. A 1973 case grew out of a search by various school and law enforcement officials over a student's complaint of her ring being missing.[94] The principal searched the room where the girl thought she may have left the ring. He and the assistant principal then requested the aid of the city police. The officers came to school, questioned the students and learned nothing about the missing ring. They then called two policewomen, employees of the county, who searched each of the eight plaintiffs and required them to undress to their undergarments. The ring was not found. No search warrant had been issued prior to the search.

The plaintiffs named eight different defendants, but the court dismissed three of them, for they were not considered as being persons under § 1983. These three included the county, the city, and the school board.

Prior to a resolution by the court on the matter of liability of the chief of police, school superintendent, principal, assistant principal, and police officers, an out-of-court settlement was reached in which each of the eight girls was awarded $800 in damages.

The first student search case to apply the good faith immunity doctrine of *Wood* was *Picha*, decided in 1976 one year after *Wood*.[95] The charge here was an illegal search. On the basis of a telephone tip, a principal requested that police be present while three junior high school girls thought to be in possession of drugs were searched. The actual search was conducted by a nurse and a school psychologist. The search uncovered no drugs and the students charged a violation of their rights under the fourth amendment.

---

94. Potts v. Wright, 357 F. Supp. 215 (E.D. Pa. 1973).

95. Picha v. Wielgos, 410 F. Supp. 1214 (N.D. Ill. 1976).

The court held that in searches like this, school officials are considered as being subject more to the constraints of the fourth amendment than they are in capacity of *in loco parentis.* A search in which school officials are protected must be "confined to an intrusion designed to discover weapons, and a citizen's inspection of a residence must not give rise to a greater invasion of privacy than is justified by the public interest the inspection serves." [96]

When the plaintiff was searched, she had a

> constitutional right not to be searched by school officials who were in contact with the police unless the extent of the intrusion occasioned by the search was justified in terms of the state interest in maintaining the order, discipline, safety, supervision and education of the students within the school. . . . Renee Picha had a constitutional right not to have the police cause a search in the absence of probable cause that she possessed an illegal material at the time of the search.[97]

The court stated that it is a misconception that school officials can have one free constitutional violation without being subject to damages.

In a case one year later, a court ruled against a school teacher who had searched an entire class of fifth grade students.[98] The teacher initiated the search on the basis of a student reporting that three dollars were missing from his coat pocket. The search included an inspection of the students' outer garments, desks, and books. The students were also taken to the restrooms of their sex and were ordered to strip to their underwear. The two-hour search did not retrieve the money.

---

96. *Id.* at 1220.

97. *Id.* at 1221.

98. *Bellnier, supra* note 91.

The court found state action to be involved but relied on the standard of "reasonable gounds" rather than "probable cause" as a justification for the search. "[T]here must be demonstrated the existence of some articulable facts which together provided reasonable grounds to search the students, and that the search must have been in furtherance of a legitimate purpose with respect to which school officials are empowered to act, such as the maintenance of discipline or the detection and punishment of misconduct." [99] The court held that the following factors may be taken into consideration in justifying a search: child's age, child's history and record in school, seriousness and prevalence of the problem, and the exigency requiring an immediate warrantless search. In applying the above standard and the special circumstances justifying a search, the court held that this immediate one was invalid. It was unreasonable because of the slight danger of the conduct involved, the extent of the search, and the age of the students. The students were not entitled to damges, however, because there was no showing that the defendants had not acted in good faith.

The second circuit ruled consistently with the above decision when it held that, the greater the intrusiveness, the more nearly the standard of "reasonableness" approaches "probable cause." [100] This standard extends to teachers who engage in an invasive search.

For being subjected to a strip search, a girl, age thirteen, sought $50,000 in actual damages and an equal amount in punitive damages.[101]

---

99. *Id.* at 53.
100. *M. M., supra* note 91.
101. *Doe, supra* note 91.

The seventh circuit rejected the notion that school officials are immune because they acted in good faith.

> It does not require a constitutional scholar to conclude that a nude search of a thirteen-year-old child is an invasion of constitutional rights of some magnitude. More than that: it is a violation of any known principle of human decency. Apart from any constitutional readings and rulings, simple common sense would indicate that the conduct of the school officials in permitting such a nude search was not only unlawful but outrageous under "settled indisputable principles of law." [102]

The court remanded the matter to the trial court for a determination of the amount in damages to which the girl was entitled.

§ 4.7. Appearance Codes.

School officials have considerable discretionary authority in regulating student behavior. This authority grows out of the notion that teachers and administrators act *in loco parentis* and may exercise reasonable authority and restraint in disciplining students. The school codes of most states explicitly provide for this.

When the students' rights movement surfaced and gained momentum in the 1960's, it soon provided students with a lever for testing the degree of authority that school personnel actually have in regulating student appearance. Students began to challenge a wide variety of dress regulations that had formerly been accepted and adhered to without question.

Over the last two decades the most litiguous area of student control has been on the question of student appearance. Well over 200 hair cases alone have been

---

102. *Id.* at 92.

litigated in both federal and state courts. Other cases have involved a challenge to a specific mode of dress. When based on constitutional grounds, this litigation has been premised on freedom of speech of the first amendment. Although appearance and dress are not stated in the first amendment, by implication, the right to speech extends to apply to one's appearance.

The appearance controversy has followed five channels in ten years, each quickly merging into a succeeding one. It began in Massachusetts in 1965 when a state court upheld an unwritten school regulation that forbade the wearing of a Beatle-type hairdo on males.[103] The import of this decision was that this court, and others entertaining similar cases, elected not to question the authority of school personnel in effecting the policies and regulations they seemed to be wise. Federal courts also took the same position as the Massachusetts court.

A second channel began shortly after the Massachusetts case. It reflected the thinking of courts that a school board's restrictions of a student's appearance must be related to the enhancement of public service. For the first time, a court held in 1967 that a hair regulation was unreasonable and unconstitutional under the first amendment.[104] In contrast, at about the same time, a California court held that a student's rights were infringed upon, but the public benefits controlled and outweighed any rights the students had.[105] The upshot of these decisions was that, as of the late 1960's a school district took a chance that its dress code policy may or may not be accepted.

---

103. Leonard v. School District, 212 N.E.2d 468 (Mass. 1965).
104. Zachary v. Brown, 299 F. Supp. 1360 (N.D. Ala. 1967).
105. Akin v. Board of Education, 68 Cal. Rptr. 557 (1968).

A third channel began in 1969 with *Breen v. Kahl,* a pivotal case.[106] Decided by the Seventh Circuit, it held that the "right to wear one's hair any length or in any desired manner is an ingredient of personal freedom protected by the U. S. Constitution." [107] Before such a right can be curtailed, the state must show a substantial justification for the restriction. *In loco parentis* does not clothe school authorities with absolute control over students; parents also share in matters such as grooming. Discipline for the sake of discipline and uniformity is inconsistent with the melting pot idea.

The fourth channel in the early 1970's involved conflicting opinions. For example, in a 1970 decision, a federal district court in Connecticut overturned a dress code for being too vague.[108] The phrases, "extreme style and fashion" and "neatly dressed and groomed" left too much to interpretation by students and too much discretion to administrators. Similarly, a federal district court in Alabama held that a constitutional right cannot be curtailed because of a reaction which the exercise of that right might produce.[109] By contrast, a dress code was upheld in California which prohibited male students from participating in extraclass activities if their hair length did not meet school standards. This code was shown to have been created to insure the young people's safety.[110]

The final channel involved a growing reluctance by

---

106. Breen v. Kahl, 419 F.2d 1034 (7th Cir. 1969); *Compare with* Ferrell v. Dallas School District, 392 F.2d 697 (5th Cir.), *cert. denied,* 393 U.S. 856 (1968).

107. *Breen, supra* note 106, at 1036.

108. Crossen v. Fatsi, 309 F. Supp. 114 (D. Conn. 1970).

109. Griffin v. Tatum, 300 F. Supp. 60 (M.D. Ala. 1969).

110. Neuhaus v. Torrey, 310 F. Supp. 192 (N.D. Cal. 1970).

federal courts to entertain hair cases. Judges have stated that they have more important issues to decide and the appearance controversy does not involve a substantial federal question. They have indicated that this matter should be resolved by local school officials and, if they are unable to resolve it, relief should be sought in state courts. A pivotal statement was made on this matter by Judge Wood when he quoted from an opinion by Justice Black who stated in 1971:

> I refuse to hold for myself that the federal courts have constitutional power to interfere in this way with the public school system operated by the States. And I furthermore refuse to predict that our Court will hold they have such power. ... There is no such direct, positive command about local school rules with reference to the length of hair state school students must have. And I cannot now predict this Court will hold the more or less vague terms of either the Due Process or Equal Protection Clauses have robbed the States of their traditionally recognized power to run their school system in accordance with their own best judgment as to the appropriate length of hair for students.[111]

The upshot of this controversy is that courts have been divided on the issue of the right of a school to regulate a student's appearance. Slightly more than half of the 200 plus cases have been decided in favor of the school board. From this number where one or more of three elements has been present in support of a regulation, the regulation will likely be upheld. These elements involved disruption, safety and health. It is also persuasive to a court for school officials to show the need for the regulation and its having been developed by a cross-section of the school community.

---

111. Hammonds v. Shannon, 323 F. Supp. 681, 682 (W.D. Tex. 1971) citing Justice Black's opinion in Karr v. Schmidt, 401 U.S. 1201 (1971).

As early as 1970 students began to premise challenges to dress codes on § 1983. The Federal District Court of the Northern District of Ohio awarded a boy nominal damages for a suspension growing out of his refusal to have his hair cut.[112] The boy had let his hair grow over the summer until it had reached shoulder length. Testimony revealed that the boy was well-behaved and courteous, created no disturbances, made no fuss over his appearance in class, and ignored snide remarks of students.

The defendants acknowledged that the rule emanated from the administration; they conceded that it was not a policy of the local board of education.

The court held that the principal had exceeded his powers in enacting the rule. Since there had been no showing that the boy had suffered any pecuniary loss or damages or had been humiliated, he was entitled only to the symbolic award of one cent.

In 1971 a court in Pennsylvania reached a similar decision.[113] It held that a plaintiff had not sustained actual or punitive damages and was not entitled to any monetary award. That dress code was also a product of the administration and not of the board of education. Although the boy's parents approved of the hair length, the principal summarily suspended him. Again there was no showing of any distraction or disruption. The court ruled that the regulation was in violation of the fourteenth amendment.

In 1975 the Third Circuit held that a student's hair length does not give rise to the level of a right protected by the federal Constitution.[114] The student had sought damages

---

112. Cordova v. Chonko, 315 F. Supp. 953 (N.D. Ohio 1970).

113. Axtel v. LaPenna, 323 F. Supp. 1077 (W.D. Pa. 1971).

114. Zeller v. Donegal School District Board of Education, 517 F.2d 600 (3d Cir. 1975).

for the school's refusal to allow him to play on the soccer team because of the length of his hair. The court dismissed the claim for damages, recognizing that the circuits were almost evenly divided on whether the right to wear one's hair at a given length is a clearly established right.[115] The court stated further its concern that § 1983 cases were covering too many rights and too many frivolous issues.

§ 4.8. Press Freedom.

In 1969 the Supreme Court of the United States held unequivocally that public school students, like teachers, have some degree of academic freedom within the school context. While academic freedom is not hinged on a specific part of the federal Constitution, it is grounded, in general, on rights that emanate from the Bill of Rights. The *Tinker* decision stands as a landmark for the protection of the right of freedom of speech for students under the first amendment.

While *Tinker* was being heard in the courts, another challenge, the freedom of the student press, was being tested also. This issue has raised a number of secondary questions on the degree of freedom that secondary school students have in publishing and disseminating materials. At the outset it must be established that student press freedom is not coequal with that of the commercial press. Student press freedom must be weighed as a balance test — the right of the students as opposed to the interests of the school in preserving order and discipline.

It has been established in recent years that school newspapers can criticize school personnel and their

---

115. The Third, Sixth, Ninth, Tenth, and D.C. Circuits have ruled that hair length is not a constitutionally protected right.

policies.[116] Further, they can take a stand on contemporary issues, for it is acknowledged that schools can and should be a marketplace of ideas for students as well as for teachers.[117] Contemporary students have been exposed to more ideas and more language than their counterparts of two or three decades ago; they are not likely to be shocked by such language.

School officials, however, can restrict the content of newspapers. That is the general holding of a majority of the courts that have been asked to rule on the issue.[118] The thinking of the judges is that it is a proper function of school authorities to restrict pornography, obscenity and vulgarity from appearing in print, as well as to avoid a libel suit. The real problem arises, however, with respect to the standards that are applied in determining what is acceptable and what is unacceptable, for there is a lack of agreement on the definitions of pornography, obscenity and vulgarity. In 1977, the Second Circuit held that school officials acted properly in restricting students from taking a survey of sexual attitudes of pupils within the school and then publishing them in the school newspaper.[119] The board of education justified its position on the ground that there was reasonable cause to believe that the distribution and publication of the questionnaire would have an adverse

---

116. Tinker v. Des Moines Independent Community School District, 393 U.S. 503 (1969).

117. *See, e.g.,* Scoville v. Board of Education, 425 F.2d 10 (7th Cir. 1970); Sullivan v. Houston Independent School District, 333 F. Supp. 1149 (S.D. Tex. 1971) and 475 F.2d 1071 (5th Cir. 1973).

118. *See, e.g.,* Zucker v. Panitz, 299 F. Supp. 102 (S.D.N.Y. 1969); Eisner v. Stamford Board of Education, 440 F.2d 803 (2d Cir. 1971).

119. Trachtman v. Anker, 563 F.2d 512 (2d Cir. 1977).

effect on some students, particularly at the freshman and sophomore levels. The court agreed:

> [W]here school authorities have reason to believe that harmful consequences might result to students, while they are on the school premises, from solicitation of answers to questions, then prohibition of such solicitation is not a violation of any constitutional rights of those who seek to solicit.[120]

The same year the Fourth Circuit reasoned differently and upheld the publication of an article on birth control.[121] The court reasoned that the newspaper was established as a public forum rather than as a part of the curriculum. The court did acknowledge that the scope of constitutional freedom varies with the environment as well as with the maturity of the individuals involved in the controversy. In this specific situation the principal had banned the article because he viewed it as being in conflict with the local school board policy on teaching about sex education. The court rejected that notion and held that the newspaper was subject to protection under the first amendment.

To date, there has not been a definitive ruling from the Supreme Court of the United States on the degree of freedom that the student press enjoys.[122] Recently, court decisions have revealed mixed rulings. In *Fransca,* a federal

120. *Id.* at 520.

121. Gambino v. Fairfax County School Board, 564 F.2d 157 (4th Cir. 1977).

122. *See* Board of School Commissioners v. Jacobs, 420 U.S. 128 (1975). Here the Supreme Court remanded the case without handing down a definitive ruling, for the class of litigants was never properly certified nor identified in the class action suit. The students had initiated the complaint on the basis of prior restraint; the circuit court found the regulations to be vague and overbroad and in violation of the test under the Tinker decision of "substantial and material disruption."

district court held that a principal acted properly in screening material and preventing its distribution when it was felt that its dissemination would likely lead to substantial disorder and disruption.[123] The principal also had concerns about possible articles being libelous. In spite of there being no school board policy on prior restraint, the court upheld the principal's actions as being reasonable. Unlike *Fransca,* a federal court in Georgia ruled that, based on the *Tinker* test, there was insufficient evidence to justify school authorities to restrict publication.[124]

In 1980 the Fourth Circuit upheld a district court ruling that forbade the distribution of any newspaper on campus that "encouraged actions which endanger the health or safety of students." [125] Two high school students published an off-campus paper and disseminated it at school. It contained a cartoon depicting a school monitor in a derogatory manner and carried an advertisement featuring the sale of drug paraphanelia. In accordance with school rules, the principal confiscated the papers and returned them to the students at the end of the day.

The court upheld the principal on the basis that the school's rules were not unduly vague. Further, because of the commercial nature of the advertisement, it enjoyed less protection under the Constitution than other forms of speech.

To date, the most definitive student press freedom case based on § 1983 is *Thomas,* a 1979 decision from the Second Circuit.[126] For publishing an underground student

---

123. Fransca v. Andrews, 463 F. Supp. 1043 (E.D.N.Y. 1979).

124. Reineke v. Cobb County School District, 484 F. Supp. 1252 (N.D. Ga. 1980).

125. Williams v. Spencer, 622 F.2d 1200 (4th Cir. 1980).

126. Thomas v. Board of Education, Granville Central School District, 607 F.2d 1043 (2d Cir. 1979).

243

newspaper and having a copy show up at school, students were subjected to a variety of penalties: (1) five-day suspensions, reduced to three days if the students wrote an essay on the topic "The potential harm to people caused by the publication of irresponsible and/or obscene writing."; (2) segregation from other students during study hall for the month of February; (3) loss of all student privileges during the suspension; and (4) inclusion of suspension letters in the students' files.

School officials suspended students under the state statute that provided for suspensions of students who are "insubordinate or disorderly, or whose conduct otherwise endangers the safety, morals, health, or welfare of others."

The students initiated a § 1983 suit, seeking injunctive and declaratory relief. Judge Kaufman of the Second Circuit ruled that this case differed from some others already decided in that almost all the activity in this one had occurred outside school. No copies of the paper had been sold at school.

> We may not permit school administrators to seek approval of the community-at-large by punishing students for expression that took place off school property. Nor may courts endorse such punishment because the populace would approve. The First Amendment will not abide the additional chill on protected expression that would inevitably emanate from such a practice.[127]

The court saw that if this kind of behavior were tolerated, it could lead to almost unlimited ends. The court remanded the case for a final determination as to the nature and form of relief the students should be granted.

In a case clearly related to freedom of the press, a § 1983 suit was initiated by parents against school officials who

---

127. *Id.* at 1051.

refused to permit children to take home a circular that parents wanted distributed to other parents.[128] Parents argued that since the school had created a public forum by permitting a wide variety of materials to be sent home by children, the parents themselves could not be denied this access.

The circuit court agreed with the district court's decision in dismissing the complaint. It quoted the district court:

> [T]he distribution via students of information concerning coming theatrical events, home safety measures, and the like, is not indicative of the establishment of a forum for First Amendment purposes. Dissemination of such material is a logical and a proper extension of the educational function of schools in our society, and such dissemination does not of itself give rise to any right of access to student distribution by parents or other concerned citizens.[129]

The court pointed out that a very different case might have been presented if the appellants had been seeking to take issue with the content of materials being distributed, but this was not the case. The court concluded that the appellants were seeking to create a forum for themselves rather than use one created by school officials.

§ 4.9. Parenthood.

Over the last two decades case law has undergone a change with respect to limitations on students who either married or became pregnant. For a number of years courts invariably supported local school district policies which placed restrictions on married students. These restrictions ranged from a prohibition on engaging in extracurricular

---

128. Buchel v. Prentice, 572 F.2d 141 (6th Cir. 1978).
129. *Id.* at 142, citing 410 F. Supp. at 1247.

activities [130] to a requirement that students withdraw from school for the remainder of the term.[131]

More recently, judges have seen the necessity of young people getting as much education as possible, and courts have modified their support of school board policies that restrict the attendance of married students.[132] Marriage, in and of itself, is not a defensible reason for denying a person the entitlement to attend school and to participate in activities available to nonmarried students.

Related to marriage as a legal question is a girl's pregnancy and the right of school personnel to restrict her attendance. Whether one is married or not, a girl who is unmarried and pregnant cannot on those two conditions alone, be deemed to be lacking in moral character.[133]

Case law based on § 1983 is very limited with respect to the right of married students or unmarried parents to attend school and to remain eligible for the various activities the school sponsors. This may be due, in part, to the changing attitude of people toward married students remaining in school. In fact, many schools now provide special accommodations for such students including instruc-

---

130. State *ex rel.* Baker v. Stevenson, 189 N.E.2d 18 (Ohio C.P. 1962).

131. State v. Marion County Board of Education, 302 S.W.2d 57 (Tenn. 1957).

132. *See, e.g.,* Board of Education v. Bentley, 383 S.W.2d 677 (Ky. App. 1964); Anderson v. Canyon Independent School District, 412 S.W.2d 387 (Tex. Civ. App. 1967); Davis v. Meek, 344 F. Supp. 298 (N.D. Ohio 1972); Holt v. Shelton, 341 F. Supp. 821 (M.D. Tenn. 1972).

133. Andrews v. Drew Municipal Separate School District, 371 F. Supp. 27 (N.D. Miss. 1973). In Perry v. Grenada Municipal Separate School District, 300 F. Supp. 748 (N.D. Miss. 1969), the court held that unwed mothers cannot automatically be excluded from school unless they were first given a hearing in which it could be established they lacked moral character, and therefore would have an adverse influence on others.

tion in child care. Further, under the provisions of Title IX, discrimination based on marital or parental status is prohibited by schools that receive federal funds. This question is therefore a Title IX or an equal protection issue and not a § 1983 matter. An illustrative case is *Shull v. Columbus Municipal Separate School District,* a 1972 decision out of Mississippi.[134] The court found that the school district's exclusion of two girls solely because they were unwed mothers was a violation of the equal protection clause of the fourteenth amendment. There was no evidence that the girls were lacking in moral character or that they had been charged with any other kind of misconduct. The only reason for their exclusion was their parental state. As a consequence, the court ruled in their favor by ordering their being readmitted to school and by being awarded attorneys' fees of $1,500, which included costs of telephone and automobile mileage.

§ 4.10. Special Education.

Special education litigation underwent two phases in the 1970's. It began with a challenge to institutionalized practices that overlooked the identification and avoided the education of young people who otherwise qualified as "special education." The first stage began in the very early 1970's with the judiciary assuming a proactive stance. A case arising in Pennsylvania provided the impetus when plaintiffs sought to insure that mentally retarded children would be entitled to the same free, appropriate education that other children received. In a historic consent agreement, the parties agreed to the stipulation that children of school

---

134. Shull v. Columbus Municipal Separate School District, 338 F. Supp. 1376 (N.D. Miss. 1972).

age classified as needing special education would be so educated.[135]

Closely following the above case was the *Mills* decision out of the District Court of the District of Columbia.[136] This case is even more significant than the Pennsylvania case above, in that it asserted that the right of exceptional young people to an education at state expense is grounded in the equal protection clause of the fourteenth amendment. Thus, for the first time, a court asserted explicitly that special education children have a right to an education under our federal Constitution.[137]

Following both cases above were a number of court cases that chipped away at established practices of avoiding the recognition and treatment of special education children as students.

In 1975, Congress passed the Education for All Handicapped Children Act, which began the second phase, that of legislative initiative.[138] The Act provided a comprehensive mandate that all handicapped children between the ages of three and eighteen were entitled to a free, appropriate education no later than September 1, 1978, and all children between the ages of three and twenty-one were entitled to a free, appropriate education no later than September 1, 1980.

---

135. Pennsylvania Association For Retarded Children v. Pennsylvania, 334 F. Supp. 1257 (E.D. Pa. 1971) and 343 F. Supp. 279 (E.D. Pa. 1972).

136. Mills v. Board of Education, 348 F. Supp. 866 (D.D.C. 1972).

137. In Brown v. Board of Education, 347 U.S. 483 (1954), the Supreme Court stated that "in these days it is doubtful that any child may reasonably be expected to succeed in life if he is denied the opportunity of an education. Such an opportunity, where the state has undertaken to provide it, is a right which must be made available to all on equal terms." *Id.* at 493.

138. 20 U.S.C. § 1401 *et seq.*

In order to be eligible for federal funds under the Act, a state had to establish a specific plan for education of handicapped children, their placement to be in the "least restrictive environment." That phrase was interpreted to mean a free, appropriate education that fits an individual's needs.[139]

The Act also mandated an Individualized Education Program (IEP) — a written plan developed by the local education agency, the teacher, the parents and the child, when appropriate. Each IEP would indicate the following: (1) present level of the child's educational performance; (2) annual goals and short-term objectives; (3) specific educational services to be provided; (4) extent to which the child can participate in regular educational programs; (5) projected dates for initiation and termination of services; and (6) objective criteria and evaluative procedures to determine the efficacy of the objectives. The Act also provided procedural safeguards for both the school district and the parents.[140] It has been estimated that approximately twelve percent of the population, ages three to twenty-one, may qualify for special education.

Since the effective implementation of the Act, a number of court cases have been initiated, most of them based on some provision of the Act. Others have been premised on

---

139. Handicapped children are defined as those who are mentally retarded, hard of hearing, deaf, orthopedically impaired, other hearing impaired, speech impaired, visually handicapped, seriously emotionally disturbed, or children with specific learning disabilities who require special education and related services.

140. Section 504 provides: "No otherwise qualified handicapped individual in the United States . . . shall, solely by reason of his handicap, be excluded from the participation in, be denied the benefits of, or be subjected to discrimination under any program or activity receiving federal financial assistance."

§ 504 of the Rehabilitation Act of 1973. A lesser number of cases have been litigated on § 1983 and cover several different issues. The cases that fall into this category have been decided since 1978.

In *Riley v. Ambach,* eighteen handicapped children brought suit in protest of three key regulations of the New York State Commissioner of Education regarding learning disabled children.[141] The regulations in dispute provided for the following: (1) requiring a learning disabled child exhibit a discrepancy of fifty percent or more between expected achievement, based on ability and actual achievement, to qualify as being handicapped; (2) removing all residential schools treating learning disabled from a list of schools approved by the Commissioner for treatment of the handicapped; and (3) issuing an advisory memorandum which stated that any school district serving over two percent of the total population of school children would be subject to an annual site visit.[142]

The plaintiffs based their suit on several federal acts, § 1983 being one of them. The court held that their claim did not rise to the level of a federal constitutional question (with one exception), and their claim for damages was barred by the eleventh amendment.[143]

In deciding the case, the court answered each of the plaintiffs' charges. On the first charge, the court held that "the use of the 50% standard interferes with the proper identification of learning disabled children . . . since it operates to

---

141. Riley v. Ambach, 508 F. Supp. 1222 (E.D.N.Y. 1980).

142. *Id.* at 1225.

143. *See, e.g.,* Stemple v. Board of Education, 464 F. Supp. 258 (D. Md. 1979); Hutto v. Finney, 437 U.S. 678 (1978); Edelman v. Jordan, 415 U.S. 651 (1974); Stubbs v. Kline, 463 F. Supp. 110 (W.D. Pa. 1978); and Ruth Anne M. v. Alvin Independent School District, 532 F. Supp. 460 (S.D. Tex. 1982).

eliminate consideration of factors and the use of techniques which do not, given the present state of the art, lend themselves to quantification." [144]

On charge two the court ruled that a residential school must be an option, in that some learning disabled children need such a facility. The third charge was rejected, for the plaintiffs had not established the lack of a rational relationship between the provision for site visitation and the legitimate purposes it was designed to serve. The court then rejected the plaintiffs' petition for tuition reimbursement for the current year in which the parents had placed their children in residential schools.

In 1979 an emotionally handicapped child successfully asserted his right to participate in interscholastic athletics.[145] He had initially been barred from participation on the basis of the state's athletic association rule which required a one-year residency for transfer students.

Doe, the plaintiff, had moved his residency from his parents' home to that of his grandparents. This had been done on the basis of a recommendation of a clinical psychologist. Doe, classified as being emotionally disturbed, had his handicap compounded by exposure to his father, who was terminally ill. The change of residence involved moving from one school district to another.

The court upheld the boy's claim on the basis that participation in sports provided him with an outlet that he needed. The injunctive relief that he sought was granted; he did not otherwise seek any damages.

For failure to provide him with an appropriate education, a secondary school student sought both injunctive and declaratory relief.[146] He charged the school district with

---

144. *Riley, supra* note 141, at 1241.

145. Doe v. Marshall, 459 F. Supp. 1190 (S.D. Tex. 1978).

146. Harris v. Campbell, 472 F. Supp. 51 (E.D. Va. 1979).

being derelict in addressing his needs and in providing adequate opportunities to meet those needs. The court rejected his claim. Evidence showed that over a four-month period the school district had made extensive efforts to assist the plaintiff. The court ruled further that before the child could maintain his suit, he must first exhaust his administrative remedies.[147]

In another § 1983 case, the father of an autistic child sought damages in the form of expenses for a full-time tutor for their child.[148] The legal issue revolved around whether the child's parents had properly requested a hearing to determine an appropriate individualized program. The court held that such a request has been made and the father was entitled to recover expenses for the tutor.

A case in New York City was litigated on the ground that children who exhibited extreme aggression because of their emotional problems had been placed in special day care schools.[149] The court held that the procedures the school district used violated due process. Further, since the students had been referred mostly to racially segregated schools, there was a denial of equal educational opportunity. The court directed that the following procedures be used in assignment of the children to appropriate schools: (1) notify by mail all parents of the possibility of reevaluation of their child's case; (2) avoid bias in discipline and referrals because of the large number of minority students; (3) train faculty about mainstreaming of special day school students; (4) establish an independent ombudsman to represent parent and child; (5) secure the

---

147. *See* Sessions v. Livingston Parish School Board, 501 F. Supp. 251 (M.D. La. 1980) in which the court ruled similarly.

148. Boxall v. Sequoia Union High School District, 464 F. Supp. 1104 (N.D. Cal. 1979).

149. Lora v. Board of Education, 456 F. Supp. 1211 (E.D.N.Y. 1978).

services of a communications expert to develop readily understandable explanations to parents and children of their choices; (6) report to the court of changes in the program to insure due process.[150]

Several special education cases have involved discipline of students, and in each case the court has overturned the school district's action. To date, courts have ruled that a special education child may be disciplined; however, if the child's misbehavior is an outgrowth of his exceptionality, he cannot unilaterally be excluded from school. Before such action can be taken, the child must first be evaluated by his placement team with respect to the cause of the misbehavior. On the other hand, if a child's misbehavior is unrelated to his exceptionality, he can be disciplined without the matter first going through the placement team. That action places a real burden on the disciplinarian to show that there was no relationship between the misbehavior and the child's exceptionality.

To date, courts have not ruled specifically on the suspension or expulsion of students as being in violation of § 1983. Court cases have been premised on the Education for All Handicapped Children Act and, to a lesser degree, on § 504 and the fourteenth amendment.[151]

---

150. *Id.* at 1294-95.

151. *See* Southeast Warren Community School District v. Department of Public Instruction, 285 N.W.2d 173 (Iowa 1979); Doe v. Koger, 480 F. Supp. 225 (N.D. Ind. 1979); Flint Board of Education v. Williams, 88 Mich. App. 8, 276 N.W.2d 499 (1979); Howard S. v. Friendswood Independent School District, 454 F. Supp. 634 (S.D. Tex. 1978); L. L. v. Circuit Court of Washington County, 90 Wis. 2d 585, 280 N.W.2d 343 (1979); Mrs. A. J. v. Special School District No. 1, 478 F. Supp. 418 (D. Minn. 1979); Sherry v. New York State Education Department, 479 F. Supp. 1328 (W.D.N.Y. 1979); S-1 v. Turlington, 635 F.2d 342 (5th Cir. 1981).

4.11. Summary.

Students have initiated legal action under § 1983 on a variety of issues, the major ones having been identified and treated in this chapter. When translated into court actions, these issues have involved a variety of remedies, including equitable relief, compensatory damages, punitive damages, and attorneys' fees. Students have named as defendants to their actions various parties, including school administrators, school board members, and school boards as corporate bodies.

The extent to which students have been successful in asserting a denial of their federal constitutional and statutory rights has varied, depending often on the subject matter. To date, the summary statements which follow in this section represent the consensus of court rulings concerning the applicability of § 1983 to a student's protected rights.

In establishing that education is not a right guaranteed by the federal Constitution, courts have disallowed assertions by parents that their children can attend a school under conditions at variance with state laws. When it is demonstrated that these laws are reasonable and are rationally related to a legitimate state objective, parents' rights and interests are subordinate to those of the state.

Section 1983 does not entitle a student to be assigned or reassigned to a school of one's choice solely on the basis of a pupil's preference for a given organizational plan. It is recognized that a local school board has considerable autonomy in determining which pupils shall be assigned to a given school.

Section 1983 also does not entitle a student to attend school in a district not his own on a tuition-free basis, even though he may have previously done so. The student may have an objective expectation of continued attendance involving no tuition, but that expectation is an insufficient basis for overturning a school board action disallowing the student's request.

Student claims over given elements of the educational program have covered a variety of issues. A number of them have focused on the degree of authority that school boards have in selecting curriculum materials, particularly when individuals or groups disagree with the board's decision. That local school boards have a right both to select curriculum materials as well as to forbid or remove certain materials has been clearly established. There is no constitutional protection for students who claim that, through board action, a school must provide them with their preferred books or materials. Likewise, students cannot claim a constitutional right to have books removed from the school list of required or acceptable materials. Unlike a faculty member, a book does not acquire tenure; it may be removed at any period of time, even though some parents or students feel it should remain in school and be accessible to pupils.

Boards of education are expected to make reasonable efforts to accommodate students who object to being exposed to curriculum materials at variance with their religious beliefs. There is a limit, however, as to how far board members have to go in this accommodation, for when students avoid a number of activities and experiences, they may not be receiving what the state expects as being a minimal education. When that point is reached, a child's religious convictions are of lesser importance than the state's interest in having an educated citizenry.

It is within the proper province of a school board to determine what courses may be required of a child rather than have a child make that determination. A student's personal or philosophical conviction is not sufficient reason or excuse

255

.aking a required course. Students have occasionally
..cted to taking specified courses on a religious ground,
out courts have just as often seen the objection as being a
personal or philosophical defense. On the other hand, where
a student is denied a course or an activity, and the reason
for that denial can be pointed to as racial discrimination,
that student has sufficient ground for a § 1983 suit.

Section 1983 does not guarantee that each child is entitled to a specified amount of time of teacher-pupil contact.
Such a consideration must be based on factors other than
some claim to a right under the Constitution or a federal
statute.

The federal Constitution does not guarantee to students
the right to participate in interscholastic athletics. Regulations governing eligibility for participation are determined by a number of forces beyond a student's control, and
these include such elements as Title IX, state laws, local
board policies and regulations of a state athletic association.

Rules of an athletic association are designed to minimize
recruiting or exploitation of young people, and those
purposes meet the rational relationship test. These rules
may at some time go beyond their intended purpose when,
for example, they restrict a young person from engaging in
competition during the summer. A school's interest in
regulating athletics during the summer is at a lower level
than when school is in session.

When a school has been penalized for violation of the
rules of an athletic association, an individual player
affected by that penalty does not have ground for a § 1983
suit. Similarly, where rules are different for boys and girls,
claims of gender discrimination have been ground in equal
protection or Title IX rather than in § 1983. Girls should be
allowed, however, the same opportunity to participate in

interscholastic athletics that boys have. Having the same opportunity does not necessarily equate with actual participation on what was a boys' team.

When students are disciplined, § 1983 operates more clearly in assuring students their rights than in some areas already mentioned in this summary. For example, an administrator may be held liable for damages for excessively spanking a child. The use of corporal punishment is not a violation *per se* of a child's rights, but the child's rights may outweigh those of an administrator when excessive or unreasonable force is used, when malice is involved, or when administrators otherwise abuse their power to correct students for misbehavior.

Today, if a student is suspended or expelled from school without first being afforded procedural due process, school officials may be liable for damages. Although the law of procedural due process is not fully mature regarding student exclusions, it is clear that, minimally, students are entitled to notice of charges and an opportunity for a hearing in a short-term suspension. The longer the exclusion, the more that procedural due process must apply.

If the procedural due process rights of students have been violated, the damages that can be collected are minimal. These damage awards will be set at not more than one dollar unless it can be shown that school officials acted with a deliberate attempt to injure a student and injury actually occurred.

Due process is flexible and must be interpreted according to a number of factors. Consideration such as the nature of the offense, the gravity of the penalty, and the objectivity of the official conducting the hearing are proper matters for determining if the exclusion was legal. Another important consideration is the clarity by school officials as to what kinds of behavior are unacceptable and lead to suspension

...on. When students know in advance what actions ...unishable and what behaviors lead to exclusion, they ...ave less chance of claiming a constitutional violation.

In maintaining order and discipline in a school, school officials have a right to search students and school lockers. For officials to act *in loco parentis* in engaging in a search, there must be a compelling state interest to justify it in terms of discipline, safety and student welfare.

When searches become highly invasive, school officials are more closely bound by the fourth amendment and its standard of probable cause than by the doctrine of *in loco parentis* and its standard of reasonable suspicion. Damages may be awarded students for a strip search. Group strip searches cannot be justified under *in loco parentis;* however, for damages to be awarded, a lack of good faith by school officials must be established.

Courts have been reluctant to include the length of a student's hair as being protected under § 1983, just as a number of courts have been reluctant to give it first amendment protection. Yet, courts have been divided on this matter. Damages have seldom been awarded students who have been required to get their hair cut as a condition for attending school.

On the issue of student freedom of the press being protected under § 1983, there has been very little litigation. Court suits have been premised more often on first amendment grounds and not on § 1983. The very limited litigation should serve only as a warning that school officials may be answerable to a § 1983 suit.

Similarly, there has not been enough litigation on § 1983 as a protection for student parents for a definitive statement. Limited damage fees have been awarded in one case where a student was excluded from school for the reason of motherhood.

Cases involving special education have been very recent, and they have established that § 1983 does protect exceptional children and their right to a free, appropriate education. A program and an activity may be open to a special education student and not to others if it can be shown that the denial of that program or activity would have a negative effect on the child and his handicap.

Where a school district has made a reasonable effort to provide a program for a special education child, the child cannot successfully assert that the district failed to meet his needs. That is, a district cannot guarantee that a child will learn, will make progress, or will progress according to some predetermined criterion. All that the district is expected to do is to make a reasonable attempt to address the child's needs.

When a school district sets special education children apart from others without ample justification for that separation or segregation, and that separation denies the child an opportunity available to others, the child will likely prevail in a suit.

Discipline of special education children is both like and unlike that of non-special education children. It is like that of other kinds of discipline in that these students are entitled to the same due process procedures that all children are whenever a school is contemplating a child's discipline for misbehavior. It is unlike that of other kinds of due process in that, first, it must be determined if the disciplinary problem is an outgrowth of the child's disability or handicap. If it is, then a change of the child's environment (placement) is the proper response rather than exclusion from school. When a special education child misbehaves and the misbehavior is in no way related to the child's handicap, then school officials may exclude that individual like anyone else.

CHAPTER 5

THE CURRENT STATUS OF THE ACT

§ 5.0. The Era of the Civil Rights Tort.

When the Civil Rights Act of 1871 was passed by Congress, its sponsors could not have envisioned the scope of its coverage 110 years later. Indeed, during the last two decades it has undergone a metamorphosis that many congressmen and judges could not have forseen even in 1961. Today its impact is considerable on those people involved in public education. Both teachers and students have been brought under the penumbra of this Act, a condition which has often made school boards and school board members wince as they see an erosion of their power and a greater likelihood of their being named as parties to suits.

As demonstrated in the previous chapters, legal challenges to school board and administrative authority have, in recent years, become more numerous. Of all the possible areas of litigation, employment matters have received more attention than any other as increasing numbers of civil rights-type complaints have been litigated in both federal and state courts. Actually having their origins as early as the mid-1960's, such cases have placed the legal decision-making prerogatives of school officials under close judicial scrutiny.

As stated at the outset of the book, a common thread running through the federal court decisions is the charge of plaintiffs that certain constitutional or statutory rights have been denied; the various courts have weighed the validity of such charges and, where the plaintiffs were upheld, the courts ultimately granted to them certain remedies for the deprivation of those rights. These cases are from a new era in school litigation — the era of the civil rights tort — that has already had and is continuing to have a profound impact on individuals directly affected by this litigation: local school board members and their administrative officers.

As the previous chapters show, the hundreds of cases filed against school officials, and the many cases treating the civil rights of students and professional personnel, indicate that no area of the country has been exempt from suit. Yet, as the case law reveals, it remains a basic rule of law that public school boards and their administrative officers possess considerable legal authority in making all policies, rules and regulations for the welfare of the school system. In their official actions, it is still presumed that school officials act in good faith. When they do so, they are generally not subject to suit.

The four preceding chapters have covered two basic elements of suits under the Civil Rights Act of 1871 and its § 1983. These elements have included a historical and analytical treatment of the Act and an explanation of its ramifications with respect to school boards as corporate entities, to school board members as individuals, and to school administrators. These chapters have also included a treatment of suits by teachers and students against these same three classes of defendants. In doing do, this study has attempted to put into focus the status of the Act and its applicability to individuals and their civil rights.

What has become very evident in the study of this Act is the evolution of judicial interpretation of its scope. As it affects educational personnel, the Act has had particular significance since 1961, as can be seen by the following sequence of interpretation of the Act, primarily by the Supreme Court.

Initially, the Supreme Court ruled that a corporate body has absolute immunity under § 1983, but an officer of that body does not enjoy immunity. The Court interpreted the Act's opening phrase "[e]very person" as meaning individuals but not a corporate body.

That interpretation held for seventeen years, or until 1978 when the Supreme Court reversed itself and ruled that local entities are not immune from suit if, out of law or custom, they violate the constitutional rights of their employees. In determining that "person" can mean a corporate body as well as an individual, the Supreme Court increased the opportunities for suits by teachers and students. These suits may be based on acts by school boards that are grounded in official policy, and they may even be based on practices that have had the effect of official policy.

The standard that determines the liability of a school board and school officials has also undergone an evolution of interpretation. Before the courts ruled that school boards as corporate bodies are subject to the Act, they held that these same boards derive greater protection from the eleventh amendment than do its members. It was recognized that school officials have a good faith immunity, later interpreted to mean qualified good faith immunity. This standard is viewed as being necessary for allowing officials to assume their jobs with a degree of discretion and without undue timidity, otherwise, they may fail to make decisions for fear of making mistakes.

263

When good faith immunity is absent, liability attaches when a board member acts contrary to settled constitutional law, is ignorant of or disregards settled law, takes action knowingly in violating one's rights, or acts with a malicious intent to deprive one of his rights.

To date, the courts have distinguished between the liability of governing bodies and their officials. Now governmental officials may enjoy the qualified good faith immunity but the governmental body does not. The governmental body (a school board) may not rely on the good faith of its officers (school board members) as a defense to its own liability under § 1983. The officers or board members are entitled to the qualified good faith immunity. This means that it may be easier to maintain a successful suit against a school board as a corporate entity rather than against school board members as individuals.

Section 1983 has also undergone interpretation with respect to the awarding of damages. When the Act was first applied to school personnel, only equitable relief was sought. Later, individuals sought compensatory damages as well. Although the Supreme Court has not addressed the specific question of compensatory damages for teachers, it has held that students are entitled to damages under special conditions. First, it must be demonstrated that one was deprived of some right and, second, that the individual must have actually sustained some injury from that deprivation. Unless the injury can be demonstrated, the student is entitled only to compensatory damages.

As of 1981, the Supreme Court has interpreted § 1983 as not intending to assess punitive damages against a corporate body for the bad faith actions of its officials. The Court recognized that such awards are against sound public policy in that they tend to penalize the taxpayers who would have to pay the damages where the more reasonable penalty would be to penalize the wrongdoer.

264

§ 5.1. Seven Cardinal Points of § 1983.

Based upon an analysis of the Act and the case law interpreting it, certain conclusions emerge. Seven cardinal points regarding the status of § 1983 can be gleaned. These points and a discussion of each of them follow.

(a) GOOD FAITH DEFENSE.

Where good faith is relied upon as a defense for taking official action, school boards and administrators must be able to show that their exercise of good faith is reasonable and that it is not used as an attempted justification for an unlawful or unconstitutional act.

In the day-to-day operation of school affairs, school personnel are subject to a myriad of laws, regulations and policies. Many of these laws, regulations and policies do not originate at the local school district level, so school officials have little choice but to assume that they are legal and must be obeyed. Beyond that, local boards of education have considerable autonomy in making policy, and administrators have considerable freedom in formulating regulations growing out of that policy.

Unquestionably, in a litigious era, almost any policy or regulation is subject to a challenge by someone. That does not mean, however, that the challenger will be successful. Courts look to the source of the authority and attempt to determine if the policymakers had the authority to enact the law, policy or regulation. If they did not possess that authority, then courts will look next to the reason for the enactment. Under § 1983, the rational basis test has been primarily used. If it can be shown that there was a rational basis for the action, school authority will unlikely be overturned. The rational basis test holds that if schools can justify the policy or regulation on the ground that it serves some legitimate interest of the school, the policy or regulation will likely be upheld. Where an enactment discriminates against an individual, it will not necessarily be declared void under the rational basis test. If the discrimination is grounded on race or if it implicates the first amendment, a higher test (strict scrutiny) will replace the rational basis test.

School officials have been required to defend their actions far more in recent years than they did two decades ago. Where they can justify their policies and decisions as being necessary in the furtherance of some legitimate educational purpose leading toward a reasonable end, chances of students or teachers maintaining a successful § 1983 suit are very remote.

The typical attitude of contemporary federal courts regarding student and teacher matters, however, was described most succinctly by the Fifth Circuit in *Lee v. Washington County Board of Education.* That court indicated the reluctance of the judiciary to interfere in local school matters.[1]

Since the mid-1970's, § 1983 has served as a primary vehicle for taking student and teacher complaints of unconstitutional discrimination into the federal courts.

Generally, the official acts of public school boards and administrators are presumed lawful, regular and necessary for the overall good and welfare of the school system. The initial judicial presumption remained in 1981 that public school officials act in good faith. The burden thus remains on the complaining party to prove otherwise. The affirmative defense of good faith has been and remains relied on consistently by school officials in § 1983 actions.

---

1. Lee v. Washington County Board of Education, 625 F.2d 1235 (5th Cir. 1980).

CURRENT STATUS OF THE ACT   § 5.1

Good faith has never been acceptable as a justification for a constitutional violation. Official actions which curtail, violate or penalize students or teachers for their exercise of a constitutionally protected right have never been and are not now considered as within the bounds of good faith immunity. Also, good faith conduct by school officials must remain within the bounds of reason or good faith itself may end up defeated.

Since 1980, qualified immunity is no longer the school board's defense; rather, it remains a defense for agents of the board (*e.g.,* school superintendents and principals). Stated another way, when carrying out non-legislative functions, a public school board (as an entity) does not have the same degree or protection as do its agents (including individual board members) acting in their official capacities. It should be pointed out, however, that public school boards still possess considerable immunity in exercising their legislative prerogatives (*e.g.,* placing a new school building while closing an old school building).

In the future, when faced with a § 1983-type suit, public school boards will most likely employ the defense that it was not the board's action that caused the problem with the plaintiff; rather, it was the act or acts of the board's agent(s). The board is not responsible for the acts of its agents. For example, a future board might state: "The superintendent went too far [on his own] in his implementation of board policy or he actually misapplied board policy and these acts caused the infraction." Thus, the board may, in effect, shift the fault and the blame over to its agents and let them stand for their own actions.

School officials have never been and will not be able to claim ignorance or mistake as a defense for disregarding a student's or teacher's constitutional rights. However, school officials will not be guilty of bad faith simply because they

267

failed to anticipate the outcome of their decision in an area of law so unsettled in which the courts themselves cannot agree.

In the 1980's the doctrine granting public school boards immunity for discretionary functions which prevent courts from substituting their judgments for those of duly sworn school officials, cannot serve as the basis for claiming a good faith defense under 42 U.S.C. § 1983.

(b) ELEVENTH AMENDMENT IMMUNITY.

Where the Eleventh Amendment immunity is claimed by school officials that immunity will be applied only where the court is convinced that the state itself is (through an overwhelming presence of state action) a party in the lawsuit.

Historically, school districts have been characterized as being an extension of the state. When a local school district engages in a function, it is the state itself which engages in that function. One advantage of this reasoning is that a local school board would receive greater immunity from suit under the eleventh amendment. Since a state cannot be sued under the amendment without its consent, neither could a school district.

That reasoning has been rejected in recent years. On several occasions courts have ruled that a state and its school districts are not one and the same. That is to say that a local governmental unit can engage in actions that are unlike those of a state. This point may not yet be fully understood by a number of school officials, for it runs counter to long-held thinking that a state and the school district are no different. It suggests a real need for school board members to be more cautious in making decisions where the action is viewed as being purely local in character.

Since 1977, the eleventh amendment as a defense is not applicable unless the state itself is shown to be an actual party to the lawsuit. Thus, when a public school district is not considered by the laws of that state to be a "state entity" but rather a local one, that school district is not entitled to an eleventh amendment immunity.

In *Mt. Healthy* the Court stated:

> The issue here thus turns on whether the Mt. Healthy Board of Education is to be treated as an arm of the State ... or is instead to be treated as a municipal corporation or other political subdivision to which the Eleventh Amendment does not extend.

The Court concluded that:

> a local school board such as petitioner is more like a county or city than it is like an arm of the State. ... [I]t was not entitled to assert any Eleventh Amendment immunity from suit in the federal courts.[2]

A similar point was made by a federal district in Montana when it recently declared that it did not have jurisdiction over a diversity matter involving the State Department of Institutions.

(c) CONSTITUTIONALLY DEFINED RIGHTS.

Where rights are clearly defined in the Constitution, these rights are more clearly protected under § 1983 than are less clearly defined rights.

Section 1983 has a hierarchy of rights which are protectable, the highest level being those rights that are specifically enumerated in the Constitution. These include such first amendment rights as freedom of speech and press,

---

2. Mt. Healthy City School District Board of Education v. Doyle, 429 U.S. 274, 280-81 (1977), *aff'd on remand,* 670 F.2d 59 (6th Cir. 1981).

freedom under the fourth amendment from search and seizure, and freedom under the fourteenth amendment to both
due process and equal protection. Even though these rights
have been clearly articulated in general as having some
degree of constitutional protection, they have not been completely brought under the penumbra of § 1983 protection.
For example, the speech and press freedoms allowed
students have not been fully and comprehensively tested in
a § 1983 context, so at this point students bringing an
action under the first amendment in general have been
more successful than students premising their case solely
on § 1983.

On the other hand, courts have not been in close
agreement that reasonable searches of students by school
officials do not violate the fourth amendment. However, if
reasonable suspicion does not exist, and if the search itself
is conducted improperly, officials will not be upheld.
Instead, they may be subject to a more rigid test bordering
on being subject to the strictures of the fourth amendment.
This is particularly true when school officials engage in
strip searches. They have been disallowed under the fourth
amendment as well as under § 1983. Further, students
have been successful in collecting damages for such highly
invasive searches.

Similarly, teachers and other professional employees in
public school systems have relied successfully on § 1983
where their complaints have centered around either the
first amendment (*i.e.,* religion, speech — public and private,
expression — in school and outside it, press and association)
or the fourteenth amendment (*i.e.,* both due process and
equal protection, especially where such matters as one's
race, handicap or professional reputation are in issue).
Moreover, as case law shows, tenure status or lack of it does
not necessarily condition the teacher's status to sue.

With respect to the application of § 1983 to the due process clause and student exclusions, courts have shown some reluctance to award damages. Judges have tended to support school officials and not award damages, even though some irregularities may have existed in the exclusionary hearing.

Section 1983 does not allow a teacher, a student or the student's parent to determine what courses will be taught, what courses must be taken, and what materials are to be used in the classroom. Regarding the use of materials in the classroom, teachers do have some limited discretion, usually set by local board policy and community social-moral climate.

These curricular decisions are proper judgments to be made by local boards of education, not by a teacher, a child and his parents. For example, parental and child interests are subordinate to those of a state and its affiliates who have the authority for determining what constitutes a basic educational program for its students. Parents have a right to object to certain books and courses, but they have no right to dictate what these books and courses will be. In voicing their objections, parents can play a variety of roles that may aid policy determinations of an educational program. As citizens, they can act as individuals in expressing their opinions to administrators and members of the board of education. As citizens, they can write, and speaking through one voice, attempt to influence board policy. It must be understood, however, that a parent's role in policy making is advisory and is relied upon only to the degree that members of the board of education wish to do so.

Where courses are required, a parent's objections carry less weight in policy making than in elective courses. After all, in electives a child has a choice of taking or not taking a subject. The more serious issue is the question of content within courses which is in conflict with an individual's or a group's belief. Courts as well as school officials will make a reasonable effort to accommodate a student's objections to some kind of course content as well as methodology. Where these objections are ground in religion, a parent has a better chance of not having the child exposed to the material and method than for some other reason. Thus, to date, § 1983 has not been of real value to parents and students who have attempted to influence the content of the educational program.

When the Act was first interpreted as being applicable to school personnel, it was teachers who initiated the litigation with students following later. Courts have seen that teachers actually need more freedom in assuming their instructional obligations than do students in receiving instruction. In particular, the freedom of the first amendment has been cited as a protection for teachers. This has involved an interpretation of the degree of freedom that teachers have in speaking out on issues, both inside and outside the school setting. Courts have shown more reluctance to acknowledge that student first amendment rights are coequal to those of teachers.

Where schools have attempted to regulate the private behavior of teachers, they have been unsuccessful unless it can be clearly demonstrated that the teacher's activities have a detrimental influence on his performance as a professional teacher at school, create some disruption of the educational process, or pose a threat to students or other teachers. To date, school officials have not tried as hard to regulate student behavior outside school, thus there has not been the same attempt to extend § 1983 to students' private behavior.

(d) PREPONDERANCE OF EVIDENCE.

Where clear constitutional questions are at issue, the acts of school officials will be judged by the preponderance of the evidence.

Where exercises of constitutionally protected rights are at issue, school officials will need to show a direct causal link between the proscribed student or teacher behavior and a compelling reason to curtail that behavior, a connection supported by hard evidence. The federal courts will carefully scrutinize the merits of the school board's case, where heretofore the emphasis might have been more on procedural issues.

Indicative of this judicial posture is a 1981 decision of the Fifth Circuit. In *Dike v. School Board* [3] the court emphasized the importance of a school board's interests in avoiding disruption of the educational process and in avoiding potential liability for accidents. However, whether these actions are strong enough to justify barring a female elementary teacher from breastfeeding her child, an activity given only minimal constitutional protection by the court, out of sight and alone in a locked room at the school during her duty-free lunch period, must be determined by the trier of fact.

It must be emphasized, however, that while § 1983 allows only for recovery of actual damages, some people believe that the statute has the potential for allowing recovery for mental or emotional distress. Recovery for such damages is not necessarily precluded by the availability of recovery under other federal provisions or under state law. This underscores the need to have hard evidence ready to defend an official act wherein a protected entitlement, no matter how minimal, is present.

---

3. 650 F.2d 783 (5th Cir. 1981).

As of now, the burden of proof in establishing a *prima facie* case of a § 1983 violation remains on the plaintiff student or teacher. Once the *prima facie* case has been established and the protected entitlement is in place, the burden for carrying the action forward will remain on the plaintiff student or teacher. However, the stronger that entitlement becomes or the more obvious the presence of an unlawful intent on the part of school officials, the more likely that the burden will then shift to school officials to show compelling and overriding reasons justifying their invading or totally forbidding the student or teacher entitlement. The key point is that, under § 1983, a civil rights violation is not presumed, it must be proved.

(e) BUSINESS NECESSITY DOCTRINE.

Where personnel decisions must be made in areas filled with potential § 1983-type litigation, the doctrine of business necessity and the Mt. Healthy standard will be applied if and when the matter is before a federal court.

The doctrine of business necessity has been and remains an available affirmative defense possibility for making personnel decisions in public school systems; it is a defense that might help school officials overcome a charge of unconstitutional discrimination. Although it is not an absolute defense of practices affecting minority employment, business necessity offers both procedural and substantive safeguards for employees. The defense suggests that the employment practice "is necessary to the safe and efficient operation of the business. . . ." [4] Its character is described by R. R. Urbach in his article.

---

4. R. R. Urbach, *Color Conscious Quota Relief: A Constitutional Remedy for Racial Employment Discrimination,* 11 URBAN LAW ANN. 333 (1976). Mitchell v. Board of Trustees, 599 F.2d 582 (4th Cir. 1979), offers an excellent example of a school case wherein a board relied on the

Business purpose is defined as having three criteria. First, it must be sufficiently compelling to override any racial impact. Secondly, no other available alternative having a less discriminatory impact can exist. Finally, the business practice must accomplish its stated purpose.[5]

The doctrine of business necessity (as developed over the last decade) implies "a careful balance between merit, on the one hand, and equality, on the other." [6] T. Devine, in his article, cautions school officials, however, that "judgments of teacher quality are at best a very crude tool. . . ." [7] Also, "when measurement of merit is not reliable, or when *qualitative* distinctions between candidates are not signifi-

---

business necessity defense. The question presented in this case is whether a school board's policy that required a pregnant teacher to report her pregnancy to school officials immediately upon discovery, and then used the disclosed pregnancy as the sole basis for declining to renew her contract for the succeeding school year violated § 703 (a)(1) or (2) of Title 7. Convinced that plaintiff had made a prima facie case under Title 7, and in view of the Supreme Court's decision in Nashville Gas Co. v. Satty, 434 U.S. 136 (1977), the Fourth Circuit remanded the case for consideration of any business necessity defense that defendants may be disposed to present on the existing or a reopened record. Said the court: "If this defense is not established, judgment should be entered for plaintiff on the basis of the prima facie violation found on this appeal." *Mitchell, supra,* at 588.

5. *Id.* For a more comprehensive treatment of "the doctrine of business necessity and teacher evaluation," see H.C. HUDGINS, JR. & RICHARD S. VACCA, LAW AND EDUCATION: CONTEMPORARY ISSUES AND COURT DECISIONS (Charlottesville, Va: The Michie Company, 1979), at 162-65.

6. T. Devine, *Women in the Academy: Sex Discrimination in University Faculty Hiring and Promotion,* 5 J. OF LAW & EDUCATION 429, 443 (October 1976).

7. *Id.* at 442.

cant, the scales tip in favor of equality, requiring an appropriate representation of minority and women employees." [8]

Since many school boards today are faced with the possibility of a § 1983-type action, it behooves board members to establish, as their primary reason for retaining certain employees (while nonrenewing, dismissing or otherwise disciplining others), the need to keep and reward the best qualified and most competent ones. In the 1980's school boards must implement carefully devised plans for evaluating the competence of their employees.

When faced with employee-plaintiff challenges to a school board policy or decision, one must ask if the policy or decision will survive legal scrutiny. For example, in a future teacher nonrenewal or dismissal challenge in a court of law, will a school board be able to show that, regardless of any single act of the teacher, it would have reached the same conclusion not to renew the contract or to fire the teacher? Also, will that board be able to produce documented, factual evidence that convinces the court of this? If not, the possibilities for remedy, where § 1983 applies, seems limitless, especially where employee first amendment rights (*e.g.*, expression, press, speech, and assembly) play a part in the matter. Today, first amendment protection extends to private as well as public expression.

(f) MAINTENANCE OF DISCIPLINE.

Where a school board's or a school official's justification for curbing student behavior is based upon a legitimate interest in maintaining order and discipline, the school's rights outweigh those of the student.

---

8. *Id.* at 443. *See* M. A. PLAYER, EMPLOYMENT DISCRIMINATION: CASES AND MATERIALS (St. Paul, Minn.: West Publishing Company, 1980) at 474-500; and its 1982 Supplement at 86-92.

Through the years, courts have recognized and supported school personnel who need to do whatever is necessary to have a climate that allows for teaching and learning. That judicial support has clothed administrators and teachers with considerable discretion in formulating regulations defining acceptable and unacceptable behavior and the punishment that follows for unacceptable behavior. Administered in moderation for the purposes of correcting a child (as opposed to being vindictive), corporal punishment is allowable unless otherwise forbidden by statute. However, in those instances where corporal punishment is excessive, is administered for a wrong reason, and inflicts permanent injury, one can collect damages under § 1983. The cases to date support this statement, although, in practice § 1983 has had almost negligible effect on the corporal punishment of students.

The degree to which school officials can exclude students from school for misbehavior has undergone more judicial evolution than has corporal punishment. Within the past twenty years courts have defined and clarified the due process rights of students in suspensions and expulsions. They have held that the greater the penalty the more due process should be accorded students. Minimally, it involves notice of charges and opportunity for a hearing in short-term suspensions. Courts have not spoken definitively on what constitutes adequate due process in expulsions, but the Supreme Court has suggested that greater safeguards must be followed. There is no question but that school officials can exclude students for misbehavior, but only on a showing of sufficient cause as determined in a due process hearing. For a denial of due process, it has been established that students can collect compensatory damages, but only of a nominal amount, unless it can be shown that the student actually suffered an injury from the deprivation.

School officials can also engage in search and seizure for the reason of protecting school personnel and school property. In undertaking this responsibility, school officials are subject to the standard of "reasonable suspicion" and must exercise some restraint in the search itself. One of the areas in which students have been most successful in collecting damages is for searches that went too far. School officials have not been upheld in forcing students to undress to their underclothing or to undress completely. Courts have seen these kinds of searches as being highly invasive and being unrelated to the school's necessity for maintaining law and order. School officials are further advised to avoid direct physical contact in searching a student.

The use of dogs as sniffers in initiating a search is unresolved at this time in that the limited number of court decisions to date have offered no definitive answer.

(g) COLLECTING DAMAGES.

Where monetary damages are sought under § 1983, it is difficult for teachers and very difficult for students to collect.

Clearly, where school officials are held liable under § 1983, the possibilities for remedy are broad. The cases demonstrate that injunctive relief, reinstatement (with tenure, where appropriate), back pay, lost benefits, expungement of personnel records, removal of letters of reprimand from personnel files, monetary damages (compensatory and punitive), attorney's fees, and the payment of other costs are all possible forms of remedy available in § 1983 cases. What makes this even more significant is that these forms of federal remedy do not necessarily preclude but are supplementary to any available state remedies. However, the exhaustion of state judicial remedies is not a fixed requirement for seeking available federal remedies under § 1983.

The Act thus far has served more as a warning to school boards and to administrators as to what could possibly happen in the way of penalties rather than actually serve as a source for the imposition of penalties. This finding may serve as a surprise to those individuals who envisioned considerable litigation following the mid-1970's. However, in subsequent litigation, the Supreme Court made it very clear that students would be unable to collect damages against school board members unless it could be demonstrated that there was proof of actual injury to a student resulting from the denial of some right. Absent that showing, a student could expect no more than nominal damages of $1 if the right were denied and no injury followed.

The *Owen* decision of 1980 [9] treated in part the issue of damages against a corporate governmental body. The Supreme Court applied the following standard as to whether one could collect damages: A local governmental body may be liable only if the constitutional violation is caused by public officers or employees in the execution of official governmental policy or custom made by the governmental body or someone whose acts may be said to represent the official body or someone whose acts may be said to represent official policy.

Presumably, a school board could be liable under the Owen standard for damages under the following conditions:

1. if it violates a teacher's or a student's constitutional rights;
2. if one or more of its members, acting in an official capacity, violate the constitutional rights of teachers or students; or

---

9. Owen v. City of Independence, 445 U.S. 622, *rehearing denied,* 446 U.S. 993 (1980).

    3. if one of its employees assumes responsibility not rightfully his and violates the constitutional rights of a teacher or student.

Even though *Owen* extended the scope of legal liability under § 1983, there is no evidence to date that it has resulted in more successful suits by teachers or students against boards of education and school board members.

Section 1983 does not, in its specific language, make any reference to punitive damages. However, the court decisions, especially the *Newport* case and those in the employment area, demonstrate that punitive damages are a possible source of remedy in situations where the intent of the school official was to wilfully, corruptly, wantonly, maliciously or recklessly harm an employee solely because of or in retaliation for his or her exercise of a constitutionally protected entitlement. Where such intent cannot be established by the employee, a punitive award will not be possible.

An example of the importance of the intent element being necessary to litigate successfully follows. Where a principal of a school was to recommend that a particular teacher be dismissed from employment, the principal's intent in doing this was to act in good faith and not violate his or her civil rights. In fact, the sole and basic reason for his recommendation was documented proof that he or she was totally ineffective as a classroom teacher. Here, not only would there be no basis for recovery of punitive damages, but there would also be no basis for suit in the first place.

Using the same scenario, what if the principal had as his motive for recommending that the teacher be dismissed that he or she was totally ineffective in the classroom, but his intent for doing this was to retaliate against that teacher for some comment that he or she had made about him and his school at a public meeting at the local community center. Under such circumstances the potential for successful litigation by the teacher and a claim for punitive damages becomes more probable.

TABLE OF CASES

A

Acanfora v. Board of Education, 491 F.2d 498 (4th Cir. 1974)
— § 3.4, nn.232, 233, 234.

Adams v. Campbell County, 511 F.2d 1242 (10th Cir. 1975)
— § 3.3, nn.126, 127, 128, 129, 130, 131.

Adams v. Jefferson Davis Parish School Board, 450 F. Supp.
1141 (W.D. La. 1978) — § 3.5, nn.331, 332, 333, 334, 335,
336, 337, 338, 339, 340.

Adelberg v. Labuszewski, 447 F. Supp. 267 (N.D. Ill. 1978) —
§ 1.0, n.5.

Aebisher v. Ryan, 622 F.2d 651 (2d Cir. 1980) — § 3.3,
nn.44, 45, 46, 47, 48, 49, 50, 51, 52, 53, 54, 55, 56, 57.

Akin v. Board of Education, 68 Cal. Rptr. 557 (1968) —
§ 4.7, n.105.

Anderson v. Canyon Independent School District, 412
S.W.2d 387 (Tex. Civ. App. 1967) — § 4.9, n.132.

Andrews v. Drew Municipal Separate School District, 371 F.
Supp. 27 (N.D. Miss. 1973) — § 1.3, n. 49; § 4.9, n.133.

Arundar v. DeKalb County School District, 620 F.2d 493
(5th Cir. 1980) — § 4.2, n.43.

Avery v. Homewood City Board of Education, 674 F.2d 337
(5th Cir. 1982) — § 3.2, n.21.

Axtel v. LaPenna, 323 F. Supp. 1077 (W.D. Pa. 1971) —
§ 4.7, n.113.

Ayers v. Western Line Consolidated School District, 555
F.2d 1309 (5th Cir. 1977) — § 3.3, n.36.

Ayers v. Western Line Consolidated School District, 404 F.
Supp. 1225 (N.D. Miss. 1977) — § 3.3, n.30.

B

Bacica v. Board of Education, 451 F. Supp. 882 (W.D. Pa.
1978) — § 1.3, nn.50, 51; § 3.5, n.321.

Baker v. Owen, 395 F. Supp. 294 (M.D.N.C. 1975) — § 4.4, n.63.

Barham v. Welch, 478 F. Supp. 1246 (E.D. Ark. 1979) — § 1.3, n.53.

Bell v. Gayle, 384 F. Supp. 1022 (N.D. Tex. 1974) — § 2.4, n.64.

Bellnier v. Lund, 438 F. Supp. 47 (N.D.N.Y. 1977) — § 4.6, nn.91, 98, 99.

Bicknell v. Vergennes Union High School Board of Directors, 475 F. Supp. 615 (D. Vt. 1979) — § 4.2, n.26.

Bicknell v. Vergennes Union High School Board of School Directors, 638 F.2d 438 (2d Cir. 1980) — § 4.2, nn.24, 27.

Bilbrey v. Brown, 481 F. Supp. 26 (D. Ore. 1979) — § 4.6, n.91.

Birdwell v. Hazelwood School District, 491 F.2d 490 (8th Cir. 1974) — § 3.3, n.125.

Bishop v. Wood, 426 U.S. 341 (1976) — § 3.0, nn.4, 5; § 3.3, n.185.

Board of Education v. Bentley, 383 S.W.2d 677 (Ky. App. 1964) — § 4.9, n.132.

Board of Regents v. Roth, 408 U.S. 564 (1972) — § 3.0, n.2.

Board of School Commissioners v. Jacobs, 420 U.S. 128 (1975) — § 4.8, n.122.

Board of Trustees v. Davis, 396 F.2d 730 (8th Cir. 1968) — § 2.1, n.20.

Boxall v. Sequoia Union High School District, 464 F. Supp. 1104 (N.D. Cal. 1979) — § 4.10, n.148.

Boykins v. Ambridge Area School District, 621 F.2d 75 (3d Cir. 1980) — § 4.2, n.39.

Bradley v. Fisher, 13 Wall. 335 (1872).

Bradley v. School Board of the City of Richmond, 416 U.S. 696 (1974) — § 1.3, n.45.

Branch v. School District, 432 F. Supp. 608 (D. Mont. 1977) — § 3.3, n.28.

Breen v. Kahl, 419 F.2d 1034 (7th Cir. 1969) — § 4.7, nn.106, 107.

C

F

G

Gurmankin v. Costanzo, 626 F.2d 1132 (3d Cir. 1980) —
§ 3.5, nn.371, 372.

H

Hall v. Tawney, 621 F.2d 607 (4th Cir. 1980) — § 4.4, nn.65,
66.

Hammond v. Marx, 406 F. Supp. 853 (D. Me. 1975) — § 4.1,
nn.9, 10.

Hammonds v. Shannon, 323 F. Supp. 681 (W.D. Tex. 1971)
— § 4.7, n.111.

Handler v. San Jacinto Junior College, 519 F.2d 273 (5th
Cir. 1975) — § 3.3, nn.162, 163, 164, 165, 166, 167, 168,
169, 170, 171, 172, 173, 174.

Hardwick v. Ault, 517 F.2d 295 (5th Cir. 1975) — § 1.5, n.78.

Harkless v. Sweeney Independent School District, 466 F.
Supp. 457 (S.D. Tex. 1979) — § 1.3, n.54.

Harris v. Campbell, 472 F. Supp. 51 (E.D. Va. 1979) — § 1.5,
nn.74, 75, 76; § 4.10, n.146.

Hickman v. Valley Local School District Board, 619 F.2d 606
(6th Cir. 1980) — § 1.0, n.7; § 1.4, n.57; § 3.4, nn.235,
236, 237, 238, 239, 240, 241, 242.

Holladay v. Montana, 506 F. Supp. 1317 (D. Mont. 1981) —
§ 3.5, n.298.

Holt v. Shelton, 341 F. Supp. 821 (M.D. Tenn. 1972) — § 4.9,
n.132.

Hortonville School District v. Hortonville Educ.
Association, 426 U.S. 482 (1976) — § 3.3, n.87.

Howard S. v. Friendswood Independent School District, 454
F. Supp. 634 (S.D. Tex. 1978) — § 4.10, n.151.

Hutto v. Finney, 437 U.S. 678 (1978) — § 1.3, n.55; § 4.10,
n.143.

I

Imbler v. Pachtman, 424 U.S. 409 (1976) — § 2.4, n.56.
Ingraham v. Wright, 430 U.S. 651 (1977) — § 4.4, n.64.

L

Lee v. Monroe County Board of Education, 640 F.2d 755 (5th Cir. 1981) — § 3.5, nn.341, 342, 343, 344, 345, 346, 347.

Lee v. Washington County Board of Education, 625 F.2d 1235 (5th Cir. 1980) — § 3.0, n.6, 7; § 5.1, n.1.

Leffel v. Wisconsin Interscholastic Athletic Ass'n, 444 F. Supp. 1117 (E.D. Wis. 1978) — § 4.3, nn.59, 60.

Lemons v. Morgan, 629 F.2d 1389 (8th Cir. 1980) — § 3.3, nn.90, 91, 92, 93, 94, 97, 98, 99.

Leonard v. School District, 212 N.E.2d 468 (Mass. 1965) — § 4.7, n.103.

L. L. v. Circuit Court of Washington County, 90 Wis. 2d 585, 280 N.W.2d 343 (1979) — § 4.10, n.151.

Lora v. Board of Education, 456 F. Supp. 1211 (E.D.N.Y. 1978) — § 4.10, nn.149, 150.

Lucia v. Duggan, 303 F. Supp. 112 (D. Mass. 1969) — § 2.3, n.55; § 3.3, nn.146, 147, 148, 149, 150, 151, 152, 153, 154, 155, 156, 157, 158, 159, 160, 161.

Lusk v. Estes, 361 F. Supp. 653 (N.D. Tex. 1973) — § 3.3, n.27.

M

Magnett v. Pelletier, 488 F.2d 33 (1st Cir. 1973) — § 2.4, nn.56, 64.

Maher v. Gagne, 448 U.S. 122 (1980) — § 1.3, nn.37, 38, 42.

Mailloux v. Kiley, 448 F.2d 1242 (1st Cir. 1971) — § 3.3, n.124.

Maine v. Thiboutot, 448 U.S. 1 (1980) — § 1.3, n.36; § 2.2, n.49.

Marlar v. Bill, 181 Tenn. 100, 178 S.W.2d 634 (1944) — § 4.6, n.85.

McGhee v. Draper, 564 F.2d 902 (10th Cir. 1977) — § 3.5, nn.281, 283, 284, 285, 286.

McGhee v. Draper, 639 F.2d 639 (10th Cir. 1981) — § 3.5, nn.282, 287, 288, 289, 290, 291, 292, 293, 294, 295, 296, 297, 298, 299, 300, 301, 302, 303, 304, 305.

Myerson v. Arizona, 507 F. Supp. 859 (D. Ariz. 1981) —
§ 3.5, n.366.

N

Nelson v. State, 319 So. 2d 154 (Fla. App. 1975) — § 4.6,
n.90.

Neuhaus v. Torrey, 310 F. Supp. 192 (N.D. Cal. 1970) —
§ 4.7, n.110.

New York City School Boards Ass'n v. Board of Education,
39 N.Y.2d 111, 347 N.E.2d 568, 383 N.Y.S.2d 208 (1976) —
§ 4.2, nn.41, 42.

Niederhuber v. Camden County Vocational and Technical
School District Board of Education, 495 F. Supp. 273
(D.N.J. 1980) — § 3.5, nn.306, 307, 308, 309, 310, 311,
312, 313, 314, 315, 316, 317.

Norton v. McShane, 332 F.2d 855 (5th Cir. 1964) — § 2.1,
n.19.

O

O'Connor v. Mazzulo, 536 F. Supp. 641 (S.D.N.Y. 1982) —
§ 3.4, n.228.

Ouimette v. Babbie, 405 F. Supp. 525 (D. Vt. 1975) — § 4.2,
nn.35, 36, 37.

Owen v. City of Independence, 421 F. Supp. 1110 (W.D. Mo.
1976) — § 2.2, n.44.

Owen v. City of Independence, 560 F.2d 925 (8th Cir. 1977)
— § 2.2, n.45.

Owen v. City of Independence, 589 F.2d 335 (8th Cir. 1978)
— § 2.2, n.45.

Owen v. City of Independence, 445 U.S. 622 (1980) — § 2.2,
nn.42, 43; § 2.4, nn.58, 65; § 5.1, n.9.

P

Panzarella v. Boyle, 406 F. Supp. 787 (D.R.I. 1975) — § 4.5,
n.74.

R

T

Tardif v. Quinn, 545 F.2d 761 (1st Cir. 1976) — § 3.3, nn.175, 177, 178, 179, 180, 181, 182, 183, 184, 186.

Tatter v. Board of Education, 490 F. Supp. 494 (D. Minn. 1980) — § 3.1, nn.10, 11.

Tenney v. Brandhove, 341 U.S. 367 (1951) — § 2.1, nn.14, 16.

Thiboutot v. State, 405 A.2d 230 (Me. 1979) — § 2.2, n.52.

Thomas v. Board of Education, Granville Central School District, 607 F.2d 1043 (2d Cir. 1979) — § 4.8, nn.126, 127.

Thompson v. Burke, 556 F.2d 231 (3d Cir. 1977) — § 5.4, n.64.

Thompson v. Southwest School District, 483 F. Supp. 1170 (W.D. Mo. 1980) — § 3.5, nn.270, 271, 272, 273, 274, 275, 276, 278, 279, 280.

Tinker v. Des Moines Independent Community School District, 393 U.S. 503 (1969) — § 3.0, n.1; § 3.3, n.100; § 4.8, n.116.

Trachtman v. Anker, 563 F.2d 512 (2d Cir. 1977) — § 4.8, nn.119, 120.

U

United States v. Brewster, 408 U.S. 501 (1972) — § 2.1, n.1.

United States v. Richardson Independent School District, 483 F. Supp. 80 (N.D. Tex. 1979) — § 3.5, n.331.

United States ex rel. Larkins v. Oswald, 510 F.2d 583 (2d Cir. 1975) — § 2.4, n.56.

United States ex rel. Myers v. Sielaff, 381 F. Supp. 840 (E.D. Pa. 1974) — § 2.4, n.64.

United States ex rel. Tyrrell v. Speaker, 535 F.2d 823 (3d Cir. 1976) — § 2.4, nn.56, 64.

Upshur v. Love, 474 F. Supp. 332 (N.D. Cal. 1979) — § 3.5, nn.373, 374, 375, 376, 377, 378, 379.

V

Valadez v. Graham, 474 F. Supp. 149 (M.D. Fla. 1979) — § 4.2, nn.33, 34.

Valent v. New Jersey State Board of Education, 274 A.2d 832 (N.J. 1971) — § 4.2, n.17.

W

Wagle v. Murray, 546 F.2d 1329 (9th Cir. 1976) — § 1.5, nn.70, 71, 73.

Walsh v. Louisiana High School Athletic Ass'n, 616 F.2d 152 (5th Cir. 1980) — § 4.3, nn.49, 50, 51.

Webster v. Redmond, 443 F. Supp. 670 (N.D. Ill. 1977) — § 1.3, n.47; § 1.4, n.57.

Welch v. Barham, 635 F.2d 1322 (8th Cir. 1980) — § 3.3, nn.79, 80, 81, 82, 83, 84, 85, 86, 88, 89.

Whiteside v. Kay, 446 F. Supp. 716 (W.D. La. 1978) — § 4.5, n.75.

Whiteside v. Washington, 534 F. Supp. 774 (E.D. Wash. 1982) — § 2.1, n.31.

Whitney v. California, 274 U.S. 357 (1927) — § 4.5, n.79.

William v. Treer, 50 U.S.L.W. 2590 (April 13, 1982) — § 2.1, n.21; § 3.4, n.231.

Williams v. Anderson, 526 F.2d 1081 (8th Cir. 1977) — § 1.3, n.46; § 1.4, n.57.

Williams v. Board of Education, 388 F. Supp. 93 (S.D.W. Va. 1975) — § 4.2, n.15.

Williams v. Spencer, 622 F.2d 1200 (4th Cir. 1980) — § 4.8, n.125.

Wisch v. Sanford School, Inc., 420 F. Supp. 1310 (D. Del. 1976) — § 4.5, n.84.

Wishart v. McDonald, 367 F. Supp. 530 (D. Mass. 1973) — § 3.5, nn.243, 244, 245, 246, 247, 248, 249, 250.

Wood v. Strickland, 420 U.S. 308 (1975) — § 1.0, n.3; § 2.1, nn.13, 22, 25, 26, 27, 28, 30, 33; § 4.0, n.5; § 4.5, nn.73, 78.

Index

A

CIVIL RIGHTS ACT OF 1837—Cont'd
Evidence.
    Preponderance of the evidence.
        Cardinal point of act, §5.1.
Fees.
    Attorneys' fees, §1.3.
    Costs other than attorneys' fees, §1.4.
Freedom of association.
    Cardinal point of act, §5.1.
Freedom of speech.
    Cardinal point of act, §5.1.
    Teachers, §3.3.
Freedom of the press.
    Cardinal point of act, §5.1.
Historical perspective, §1.2.
Introduction to chapter, §1.0.
Remedies.
    Exhaustion of state remedies, §1.5.
Summary of chapter, §1.7.
Teachers.
    Racial discrimination, §3.5.
    Rights under act, §3.1.
Torts.
    Era of the civil rights tort, §5.0.

CONGRESS.
Civil rights act of 1871.
    Post-civil war congressional acts, §1.2.

CONSTITUTION OF THE UNITED STATES.
Amendments.
    Eleventh amendment.
        See ELEVENTH AMENDMENT.
    Post-civil war constitutional amendments, §1.2.
Rights under constitution.
    Cardinal point of civil rights act, §5.1.

CORPORAL PUNISHMENT.
Students, §4.4.

COSTS.
Actions under civil rights act.
    Fees other than attorneys' fees, §1.4.
Fees generally.
    See FEES.

D

DAMAGES.
Actions.
School boards and administrators, §2.4.
Cardinal point of civil rights act, §5.1.
Civil rights act of 1871.
Collecting damages.
Cardinal point of act, §5.1.
Liability.
Collecting damages.
Cardinal point of civil rights act, §5.1.
School boards and administrators.
Corporate bodies, §2.4.
Individual board members, §2.4.
School boards and administrators.
Corporate bodies.
Assessments, §2.4.
Individual board members.
Assessments, §2.4.
Torts.
School boards and administrators, §2.4.

DEFENSES.
Cardinal point of civil rights act, §5.1.
Civil rights act of 1871.
Cardinal point of act, §5.1.
Good faith defense.
Cardinal point of civil rights act, §5.1.

DEFINITIONS.
Constitutionally defined rights.
Cardinal point of civil rights act, §5.1.

DISCIPLINE.
School boards and administrators.
Maintenance of discipline.
Cardinal point of civil rights act, §5.1.
Teachers.
Maintenance of discipline.
Cardinal point of civil rights act, §5.1.

DRESS CODES.
Freedom of speech.
Students, §4.7.
Teachers, §3.3.
Students, §4.7.
Teachers, §3.3.

303

305

P

PARENT AND CHILD.
Students.
Parenhood, §4.9.

PARTIES.
Fees.
Prevailing parties, §1.3.

PICKERING STANDARD.
Teachers.
Freedom of speech, §3.3.

PRESS, FREEDOM OF.
See FREEDOM OF THE PRESS.

R

RACIAL DISCRIMINATION.
Students.
Assignment to school, §4.1.
Teachers, §3.5.

REMEDIES.
Actions.
Exhaustion of state remedies, §1.5.
Civil rights act of 1871.
Exhaustion of state remedies, §1.5.

S

SCHOOL BOARDS AND ADMINISTRATORS.
Damages.
Corporate bodies.
Assessments, §2.4.
Individual board members.
Assessments, §2.4.
Discipline.
Maintenance of discipline.
Cardinal points of civil rights act, §5.1.
Eleventh amendment.
Immunity, §2.1.
Good faith immunity, §2.1.
Immunity.
Administrators, §2.3.
Due process issue, §2.1.
Eleventh amendment immunity, §2.1.

307

3169